Keeping the Family
Business Healthy

*How to Plan for Continuing
Growth, Profitability,
and Family Leadership*

John L. Ward

Foreword by Léon A. Danco

Keeping the Family Business Healthy

How to Plan for Continuing Growth, Profitability, and Family Leadership

Jossey-Bass Publishers

San Francisco   •   London   •   1987

KEEPING THE FAMILY BUSINESS HEALTHY
How to Plan for Continuing Growth, Profitability,
and Family Leadership
    by John L. Ward

Copyright © 1987 by: Jossey-Bass Inc., Publishers
                     433 California Street
                     San Francisco, California 94104
                                &
                     Jossey-Bass Limited
                     28 Banner Street
                     London EC1Y 8QE

Library of Congress Cataloging-in-Publication Data

Ward, John L.
    Keeping the family business healthy.

    (A publication in The Jossey-Bass management series)
    Bibliography: p. 255
    Includes index.
    1. Family corporations—Management. I. Title.
II. Series: Jossey-Bass management series.
HD62.25.W37   1986   658'.045   86-45624
ISBN 1-55542-026-5 (alk. paper)

Manufactured in the United States of America

JACKET DESIGN BY WILLI BAUM

FIRST EDITION
        First printing: November 1986
        Second printing: September 1987

Code 8645

The Jossey-Bass Management Series

Consulting Editors
Management of Family-Owned Businesses

Richard Beckhard
Richard Beckhard Associates

Peter Davis
*The Wharton School
University of Pennsylvania*

Barbara Hollander
The Family Firm Institute

Contents

ix

Tables and Figures

A Note to the Reader

Over 95 percent of all businesses in the United States are family owned. Although many family businesses are small, a substantial proportion are major corporations, including about 175 of the *Fortune* 500. Family businesses produce almost half the gross national product and generate about 50 percent of the total wages paid in this country. The effectiveness of such companies and the quality of their management are clearly significant for the economy and the society.

Family business is without doubt the predominant form of organization in the modern economy, yet little has been written about it until recently. Interest in the subject is growing dramatically, partly because large numbers of founders who established their businesses after World War II now face retirement. These entrepreneurs are vitally interested in succession planning. In addition, many younger people are entering their families' businesses because they see opportunities to advance rapidly and to make a more significant impact than they could in nonfamily firms. Moreover, entrepreneurial starts increased from 90,000 in 1951 to 900,000 in 1984. A large number of these are or will become family firms. With this economic shift toward entrepreneurialism, the welfare of the family firm is more important than ever.

Family businesses tend to have relatively short life spans. Problems such as succession, the interplay of family issues and business decisions, the professional development of family members, the transition to nonfamily management, the retention of competent nonfamily employees, and the balance of personal and corporate finances are all factors that make the survival of the family firm perilous.

New information about family-owned firms has emerged
in recent years from such diverse fields as family theory and
therapy, sociology, psychology, business, organizational behavior and development, finance, and law. The family firm is now
recognized as a highly complex entity involved in a system composed of three major parts—the family, the business, and the
marketplace. Events in one part of the system, we now know,
are likely to have ramifications for other parts.

The Jossey-Bass series on management of family-owned
businesses is dedicated to providing readers with practical, applicable state-of-the-art information about these businesses. It
is designed primarily for people actually involved in family businesses—owners, managers (both family and nonfamily), and
board members—who are committed to increasing their firms'
effectiveness. Each book will examine new concepts in the management of family firms and will support the systematic development of knowledge and skills managers need to develop
healthy family businesses.

Factors critical to the survival of the family business will
be addressed—such as understanding family dynamics and their
effects on the business, planning for succession, implementing
strategic decision-making methods, selecting and managing employees, developing the culture of the organization, ensuring
continuity, providing for career development within the company, and developing and utilizing a board of directors. While
many of these ideas have been addressed in other more general
books, this series will consider each one in the unique context
of the family firm, where family issues and business concerns
overlap.

Books in the series will also be of value to professionals
who serve family firms: accountants, lawyers, family therapists,
financial planners, bankers, and management consultants. An
individual in any one of these areas may find it difficult to cope
with the complexities of a family firm's mode of operation. Accountants, for example, often report frustration when the emotional processes of the family impinge on their work with the
business. This series of books will enable such professionals to
increase their familiarity with all areas that relate to family busi-

ness matters and to identify resources for handling those not within their purview.

Academics, students, and researchers will also find this series useful. To date, the literature and research has been sparse, particularly in light of the numbers of family firms in the United States and their impact on the economy. There are, for example, no texts available on the family business. Several universities now offer courses on the family business, however, and research on the topic is increasing. In response to obvious need, we hope that the Jossey-Bass series on family business will serve as a foundation for researchers, students, professors, and professionals who are exploring theory and developing applications that will enhance the family-held business as a distinct economic form.

The series editors, all of whom have been both consultants to and researchers on family businesses, have identified the main topics the series will treat and have recruited experts to write on them. It is our hope that the Family Firm Series will become a significant and useful resource for all who are dedicated to ensuring the effectiveness of the family-owned business.

September 1986   Richard Beckhard
                                    New York, New York

                                    Peter Davis
                                    Philadelphia, Pennsylvania

                                    Barbara Hollander
                                    Pittsburgh, Pennsylvania

Foreword

Contrary to popular opinion, America's family-owned and privately held corporations are not being destroyed by confiscatory taxation, ruthless competitors, unproductive labor, technological change, or insidious regulation—to name only a few of the more common scapegoats for the demise of once-thriving businesses.

Family businesses fail because they allow themselves to be destroyed, slowly but surely, by the action—or more accurately, the inaction—of their owner/managers. The businesses fail because, more often than not, these people never make the decisions needed to ensure the vitality of their companies in an ever-changing, ever more complex world.

Why?

Because family business owners typically fail to *recognize the needs of the future* in managing their businesses. Instead they prefer the comfort of past visions, the safety of old routines. They enjoy the fixed power of their positions. And when it comes to the future, they choose the refuge of ambiguity—instead of the risk of a new plan, purpose, or review.

What a shame!

To be magnanimous, perhaps the attitude of the business owner is understandable. By the time we are in our fifties, many of us feel our accomplishments are apparent. We've been at it a long time by then, longer than we'd care to remember. And we're tired of the struggle. We'd mostly just like to coast—while reaping the rewards for all our work. We want all the good things, and we dream of carrying them off into some permanent nirvana. We want peace, quiet, enjoyment, and love. What's more, we think we deserve it.

To the outside world, we continue to say "Never felt better!" But inside, we fear our increasing irrelevance. We fear that the precious mixture of stamina, creativity, drive, and need that once fueled us won't be renewed. We fear our decline. And so we reassure ourselves with expensive toys (deductible, of course), pontificate in front of people we pay to applaud, and exercise our managerial "muscle" without the discipline imposed by our once-Spartan circumstances. Often, we hide our lack of true accomplishment with a flurry of activities in marginally useful areas. We hope only that the golden goose will keep on producing those golden eggs, proving—against all our fears—that we are still the successful men and women we'd like to be.

But while we as business owners insulate ourselves with such thoughts, the world is busily changing. And unless we wake up from our reverie and respond to those changes, the world will pass us and our companies by.

Clearly, what we need is some revitalizing force that will allow us to *see* change and adapt to it. We need to know how to renew our companies as well as ourselves. We could use someone who, by commitment and example, will point to the problems ahead and help us find the tools for their solution. We need guidance that can help us see that the problems of the future are not only solvable but worth solving.

In *Keeping the Family Business Healthy,* John Ward has provided this guidance. He brings more than a decade of experience to bear on the topic of family business and the need for business owners to examine future change. He urges us to make this assessment not only for the benefit of society but for ourselves and our *families*—for those of us who run our own businesses and who have dared to involve our families in them. Only by such care may we fulfill our dream of keeping our companies healthy and alive, generation after generation.

John Ward's book is refreshingly different from the scores of business books. It involves the reader. It encourages the reader to think through problems and to become a participant instead of a spectator. The book's powerful ideas sweep away the fears that can cloud a business owner's perspective and provide renewed hope for the future.

A teacher can do no more!

Cleveland, Ohio   Léon A. Danco, Ph.D.
September 1986   *President*
                                          Center for Family Business

To my family, Julie, Jeffrey, and Gail — with
excitement and commitment for our future

Preface

"This Business Shall Last Forever."

That motto—promoted by Léon Danco, president of the Center for Family Business—is every family business owner's dream, and at no other time in our nation's history have so many men and women dreamed it. Founders of the companies that mushroomed after World War II are reaching retirement age. Their sons and daughters see the entrepreneurial opportunities inherent in running the family firm. Both generations long for the independence and freedom that a family business can provide.

Yet for many, this dream will die. Their companies will be sold, closed, bought out, or merged with others—lost to the families that led them for so many years.

The purpose of this book is to show family businessmen and women how to keep that dream alive and realize it through good planning, which is the key point of this work. Good planning is much more than merely thinking ahead. It is a comprehensive, step-by-step approach that can help family business owners to (1) maintain growing, healthy, and profitable companies, (2) shape future business directions, (3) prepare new family leadership, (4) ensure the support of family members who do not work for the company but who significantly influence its fate, and (5) guide future generations via thoughtful philosophies.

This book is unique in that it reflects the special choices and challenges faced by family businesses. Business planning books (such as Steiner, 1969; Andrews, 1980; and Aaker, 1984) ignore the intricate family issues that fundamentally influence a company's future. And those books designed to address family issues (the best are Danco, 1975; Alcorn, 1982; and Rosenblatt and others, 1985) fail to examine the role of formal business planning. The reader is left without aid to integrate family and business planning issues. This book is designed to help the reader integrate these two realms, and it does so in a complete yet concise manner.

Family businesses need help developing perspectives and methods for planning and for family issues. Fewer than 30 percent of successful family businesses make it *to* the third generation, and fewer than 15 percent make it *through* that generation, chiefly because many family businesses lack a clear framework for thinking about the future of their businesses and their families. Lacking certain important analytical tools and methods, these businessmen and women are unaware of the available alternatives and make mistakes that increase tension and heighten family conflict. This conflict then becomes the focus of trouble within the family business that can result in the dissolution of the company.

The focus in this book is on the business, although full recognition is given to the family foundation that undergirds it. Many business fundamentals are provided, including the tools for market and financial analysis, a step-by-step process of developing a business plan, and a framework for selecting a business strategy that emphasizes the special advantages of a family company. Similar methodology is used for exploring family interactions to help family business owners develop and carry out a "vision" for their families as well as for their companies. Since successful family businesses balance the needs of the business with the needs of the family, planning is necessary to reconcile differences.

The goal of this book is to present skills and ideas crucial to revitalizing the family business so that it may continue generation after generation. As such, this book will be a useful resource for companies at any stage of development but will be especially helpful to mature businesses run by healthy families—businesses with over $3 million in sales whose basic product or service has already proven itself in the marketplace and whose organization has reached more than twenty employees. The owners of these businesses as well as the sons and daughters who will succeed them in the business are the primary readership for this book. However, key business employees who are not members of the family—and key family members who are not employees of the business—will also find the book useful in gaining a better appreciation for the unique issues that commonly affect family businesses.

This book is also directed toward advisers to family businesses—bankers, accountants, lawyers, and investment and family counselors—who, as trusted professionals, are most likely to see the need for more formal business and family planning. The book offers these professionals a strategic perspective on how family businesses operate.

Academics will find this treatment of interest, as it includes many common family business issues worthy of more research and also presents the formal results of the author's original research. This work includes research on (1) critical issues facing siblings who work together, (2) successors' rationales for staying in the family business, (3) contrasts between public and private companies' performances and strategic choices, (4) the relative aggressiveness of family business strategies, and (5) the life expectancy and survival rate of family businesses. The information presented here is based on surveys of various groups (typically between 75 and 200 family business owners), analyses of a data base on business performance and strategies, and a historical study of 200 family businesses. Although these research efforts have been supported by the work of many others, this work is not intended to provide a formal summary of all family business research. Rather, it presents an overall view of family and business that provides opportunity for further research. As such, it is an ideal introductory text and will be useful in courses and seminars on the rapidly growing field of family business.

The chapters of this book are organized as a series of "building blocks" that business owners, their key managers, and their families can use in attaining family and business goals.

In Chapter One, the basic challenges of keeping the fam-

ily firm alive and the reasons behind business failure and success
are outlined. The value of planning is emphasized and a basic
planning checklist, whose details are elaborated throughout the
book, is provided. Chapter Two covers the stages of growth
within a business and family, including changes in the business
life cycle, the organization, the chief executive, and the financial constituencies served. Ways that family business owners
can use their understanding of these natural evolutionary stages
to overcome the barriers to long-term business health are described.

The growth of the family alongside the business is explored in Chapter Three along with ways the family business
owner can ensure family interest and cooperation. The fundamental beginnings of strategic planning—assessing the firm's
financial and market situation—are analyzed in Chapter Four,
with a focus on the prevalent practice of "harvesting" the business for current profit at the expense of future viability.

Chapter Five deals with strategic business planning, as
tailored to the unique needs of a family business. A plan for the
family is developed next in Chapter Six, and such questions
as how the family can work together in the business and how
the family can share in the benefits of the business are considered. To guide family planning, a series of conceptual models
and the underlying assumptions are discussed and topics for
family meetings are suggested.

Chapter Seven focuses on the final selection of a comprehensive corporate strategy, outlined in the previous two
chapters, that includes consideration of the business and the
family. The potential competitive advantages of family businesses are also pointed out. Chapter Eight shows how to prepare for the transition to new leadership. This chapter provides
substantial guidance on how successors can best prepare for
future business leadership in order to promote a revitalized
business vision and strategy and specifically discusses the following:

- A special approach to analyze the future financial and market health of a business
- A comprehensive list of business strategy alternatives

- A methodology to select the best alternative direction for in-dividual circumstances peculiar to each family business
- An innovative, integrated business strategic planning process
- An overview of the family's options
- An outline of the competitive advantages and disadvantages of family firms.

Several resources are included as appendixes, which fur-ther clarify the planning framework outlined in the book. These appendixes include model business and family plans, a sample business analysis, a questionnaire on business values, a discus-sion of the family business research, and suggestions for future research directions.

Readers may approach this book in several ways. Active family business owners and professionals may use it to learn and can apply its analytical tools to calculate market share, evaluate reinvestment rate, or identify market segments. Or readers may use the book as a stimulus for a new way of thinking strategi-cally about their businesses. Those readers who wish to imple-ment comprehensive planning methodology within their family companies will find that this book provides an easy step-by-step guide. For these readers, many sections of the text are like a workbook, with checklists and worksheets to help them analyze their businesses and record their insights.

Sharing this book within the family or the business is use-ful for stimulating discussion. Open, frank talk is crucial to planning. This book can aid in that process. It is hoped that this book may also persuade family business owners to share their dream of perpetuating the business and to guide their com-panies and families in ways that will make that dream possible.

I am grateful to those who have shaped my thinking and my enthusiasm for the subjects treated in this book. Sidney Schoeffler, of the Strategic Planning Institute and, recently, Mantis Associates, both based in Cambridge, Massachusetts, has taught me much about the value and techniques of strategic planning and analysis. He also has proven the power of research-ing business analogies.

Léon Danco, of the Center for Family Business in Cleveland, Ohio, has generously shared with me his more than twenty years of absolutely unique experience and insight on the issues of families in business. In many ways, he has made this book possible.

I am also thankful to my literary partner, Laurel Sorenson, who has mentored the writing of this book. As a colleague, she has repeatedly challenged its logic. As a writer, she has contributed her considerable skill to better convey the thoughts expressed in these pages.

Others have helped shape the book through their thoughtful review of earlier drafts. I appreciate the wise counsel of Richard Beckhard, Jeffrey Hawk, Barbara Hollander, Walter Horwich, Earl Johnson, Ivan Lansberg, Robert Neff, and Scott Wimer.

While Sidney, Léon, and Laurel have made this book possible, I, of course, accept full responsibility for its content.

September 1986   John L. Ward
                                                        Chicago, Illinois

The Author

John L. Ward is Ralph Marotta Professor of Free Enterprise at Loyola University of Chicago. He received his B.S. degree (1967) in economics from Northwestern University and his M.B.A. degree (1969) and Ph.D. degree (1973) in management from the Stanford University Graduate School of Business. He also studied economics at the Sorbonne, University of Paris (1967).

Ward's main research activities have been in the field of family business, as well as in business and marketing strategies. He is widely known as a consultant to family businesses, specializing in owner-managed firms interested in business and succession planning. He is a partner himself in two small business ventures (retailing and real estate) and sits on the boards of seven private businesses.

In addition to teaching at Loyola, Ward has also served as associate dean of Loyola's business school and as a senior associate with the Strategic Planning Institute (PIMS Program), a research and consulting organization in Cambridge, Massachusetts. He is a regular member of the faculty of the Cleveland-based Center for Family Business and has conducted numerous seminars and workshops on family business topics. He lives with his wife, Gail, and their two children, Julie and Jeffrey, in Evanston, Illinois.

Keeping the Family Business Healthy

How to Plan for Continuing Growth, Profitability, and Family Leadership

ONE

The Challenge of Keeping
a Family Firm Alive

Keeping a family business alive is perhaps the toughest management job on earth. Only 13 percent of successful family businesses last through the third generation (see Table 1 and Appendix G). Less than two-thirds survive the second generation. And,
as indicated by other studies (Blotnick, 1984), fewer than 5 percent of all businesses ever started actually become family businesses through appointment of a successor from the next generation.

The dying family business so permeates our business culture that it has become legendary. Expressions such as "shirt-
sleeves to shirt-sleeves in three generations" and "rags to riches
to rags" are common in this country. Similar phrases occur elsewhere: in Italian, "dalle stalle alle stelle alle stalle" sends the
family "from [barn] stalls to stars to stalls"; and in Spanish,
"quien no lo tiene, lo hace; y quien lo tiene, lo deshace" pre-
dicts that "who doesn't have it, does it, and who has it, misuses
it." All these phrases suggest the same story. The first generation builds the business, the second generation "milks" or "har-
vests" it, and the third generation must either auction what is
left to the highest bidder or start all over again.

Why Family Businesses Fail

To be sure, all businesses—family or otherwise—find it
difficult to last a long time. The evolution of the *Fortune* 500
list is a case in point: since 1955, only 188 companies have kept
their status on this list as independent concerns. More than 60

1

Table 1. Life Expectancy of 200 Successful Manufacturers, 1924-1984.

Percentage No Longer Surviving	80%
Percentage of Same Name Still Surviving as Independent Companies	20%

    Of these 20% . . .   5% were sold to outsiders

                              2% went public and were no longer controlled by founding family

                        13% are still owned by same family as in 1924

                - - - - - - - - - -

    Of the 13% still owned by the same family . . .

                  3% grew significantly[a]

                  3% did not grow

                  7% declined

                - - - - - - - - - -

    Of the 80% of the companies that no longer survived . . .

              33% ceased   0 to 29 years old

              35% ceased 35 to 59 years old

              16% ceased 60 to 89 years old

              16% ceased 90 years old and over

Note: Each business studied had twenty or more employees and was at least five years old in 1924. Businesses that are said to have grown increased employment by more than 10% from 1924 to 1984. Businesses that are said to have declined had decreased employment by more than 10% from 1924 to 1984. For more discussion on this research, its methodology, limitations, and implications, see Appendix G.

[a]Growth was measured by change in employment over sixty years by more or less than 10% of 1924 levels.

percent have been sold or acquired or have watched their sales decline significantly in the past thirty years. The reasons for this are many. Businesses mature. Markets and technology change, eliminating the need for various products and services. Suppliers and customers alter the "rules of the game," or competitors quickly copy successful strategies. Any of these changes can take the company by surprise, decreasing its sales and profits. Sometimes an outside buyer is simply willing to pay more to acquire the company than it is worth. Owners are unable to resist the premium and sell out.

Beyond these typical business pitfalls, however, family businesses face special challenges. Many family businesses are also private, small businesses. They lack the financial capabilities or staff skills of larger concerns. A study by the Wharton Entrepreneurial Center (1975) indicates that nearly half of the twenty-eight family businesses under review were sold because they lacked the necessary funds or marketing expertise. Other respondents claimed that suppliers, through refusing to deal with companies they considered "too small," virtually forced them to sell out. Still others cited a lack of management depth as the cause of sale. Thus it would seem that status as a small or private company may become untenable at some point for many businesses.

Second, many family businesses find that the family itself becomes a stumbling block. In later years, the family's growing financial demands tempt owners to harvest the company's profits rather than reinvest them in additional growth. The rigors of business also sharpen such typical family problems as sibling rivalry or competition between the generations. Human emotions such as pride or jealousy may become enlarged when work and home are intertwined. The natural desire of a child to steer a course independent of his or her parents can also nip succession plans in the bud. These are emotionally trying issues for all concerned. As a result, many families abandon the effort at succession because they feel it will destroy the family. The Wharton study, in which 35 percent of all companies sold cited lack of management depth or successors as a key reason for selling out, confirms this view.

Yet there is a final reason for failures in succession, and it is a more important one than those already given: many family businessmen and women lack a clear conceptual framework for thinking about the future of their businesses. Thus, they often lack some of the modern analytical tools that might allow them to conquer business and family challenges.

The most critical of these tools is a *plan* to guide both the company and the family. Such a plan will help the business owner focus on the business itself—specifically, on the need for reinvesting in new strategies that will revitalize the company and promote future growth. This need is often ignored as the business matures and the family's financial demands grow. Business owners and their families must instead appreciate and address business needs; a business plan ensures that they will. Inevitably, the process of preparing the plan will spark examination of the family's own needs. That opens the door to addressing family goals as well.

At the same time, however, formal or even informal attempts at planning often threaten business owners. Many entrepreneurs think of planning as a straitjacket that will constrain instinctive survival skills and limit business flexibility. The nature of the planning process also requires these independent business owners to share decisions—and private financial statements—with others in the company. That is power and information that many owners would rather keep to themselves. Other owners object to planning because they think the future is too full of uncertainties to make the effort worthwhile. Rapidly changing markets, an unpredictable economy, and offsprings' unclear career interests are just a few of the uncertainties they foresee.

But perhaps the greatest threat of all is that planning is associated with change. For business owners, that creates nearly unresolvable dilemmas because of the inherent compromises that change always seems to require. For example, satisfying customers' demand for a new product may require that the business take money from successful projects (with a guaranteed return) and spend it on experimental activities (whose return is unknown). Again, performing the new tasks associated with change forces business owners to spend more time on activities they know less about (and probably perform with less skill). Finally, executing the changes suggested by planning often requires business owners to tailor their products to specific customers in specific markets, thus destroying the "Be All Things to All Customers" principle that guides so many businesses in their early years.

Working through such compromises is painful and, to many business owners, unnecessary. They reason that past successes mean change is not needed. They are understandably reluctant to trade proven theories for ideas that are less sure.

We have summarized these and other objections (along with our rebuttals) as follows:

Objection	*Response*
• Planning is a "straitjacket" that limits flexibility.	• Planning expands options and ability to respond to change.
• Too many uncertainties make planning impossible.	• Planning generates more information and reduces uncertainty through better understanding.
• Planning requires sharing sensitive information with others.	• Planning motivates, increases the ability of the organization to understand how the business performs, and reduces unconstructive guessing as to what is going on.
• Planning makes an owner "go public" with ideas and prohibits him from changing his mind.	• Planning allows others to better understand the need for change; "going public" increases the ability of the organization to reach its goals.
• Planning implies change from the comfortable (and successful) to the uncomfortable (and unknown).	• Planning *anticipates* inevitable change and better *implements* required change.
• Planning often increases "focus" on certain markets at the expense of a broader strategy.	• Planning helps conserve valuable resources.
• Planning suggests changes that may "cannibalize" past success.	• Planning suggests options to minimize that possibility while encouraging the business to compete.
• Planning identifies changes that require moving managers beyond their current skills; therefore, it increases	• Planning helps perpetuate the institution beyond the lives of key managers.

Objection	*Response*
their dependence on others who can contribute or teach those skills.	
• Planning challenges business assumptions that contribute to clarity, consistency, and effectiveness.	• Planning confirms many assumptions while addressing those that must change with the times.

All lead to the same decision: the owner rejects planning in favor of a more intuitive, spur-of-the-moment approach to making decisions. Unfortunately, as the business matures, that approach often strangles the ability of the business to anticipate challenges. Other observers have also noted the lack of business planning by family companies (Christensen, 1953, and Trow, 1961). Lansberg (1985) has even suggested that family businesses, by their very nature, have almost insurmountable incentives to avoid planning. He explains that planning causes key members of the family business to expose themselves to uncomfortable issues. For example, parents and offspring must consider the prospects of succession. Key managers must contemplate a change in organization. And paid outside advisers must risk offending the desires of the president.

Value of Planning

Yet planning expands the options and alternatives that a business can pursue. It allows businessmen and women to anticipate opportunities and pursue potential resources or contacts. Planning also generates new, important information. Its prescribed inquiries are designed to unlock information about and insights into the company and the world in which it operates. If these inquiries are not made, new alternatives might not even be considered, let alone pursued.

The process of planning requires that certain questions be asked of family members and key business managers. Doing this not only yields new ideas but establishes a common understanding of the needs of the business and the pros and cons of alternative business strategies. This increases the organization's ability to accept required changes, such as entry into a new market or revision of current manufacturing systems. It also increases everyone's ability to execute changes. Managers and family members who understand issues and trade-offs are far more likely to successfully implement new programs than those who do not. Such participation also builds commitment, motivation, and a sense of ownership among the key employees and family members.

If formally executed to the fullest degree, this process results in a set of written plans for the business and the family. Yet the real value of planning does not lie with these documents in themselves. Rather, it lies with the mental activity they provoke. The process of planning creates a golden opportunity to *think* amid the daily pressures of business activity. Through planning—one could just as easily call it *strategic thinking*—business owners can deliberate about larger, more abstract issues. Through planning, they can build a common understanding of business and family goals among the key players of each unit. And through planning, they can increase the odds of persuading those players to pull in one direction instead of several. That increases the chances of achieving their goals.

Of course, it is possible for businesses to survive without these revolutions, and without planning. The languishing, no-growth businesses in our life-expectancy research (Table 1) prove it. They managed to "succeed" simply by serving markets that were sheltered from competition in some way or by putting in a great deal of hard work.

But that approach leaves a lot to luck, and luck is much less likely to work in the future. For example, new technologies such as telecommunications, biochemistry, and computers are rapidly altering many methods of production, selling, and distribution. Moreover, competition has increased as traditional boundaries between industries fall; telephone companies branch into computers, soda makers expand into potato chips. The new wave of entrepreneurs (between 600,000 and 700,000 new businesses form every year now in the United States) is further intensifying competition for the buyer's dollar. At the same time, there are fewer of those dollars to go around, since the rate of economic growth in the United States has declined. Finally, participation in a worldwide economy means that standards for competition are globally determined.

The upshot of these trends is that business or product life cycles are shortening dramatically. Once lasting sixty or more years, these cycles, which are created by the laws of supply and demand, have now been reduced to twenty years (Fraker, 1984; Davidson, Bates, and Bass, 1976). They are even briefer in certain high-technology industries. This means that business change in many industries now occurs much more rapidly than in the past. The ability to adapt to such changes, successfully revitalizing or regenerating a business so it thrives from cycle to cycle, will depend on the thought processes sparked by strategic planning and management.

Strategic Thinking and Planning

The strategic planning process, elaborated throughou. this book, recognizes several basic truths. First, the successful business of tomorrow will not look like the successful business of today. Second, forces are already at work influencing the future. Third, actions undertaken today will shape the business of tomorrow.

To address these premises, owners must constantly ask certain questions. This calendar of systematic inquiry provides an organized framework that helps control the destiny of both company and family. As a result, nearly all the general questions involved in planning are as appropriately asked of the *family* situation as of the *business* situation. That means involving both family members and key managers in the planning process and in developing answers to key questions. This reflects a fourth basic truth that we will return to again and again, namely, that family circumstances critically influence the choice of business strategy.

Some readers may be surprised by our insistence that the family be involved in this process. They may subscribe to the popular wisdom that suggests that focusing on the business instead of the family will solve many typical family business problems. And, to be sure, there is some truth to that view. Yet if the company is developed to the *exclusion* of the family, potential problems—and opportunities—may be overlooked. Family members are one of the family business's most important natural strengths. Ignoring them inevitably weakens the business. Lack of consideration of the family's interests can also lead to lack of commitment to the future of the business.

Family plans ensure that the family's interests are taken care of along with those of the business. These plans may begin with something as simple as parents asking children if they are interested in joining the business or asking them what roles they envision for themselves in the company. They may conclude with something as complex as an estate plan, covering the financial interests of all offspring. In this manner, planning helps ensure that both the family and the business recognize critical issues. And it can help the family "regenerate" its leadership along with the business.

For both the family and the business, then, the general questions involved in planning are:

- What are the forces already shaping our business and family?
- How do they influence our current business performance and behavior?
- What has made us successful so far?
- What are the keys to future success?
- What alternative directions might we consider?
- What lessons can we learn from the experiences of other families and businesses in situations similar to ours?
- How should we try to shape our future success? Should we build on our strengths? Attempt to overcome our weaknesses? Take full advantage of our resources? Seize opportunities? Adapt to threats? Exploit our motivations, values, and goals?
- How do we prepare future leadership?

Through family meetings and business planning, the following plans may be developed. They are essential to keeping the family business alive through the generations. Except for the Estate Plan, which we will leave to such legal experts as Becker and Tillman (1978) and Chasman (1983), we will discuss the following plans in detail throughout this book:

1. Plan for Family Participation in the Business:
    • To educate the family about the business and its needs
    • To foster the values of entrepreneurship, savings, and risk and to emphasize the importance of business success to the family
    • To welcome family interest in the future of the business
    • To develop future family leaders
    • To shift leadership from one generation to the next
2. Business Strategic Plan:
    • To address how well the business is performing, where it is going, and how it is going to get there
    • To identify the fundamental assumptions of the business for discussion and monitoring
    • To identify the basic values of the key owners and/or managers that influence the direction of the business
3. Family Strategic Plan:
    • To express the family's commitment to perpetuate the business into the next generation
    • To develop a collective vision of how the family and the business will work together
    • To propose means to encourage future family cooperation and leadership
    • To identify objectives needed to make the plan work
4. Estate Plan:
    • To provide lifetime security for the business owner and his or her spouse
    • To resolve the question of who will share in business ownership and financial growth
    • To specify who controls the business decision-making process
    • To provide continuing challenges and opportunities for those who retire

5. Successors' Leadership Development Plan
    - To prepare the successor or senior team of family managers for business leadership
    - To ensure the successors' ability to effectively promote and revitalize the strategy of the business
    - To provide successors with opportunities to make meaningful contributions and to receive recognition
    - To evaluate successors' performance

Such plans may seem to require an impossible amount of labor. Yet successful multigeneration family business leaders say that such plans are critical to success. They do not see the process of preparing them as complicated or time consuming. Instead they see these plans as an integral part of the management process and, therefore, of the business day—much like budgets and performance reviews. Such leaders tend to be those who have successfully graduated from the role of entrepreneur-as-streetfighter to that of entrepreneur-as-manager. They are no longer motivated purely by action, their days filled with calling on overdue customers, negotiating with suppliers, and telling employees what to do. Instead they are absorbed with the more abstract duties of *managing*: analyzing market strategies, clarifying organizational responsibilities, and leading the assembled management team.

Who Survives and Why: General Strategies

Planning is not the only key to survival, of course. *How* plans are implemented also counts. Readers will recall our study of 200 firms, discussed at the beginning of the chapter (Table 1). The more successful companies in that group exhibited several common traits. We believe that those traits help to explain why some family businesses managed to survive sixty years, while others collapsed in much shorter periods of time. The traits include (1) pruning the family tree, (2) regenerating business strategy, and (3) regenerating business leadership.

Pruning the Family Tree. Some two-thirds of the family

businesses had either stayed at the same number of employees as at the beginning of our survey or had shrunk. This may sound like a lackluster performance, and by some standards it is. But in other ways it is a remarkable achievement, since only 15 percent of the family firms survived at all. These no-growth survivors are even more remarkable because the size of the families involved tended to grow rapidly from generation to generation. This apparent contradiction indicates that these families resisted the temptation to include a large number of family members in the management and ownership of the business. Instead, they "pruned the family tree." They put ownership and management in the hands of a few persons or even just one person. That limited sibling rivalry and subsequent managerial conflicts. It also concentrated the money of the business in the hands of those who directly affected its destiny: a responsibility carrying with it some powerful motivations.

In many cases, families developed this simple ownership structure through sheer luck. They had only one son instead of several, or a bachelor uncle was one of the original business partners. A few, however, deliberately used one or more of the following devices to concentrate management and ownership:

- A tradition of allowing the oldest son to inherit the business
- Financial inducements meant to persuade certain offspring *not* to participate in business ownership
- Creation of independent business units for each child
- Buy-sell options whereby one child agreed to sell his or her share of the business to the other children at some point, perhaps during a period of conflict
- Leveraged buyouts in which those who stayed with the business actually took the risk and raised the capital to do it themselves, yet also continued to provide capital for their parents and/or siblings no longer in the business

Whatever the approach, the result was the same for most of these long-lived companies: the family business was owned by a small number of heirs who actively managed the business. That helped the business survive.

Regenerating the Business's Strategy. Pruning the family tree is one way to keep the company alive. However, there is far more to success than survival. Surviving businesses may last but do not necessarily prosper, especially if they fail to *think strategically* and *plan ahead* and so miss key developments in their markets or manufacturing technology. Such businesses pay a price for these failures. That price is lackluster performance and perennial existence on a no-growth plateau.

Only a handful of family-owned companies in our study (3 percent) went on to prosper, as evidenced by an expansion of their employee base by more than 10 percent between 1924 and 1984. They usually did this by breaking out of the first major growth or profit plateau on which all businesses eventually find themselves. The study was not intended to reveal how each business achieved this. Typically, however, such a breakthrough results from a "strategic regeneration," which alters the character of the business in some way. This could mean expanding into a new geographical territory, adding complementary products, or integrating into retail operations (forward integration) or production (backward integration). Strategic regenerations may even mean branching out into a new business altogether. Most of the time, however, regenerations follow strategies that simply extend past strategies in a logical way. They are sparked by arrival at that initial plateau, which owners interpreted not as a signal of inevitable decline but as a need for new ideas. Consider these typical examples of regenerative efforts:

An umbrella manufacturing business, founded in 1929, had made its owners a comfortable living for about forty years. Suddenly, however, its market was threatened by a flood of imported umbrellas. To recoup, the business—then in the hands of the second generation (the founder's son)—began manufacturing higher-priced designer umbrellas for exclusive department stores. Sales rebounded for several years but eventually slumped when a second wave of less expensive designer umbrellas came onto the market. The founder's grandson, who had just entered the business, then developed yet another strategy: umbrellas as business gifts featuring the corporate name, logo, and colors. The company also began manufacturing and importing beach

and patio umbrellas. This repositioning increased sales sixfold
between 1979 and 1984 (Richman, 1985).

A ninety-seven-year-old bottle distributor had its humble
beginnings with one man who collected used bottles (bottles
were costly at the time) door-to-door for resale to breweries and
other large users. The founder's sons entered the business and
seized the opportunity to act as distributors between leading
bottle manufacturers and dozens of local breweries. Later, the
company began distributing plastic containers—a move implemented by a third-generation son. Each incarnation of the company brought a new surge of sales and profit. The latest twist,
generated by the founder's great-grandson, involves supplying
plastic spray bottles to mass retail merchandisers for marketing
to consumers (Posner, 1985).

A food service distributor began in the early 1900s with
its founder selling fresh fish to restaurants off the docks of an
Eastern seaport. The business grew and prospered. Then the second generation, observing the "new technology" of refrigera-
tion during World War II, outfitted storage facilities with cool-
ing equipment. They began distributing fresh fish and then
frozen vegetables to restaurants. Such moves were also successful. The next generation expanded the product line to include
a full line of dry, fresh, and frozen food products. That generation also moved the business into three new states, taking full
advantage of the economies of a large warehouse and the trend
toward eating away from home.

These examples illustrate several common tendencies.
One, business ownership and management remained in a few
hands. Two, new strategies continually emerged after periods of
slow or no growth. Finally, these strategies not only logically
extended past business activities but also responded to changing
times.

Regenerating Leaders. Astute readers will have noted another parallel in these examples. In each of the businesses discussed above, the strategic "regenerations" were accomplished
as new leadership took over the business. This is quite possibly
the most important lesson that successful family businesses
teach: the need to combine strategic revolutions with changes

in leaders, be they sons, daughters, or outside managers (Hershon, 1975; Miller, 1982). These new leaders, arriving every twenty to twenty-five years or so, naturally bring their own ideas to the business. They have the passion to contribute and are more willing to challenge traditional assumptions than are their elders. As a result, they are capable of bringing the business to new heights.

Preparing new family leadership to revitalize corporate strategy is thus a critical dimension of continuing growth and profitability. To be sure, this approach has its risks. Perhaps the new blood coming into the business will be less capable than the old. New territories may not prove as fruitful as expected. Expansion costs can chew up profit. Yet when the inevitable challenges are addressed, the combination of fresh leadership and new directions seems almost unbeatable. It appears to be the key to keeping the family business alive through the years.

Proper planning helps achieve this. For planning provides the conceptual framework needed to successfully combine the needs of the business with the needs of the family. It provides opportunities for successors to learn the business, and it identifies the strategic needs and opportunities for the future.

Why Take on the Challenge of Perpetuation?

When businesses are founded, they are rarely conceived of as "family businesses." Instead, they are typically expressions of an entrepreneur's desire for independence. He or she views it as "my business" or "my company." The family, while a source of support and perhaps even of employees, remains in the background. Yet there eventually comes a time when these same entrepreneurs yearn to leave their business as a legacy to their children. That dream usually begins to form when their sons and daughters enter their teen-age years, ask questions about the business, perhaps begin to work in it part time. The dream becomes more compelling as the business owner matures, and failing to achieve it becomes highly painful. "Letting go of my business is like losing a member of the family," said one seventy-two-year-old Vermont retailer just a few hours after he

had sold his store to a large retailing chain. Previously he had
dreamed of bringing his four daughters into the business. Yet at
the critical moment, none were ready. He had not groomed a
successor. And at seventy-two, he was past the point of trying
(Gilman, 1985).

Why do business owners eventually so yearn to pass on
the family business? We asked that question of seventy-five family business owners and spouses who were working hard to ensure family perpetuation of their businesses (Ward, 1986a). The
results of our survey are outlined in Table 2. Many of these rea-

Table 2. Why Perpetuate the Family Business?

(34%)	1.	Pass on opportunity to children
		• Provide opportunity for freedom, control of their destiny, and autonomy
		• Provide opportunity for personal growth, creativity, and expression
(21%)	2.	Perpetuate heritage
		• Build tradition, history, and roots
		• Create living memorial
(15%)	3.	Keep family together
		• Help family work together
		• Strengthen family bond
		• Allow more family time together
(10%)	4.	Generate financial advantages and wealth
(8%)	5.	Ensure own retirement and personal purpose past sixty-five
(6%)	6.	Protect loyal employees
(5%)	7.	Provide family with financial security
(1%)	8.	Benefit society

sons indicate a belief that the family business benefits the family. Founders felt that their children, by entering the business,
could enjoy the same opportunity for freedom and growth that
they had had. Or they saw the business as a way to perpetuate
the family's tradition and business heritage.

We believe that a family business offers many other defi-
nite advantages, aside from the reasons given in our survey:

• A sense of identity ("that's our name on the truck delivering
  goods to the church!") and family pride

- Common family interests and interaction
- Opportunity to develop future family leadership
- Living evidence of the family's potential power of working together
- Security to take chances in other careers or ventures
- Opportunity for philanthropy
- Excuse to begin developing family goals and plans
- Great "educational" opportunities for family—to meet and work with many kinds of people
- Opportunity to stress and demonstrate the values of sacrifice, saving, investment, and risk

Whatever the reason, the desire to pass on the family business has never been more compelling. The numerous businesses founded in the wake of World War II are now coming of age along with their founders; they are becoming available just as hordes of college graduates have come to consider careers as "entrepreneurs" more challenging than many others. Thousands of families now attend seminars and courses on family business succession at trade association meetings, business groups, and universities. Those institutions that have begun offering regular seminars and courses in family enterprises just in the last few years include Harvard University, Loyola University of Chicago, the University of Pennsylvania, the University of Southern California, and Yale University.

Planning to successfully perpetuate the family business also benefits society as a whole. According to the U.S. Small Business Administration, four million small businesses in this country (excluding farms) provide nearly half of our eighty-eight million jobs. They create nearly two-thirds of all new jobs, and they produce two and a half times as many innovations as large firms on a per capita employed basis (Small Business Administration, 1983b). Other studies (American Institute of Certified Public Accountants, 1984) suggest that smaller companies are more likely to employ women, younger people, older people, and part-time employees. Since the vast majority of family businesses are also small businesses, we can safely assume that family businesses make many of these same contributions.

Family businesses are less likely to uproot employees. They will probably stay—at least geographically—right where they started. The owning families typically join local church boards, temple boards, hospital boards, school boards, and charities, contributing in important ways to the stability and well-being of the local community. Family-owned businesses also more consistently invest their money for long-term returns, according to our research into some 300 similarly sized public and private concerns (Ward, 1983). They are not pressed by the need to show stellar earnings each quarter—a need that often forces publicly owned companies to sacrifice future gains for short-term results.

Family businesses are also essential to our free enterprise system. They add the economic and political diversity that makes the system strong. And they exemplify the economic principle of private property, the political principle of pluralism, and the social principle of family. As the English statesman Edmund Burke is credited with saying: "The power of perpetuating our property in our families is one of the most valuable and interesting circumstances belonging to it, and that which tends the most to the preservation of society itself."

Summary

Strategic planning involves more than just a thoughtful review of business problems. Over the past ten to fifteen years, corporate leaders and researchers have developed valuable insights into what planning actually involves and the ways in whch it leads to business success. These insights offer family businesses guidance on how to think about their challenges. They are based primarily on three propositions about business behavior and performance:

1. Most businesses follow predictable, evolutionary life cycles.
2. It is possible to learn a great deal from the experiences of other businesses and families.
3. The culture of the family business—its leadership and its organization—influences the achievements of the business far more than any other factor.

These propositions form the core concepts of this book. In the following pages we will explore the barriers to long-term health that face almost all mature family businesses. We will share the lessons of other families and businesses through empirical research and observation. We will demonstrate how personal values and family goals eventually shape the alternatives that family businesses consider and the decisions that they make. This leads to the ultimate management challenge: keeping the family business healthy into the next generation and beyond, while bringing it to new heights of sales and profit. Few things are more rewarding than that. And in the end, nothing will strengthen the family more.

TWO

Overcoming Barriers to Long-Term Business Health

A healthy company is the foundation of family business continuity, and long-term health is based on the ability to anticipate and respond to change. Specific changes vary with each industry, of course. But certain developmental changes are common to most businesses. They are triggered by forces that are a natural part of the evolution of the family-owned business; these forces steer each company through a predictable pattern of growth and change. These include developments in (1) the nature of the business, (2) the character of the organization, (3) the motivations of the owner-manager, (4) family financial expectations, and (5) family goals.

Changes in these areas have implications for manufacture of the company's product as markets mature; managing the business as it grows in size and complexity; leading the business through the owner's own maturation; satisfying the increasing number of claims upon the company's financial resources; and balancing the demands of family and business. These implications are illustrated in Table 3, which sets forth the natural stages of growth experienced by family companies, whether they are manufacturing or service concerns.

This developmental model is particularly descriptive of an entrepreneurial business in its early stages. But its underlying principles also pertain to the more mature family business that chooses to enter a period of regeneration (see Chapter One). This is a period when new leaders bring new strategies to the business.

The model suggests that there is a great deal of *consis-*

Table 3. Stages of Family Business Evolution.

	Stages		
	I	II	III
Timing (in years):			
Age of Business (or Business Renewal)	0 to 5	10 to 20	20 to 30
Age of Parents	25 to 35	40 to 50	55 to 70
Age of Children	0 to 10	15 to 25	30 to 45
Challenges:			
Nature of Business:	Rapidly growing and demanding of time and money	Maturing	Needing strategic "regeneration" and reinvestment
Character of Organization:	Small, dynamic	Larger and more complex	Stagnant
Owner-Manager Motivation:	Committed to business success	Desires control and stability	Seeks new interests or is "semiretired"; next generation seeks growth and change
Family Financial Expectations:	Limited to basic needs	More needs, including comfort and education	Larger needs, including security and generosity
Family Goals:	Business success	Growth and development of children	Family harmony and unity

tency between the needs of the business and the needs of the family in Stage I. However, by the time Stage III appears, the two units are in considerable *conflict*. This inevitable contradiction and conflict between the needs of the business and those of the family is a special barrier to long-term business health for family companies. Resolving that conflict in ways that meet the needs of both family and business is the aim of family business planning.

Business Life Cycle

As we have just indicated, successful family businesses pass through evolutionary stages of development. One force behind these stages is the product life cycle (Salter, 1970; Peiser and Wooten, 1983; Adizes, 1979; Greiner, 1972). Each stage changes the nature of the business. Therefore, each stage demands a new style of management and strategic emphasis.

The movement from stage to stage is driven by many forces. These forces combine the influences of the product life cycle (Kotler, 1976) and the industry's evolution (Porter, 1980). They include market growth and size, competitive entry and aggression, and the customer's desires and sophistication. These forces are unavoidable. No business owner, no matter how successful, is beyond their influence.

The cycle begins when the business is young or in the early phases of its regeneration. Its product or service is then new. If it is a good product or service, customers will want it. Competition is limited, and keen demand keeps supply short and, as a rule, prices high. But as the idea gains acceptance, competitors enter the market. They begin to siphon off customers as they expand their capacity to serve the growing market. And as competition intensifies, everyone attempts to identify more precisely what the customer wants and needs.

Meanwhile, customers grow more sophisticated. They begin to realize that they have choices among various producers who can be pitted against each other. Eventually, the market's rate of growth declines as more of the customers' needs are met and as competitors begin to serve more of the market potential.

Customers become even more demanding, and competitive battles increase.

To put all this another way, early in the life of a business, demand in the marketplace exceeds supply. Consequently, prices and margins are high, and competitive demands are low. Later, however, as the market matures and competition appears, supply begins to exceed demand. Prices and margins narrow. Customer and competitive demands increase. In order to improve its competitive abilities, each business adds considerable capital investment to decrease costs and increase output. Consequently, fixed costs increase as margins decline, and the break-even point becomes much higher than when the business began. Eventually, some competitors fail or exit. "Better mousetraps," created by new entrepreneurs or established entrepreneurial companies, appear on the scene. And a new business life cycle begins.

This final phase of intense competition and market exits is particularly trying for family businesses. That is because family businesses are very likely to populate industries made up of many other family businesses: industries such as printing or machine tooling. Usually these companies have only one business interest or line. And usually, their owners want to keep them alive as long as possible in order to permit participation by family members and protect loyal employees. In short, mature family businesses are reluctant to close down. When such reluctance permeates an entire industry, competition becomes fierce indeed. This intensifies the consequences of decline in the business life cycle.

The length of this cycle varies by industry. Typically, business cycles are about twenty years long for the kinds of industries that attract family businesses—retailing, wholesaling-distribution, service, and component manufacturing. Yet as we noted in the last chapter, this twenty-year-cycle is likely to shorten due to technological change, the increasing number of competitors, and global standards for competition. Thus, emerging family business leaders will probably witness two or more life cycles during their time at the helm.

As the market, competitors, and customers change, the

nature of the business will also change. Owners should therefore consider revising their approaches to products, pricing, distribution, marketing, selling, promotion, production, and operations. In short, they should consider revising their business
strategies (see Table 4). The following tale from the twenty-first
century illustrates strategies suited to early, middle, and late
stages of the business cycle and exemplifies the sort of changes
managers may be required to make as their businesses evolve.

Early Stage

Let us say that you have developed a fantas-
tic concept: the first garage-sized vehicle for solo
space travel, the so-called SpaceJet. Customers who
have lusted for the moon all these years are agog.
You spend nights scheming in your basement
workshop. You spend days calling on potential accounts, advertisers, and product designers. You
hone your sales pitch: yes, space travel is safe, no,
you will not explode as you return to earth. Orders
mount. You estimate that as soon as you hoist
your project off the basement floor and onto an as-
sembly line, sales will spurt ahead some 30 to 50
percent annually, even after adjustment for inflation.

At this point, you have no competitors and
no other products. What you do have, for all its
glamour, is a relatively unsophisticated product
that you have knocked together with your own
sweat. Your sole mission in life is to spread the gos-
pel of solo space travel. You do. You gain converts,
build a little manufacturing plant, and start chum-
ing out SpaceJets. Demand exceeds supply. Sales
soar. Profits start to flow.

Middle Stage

Because yours is a good idea, others soon decide they can turn out a better or cheaper model.
New versions of the SpaceJet develop—versions

that do not lose that troublesome rear rocket in a rough tailwind, as yours often does. Competition sets in. Copycats flourish. Price wars develop. People are suddenly selling solo spaceships like cars. Now you spend your nights searching for a little segment of the market—the market *you* created—that you can still have to yourself. You craft new advertising campaigns. You tell your advertising firm to ditch the plaid polyester astrosuits for black silk mooncapes. You put little ornaments on the SpaceJet's hood. You offer free tanks of oxygen with every sale. Instead of seeking to sell to the world, you seek special customer groups: government officials or the over-sixty crowd with retirement homes on Mars. You struggle to cut production costs and increase the efficiency of your distribution. For all your efforts, however, sales still slow. Your accountant charts figures that show growth of no more than 10 percent annually.

Late Stage

Still more competitors enter the fray, from places you had never dreamed of as a cellar visionary. Japan, Germany, Brazil—all of a sudden you are buffeted by a world market. So is everybody else. Substitutes are even developing; the Space-Traveller, for example, installed right in your jetport, can beam a body up in the twinkling of an eye. The market is flooded with your product. SpaceJets gather dust on used jet lots. Sales decline. Competitors begin to crumble. You decide to hang in there, but it is clear that a simplified product, targeted to a few key customer groups, is your only hope. You sell now chiefly to senior citizens and honeymooners who want to travel slowly, as they did in years gone by, gazing at the stars.

Maturity has struck.

And you begin to dream of new ideas.

Table 4. Strategic Implications of Business Life Cycle.

	Early	Middle	Late
Product	Full line of price points and styles	Improved and new products	Product line simplification and standardization; emphasis on "spares and repairs" and after-market
	"Debug" product and educate customer	Customize product and respond to customer	Respond to competitors' product
	Easily identifiable packaging	Fresh packaging to attract attention	Efficient packaging to minimize costs
Price	Fair, stable price	Defensive pricing	Maintain margins even at expense of volume
Distribution	Gain first distributors	Gain more intensive, extensive distribution; build incentives and loyalty	Be more selective, efficient in distribution
	Rent logistical support (for example, trucks)	Own logistical support	Rent logistical support
Marketing	Heavy personal selling, personal service, and word-of-mouth advertising	Fresh promotional efforts; more use of media	Consistent, efficient mass marketing
	Build strong brand image	Stress product improvements, new products, and style	Stress competitive advantages—maybe comparative advertising
	Promote that product through public relations and personal appearances	Promote product availability, usage, frequency, and new users	Target heavy, large users—private label
	Encourage trial of product or service	Segment market	Redefine and consolidate market into fewer segments
	Build sales force	Target sales force to high-potential accounts	Gain more sales per salesman

Product Operation

Sales force commissioned to penetrate market	Sales force salaried and trained to be "professional"	Sales efforts and rewards re-organized to maximize efficient
Market research to learn product weaknesses and rate of product acceptance	Market research to learn how to forecast sales and segment market	Market research on competitive moves and strengths and weaknesses
Cope with crises and changing product design	Gain economies of scale	Keep fixed capacity busy
Get product out on time	Gear production to demand forecasts	Make product as simply and homogeneously as possible
Stress high and consistent quality	Get faster production, stress labor efficiency, remove production bottlenecks	Look for materials substitution and stress operating efficiency
Job shop system likely	Batch shop system or assembly line likely	Mass production system likely
Seek timely supply of raw materials or components	Control finished goods to market demand	Minimize finished and work-in-process inventories
Seek multiple suppliers—possibly put some in business	Backward integrate as possible	Subcontract as possible

The lessons of Table 4 and the preceding example may be summarized as follows:

First, within the business life cycle, make adjustments. As a product or service matures in the marketplace, changes will be required to keep pace with customer demands. The product itself may need alteration, or perhaps prices should be changed. Distribution, marketing, and operational systems may require development.

Second, between cycles, regenerate the business. Because of competitive forces, virtually every product and service will reach a point of decline. At that point, the business absolutely requires renewal if it is to continue growing. This renewal may require significant reinvestment in the company; that, in turn, often requires advance planning to ensure that the reinvestment is made in the right areas.

Third, develop the necessary managerial skills to accomplish these tasks or assign them to successors. As a product matures and the industry evolves, business owners must deal with tougher competition and more demanding customers. They will probably have to renegotiate relationships and arrangements with suppliers, customers, distributors, and employees, particularly the sales force. They must also orient themselves more toward marketing and less toward manufacture of their product. This includes the realization that marketing covers more than mere selling; it includes determining customers' changing needs, addressing those needs through advertising and promotion, and anticipating competitors' actions.

But no matter how obvious these needs are, many business owners and entrepreneurs will resist meeting them. They loved the aggressive excitement of the early days; now, as they must move more defensively and plan more systematically, many lose the enjoyment they once took in business activities. Hence, the solution for many companies will lie in the next generation. In such cases, successors will be the ones to foster a new business life cycle. They will be the ones to develop the organization professionally. Business owners who accept this potential contribution are likely to have an easier time handing responsibility over to the next generation. Since the contributions of each generation are clearly recognized, power struggles are more easily avoided.

Organizational Life Cycle

As an industry and its products evolve through their life cycle, so too will the way in which businesses within the industry are organized. Methods of organization evolve partly because growth requires more employees. But they also evolve because bigger, more mature businesses are simply more complex than fledgling ones. They are likely to have a greater variety of products and customers and, as a result, to require different managerial skills. With these developments also come more stable and formal commitments to the people who work within the organization. That means changes in managerial style, too.

At any stage, management is a process to ensure the effectiveness and efficiency of an organization. Its tools include:

- Setting goals
- Directing organizational forces or attention
- Determining who makes what kinds of decisions
- Structuring the organization
- Selecting measures of performance
- Establishing reward systems
- Deciding how to control for results

But the way in which these tools are applied must develop as the organization matures, as outlined in Table 5. In the early days of the business, for example, its rapidly changing character and small size not only *permit* but *require* more flexibility and personal, hands-on control from the business owner. At this stage, the company is the classic one-man show. Gradually, however, its increasing size will require that the owner do more and more managing through subordinates. This shift from direct to indirect management requires the development of information systems, performance review systems, budgets, policies, compensation systems, and so on. Owners will perceive

Table 5. Managing During the Different Stages of Organizational Development.

	Early	Middle	Late
Goals	Survival and flexibility	Cost control and stability	Market control and organizational efficiency
Focus of Attention	The owner	Team building and market needs	External needs—technology, suppliers, substitutes, competitors
Degree of Decentralization	None	Operating decisions decentralized	Some strategic decisions decentralized
What Decisions Made by Owner	All, including technical decisions	Strategic and human relations decisions	Mostly strategic decisions
Organizational Structure and Communications	Informal		Formal
Performance Measures	Sales objectives: volume and orders	Operating objectives: budget vs. past; actual vs. plan	Strategic objectives: investment returns and market share
Rewards	Subjective, individualistic, and changing		Objective, formal, and uniform
Control Systems	Cash flow	Budgets and forecasts	Asset utilization, strategic planning, and setting of strategic objectives

changes in many dimensions of their organizations, including methods of coordination and communication. They will likely sense a loss of personal power over employees' behavior. They will probably no longer know everyone's family and individual circumstances or even everyone's name. Formalization of management will have set in.

These developments become pronounced only as an organization grows past thirty to forty employees, as a noted by social scientists for more than a century (McNeill, 1968). That is when effective informal communication begins to suffer and when the organization needs to replace the leadership of a powerful individual with the leadership of powerful management systems. Managerial talent lies in the ability to accomplish this transition from one stage to the next. But this is not an easy shift to accomplish, as data from the Small Business Administration (1983a) affirm. Its studies show that there is a rapid drop-off in the number of businesses past the twenty-employee mark.

Number of Employees	1 to 4	5 to 19	20 to 49	50 to 99	100 to 499	500 plus
Number of Businesses (in thousands)	2,300	1,200	300	100	65	15

Why is the shift so difficult to make? As we have already noted, some business owners and entrepreneurs simply may not possess the new skills that more sophisticated management requires. But it is also because the very success of past management practices seems to preclude the changes that growth demands. Business owners' efforts to delegate power is a good example of this. Early on, owners make all the important decisions. Consequently, employees neither gain experience in making decisions themselves nor feel responsible for doing so. Thus, when owners first try to delegate decisions, failure is almost certain. Often they compound their troubles by expecting success too soon and too dramatically; they do not coach and encourage employees as they should. Nor are they consistent in their delegations. Employees are therefore reluctant to assume authority, correctly fearing that the owners may resent their presumption. As employees continue to turn to the boss for guidance and resolution of problems, owners find it increasingly difficult to deflect inquiries back to them, that is, to allow employees to struggle with their own decisions and even to make some mistakes.

Hiring and promotion practices are other good examples of the way past successes sometimes beget future troubles. Early in the life of businesses, owners often hire their peers: people of similar age whom they consider talented or whom they like. Early business victories confirm their judgment. But since they continue to promote from within, often on the basis of loyalty, those whom they promote eventually reach their managerial limit. These early employees have little experience in managing a larger organization, and they frequently have little skill in effecting change. Their decisions might then reflect their inexperience. And yet business owners, loyal to them, rarely move to fire them or to bring fresh talent into senior positions.

Stagnant Organizations

As these managerial issues accumulate, the rate of growth of the business begins to slow due to the natural evolution of the product cycle. As a result, the rate of new hiring also begins to decline. Since the owner's earlier personnel practices have likely made the organization top-heavy with older, trained-in-the-business managers, there is now little opportunity to hire ambitious new employees for fast-track promotions to the upper ranks. The age distribution of management thus makes the organization look like an inverted pyramid—many more oldsters at the top than youngsters at the bottom—instead of like the normal pyramid one would usually want to see (Figure 1). Typically, the inverted pyramid is found in a stagnant organization. Such an organization finds it difficult to develop new ideas or to generate the excitement so necessary for business success.

Stagnant organizations exhibit other symptoms, too. In most of them, the owners have many people reporting to them,

Figure 1. Age Profile of Organizational Hierarchy.

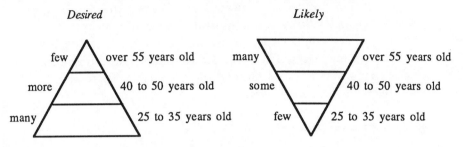

but these people, in turn, receive very few direct reports themselves. This means that owners must spend too much time digesting reports and too little time on tasks critical to the organization's development—tasks such as coaching, thinking strategically, and studying the market. It also usually means that they have not developed two or three outstanding people who can replace them in a crisis. Nor will they develop those people for the future. Their immediate subordinates get too little management experience.

More than likely, in this kind of company few employees will be offered positions in other firms. That is a bad sign. A company should pride itself on developing people good enough to attract offers from others. But if good managers leave not because they are offered better jobs but because they are frustrated with lack of upward mobility and progress, chances are they have been working for a stagnant organization. Companies should regularly review their organization for symptoms of such stagnation. Adizes (1979) suggests that a good way to begin is merely to observe the office setting for a few minutes. In the early stages of a business, for example, employees may dress casually in shirt-sleeves and greet one another by nicknames. In the later and potentially stagnant stage, managers tend to wear three-piece suits and address one another much more formally.

Organizational stagnation is quite destructive. Stagnation slows the ability of a business to adapt to new market conditions and leaves the next generation without a well-developed management team for the future. The large proportion of older managers makes it difficult to implement new standards, new reward systems, and new expectations. Stagnation creates low turnover, which allows few opportunities to hire people with new perspectives and experiences. And it makes mobility low for younger managers. That precludes rapid promotion and frequent changes in responsibilities, which are essential to the development of these managers.

What the Family Business Can Do

To avoid such stagnation requires a good deal of attention and advance planning by business owners. They must stop long enough to think about how to organize their companies. This so-called "pause" is difficult to achieve, especially in the early stages when growth is rampant. But owners must persuade themselves to invest time in developing the organizational systems and management superstructure. *Their chief goal should be to give the organization a longer life than that of any of its managers.* The managerial tasks of this "pause" are very specific. They include:

Establishing Formal Management Systems. Such systems direct, reward, evaluate, and inform people. Without these systems a manager is unable to control the total organization.

Delegating Authority. As such systems are established, employees' responsibilities will expand. They will need more authority to do their jobs. The owners' task, once they have delegated authority, is to coach those managers now acting in their stead.

Hiring New Employees from Outside. One of the hallmarks of a well-run, well-managed mid-sized company is a group of younger, highly competent, and up-and-coming employees. This group serves two roles. Early on, they act as peers of the owner's offspring, competing against them for recognition and stimulating their development. Later, they will become candidates for the offspring's own management team. The existence of such a group enables successors to look within the company to fill key positions.

Developing a Senior Manager to Replace President in Emergencies. This temporary successor should be accustomed to broad responsibilities, which in turn should qualify him for a number of other roles. For example, his skill and authority may make him an excellent mentor for the owner's offspring. Or he may be qualified to serve as a nonfamily interim president between family generations—an excellent tactic if offspring are not yet ready to assume the presidency.

Business owners can come up with a number of arguments against this "pause." They like fast-growth action; time spent managing may seem like time lost to the real business of the company. But eventually the pause will be mandatory for the organization. Carrying it out successfully means compounding growth—growth through the efforts of all employees, not just growth that results from the owner's personal energy. But this effort requires a different set of skills from those needed to start a business. And business owners who wait until stagnation forces the development of these skills will find the task extremely difficult. Then they will need to reignite the company with exciting new visions and plans. Their primary job will be selling the organization on new aspirations and expectations. But they may find it difficult to do this because of the older cadre of employees that has formed within the organization.

Owners may handle this group in any one of several ways. They may, for example, simply wait to make any major moves until the older employees retire. Typically, many leave at about the same time, allowing for the hiring and promotion of new managers. The price owners will pay for such delay, however, is that simultaneous departures among top people tend to destabilize a company. And this natural attrition may come too late in the life cycle of the company for it to be saved. A new spurt of business growth is a second way to create new opportunities for people. While this alternative is ideal, it is available all too infrequently. Finally, an owner can make the difficult decision to retire some senior managers, thus making room for outsiders at the middle-management level. For most family business owners, this means taking a tough, critical look at managers in their forties and fifties and deciding whether they should become permanent members of the organization. In fact, however, releasing people who are past the fifty-year mark is rarely an acceptable choice to most business owners.

Business Owner's Life Cycle

The character of individual business owners profoundly affects the company's future. Their values will significantly shape the business strategy (Andrews, 1980; Steiner, 1969) and will also be reflected in the organization's own personality, priorities, and beliefs. This intricate, symbiotic relationship between chief executives and their companies is made even more complex by the fact that executives' values, even their personalities, will change as they age (Levinson, 1978). As a result, so will the values and personalities of their organizations.

Nowhere is this more true than in the family business, where ownership and leadership are often synonymous and traditions are deeply entrenched. And nowhere are the effects of organizational change—stemming from changes in the business owner himself—more powerful. A family business ordinarily represents most of the owner's assets. This tightly links the owner's personal financial needs to the decisions he or she makes for the business. Furthermore, in most family businesses, the owner serves as president for a very long time. The average tenure of the president in a privately held company is likely to be twenty to thirty years, three to four times longer than that of his or her counterpart in a publicly held company. That is more than enough time for him or her to grow and change. Consequently, the family business will be deeply influenced by the owner's personal development over the years. As business owners mature, several dimensions of their characters will influence their companies: (1) their personal management skills, (2) their leadership style, and (3) their motivations.

Management Skills

As we noted earlier, beginning a business requires different managerial skills from those needed for running an established concern. In fact, one could argue that these two sets of skills are almost the opposite of one another, as the following list indicates:

Entrepreneurial/ *Growth Stage*	*Larger/* *Maturing Stage*
• Innovative decisions	• Responsive decisions
• Bold new strategies	• Fine tuning of current strategy
• Personal, hands-on involvement	• Manage through other managers
• Deal with tangible results	• Deal with intangible, abstract results
• Lead by action	• Lead by philosophy
• Take big personal risks	• Take repetitive, small risks through others
• Stress utilitarian, practical values	• Stress perceptions
• Develop new relationships	• Renegotiate old relationships
• Personally identify with every activity	• Analyze activity through information reports

In the best of all possible worlds, effective managers would be strong in both sets of skills and attitudes: those needed in the entrepreneurial, growth stage and those needed in the larger, maturing stage. Realistically, however, people have only so many abilities. Any given manager will likely be stronger in one set of skills than in the other. This can lead to difficulties as managers try to move their businesses from one phase to the next. Superior entrepreneurial skills may cover up managerial weaknesses until the business begins to mature and margins tighten. Moreover, in the early phase of a business, the tasks that excite owners and the tasks necessary for the business are often one and the same. Later, this will not be so.

Of course, this generalization is not true in every case. We have seen many successful entrepreneurs make the transition, becoming excellent managers and enjoying the challenges of that stage as much as those of the early stage. In fact, as Drucker (1985) suggests, it is possible that the better the manager, the more likely he or she is to be an entrepreneur in the first place!

The important question, therefore, is this: Why are some entrepreneurs better able to overcome the limitations of their interests and skills than others? Why do some business owners call a halt when their companies reach the twenty-employee mark, while others keep marching on?

It seems that there are three reasons. First, some new businesses have such powerful strategies—and thus grow so fast and so strongly—that managerial skills are not a key factor. In such businesses, the entrepreneur has no choice but to hire a large number of people, fast, merely to keep up with orders. Before the entrepreneur realizes the full extent of the managerial talent this growth requires, he has a group of good managers already in place. These business owners never had much of a chance to reflect on what they were losing through the lack of tight personal control. They were working too hard just to keep up! And fortunately, they had the good sense—the good faith and commitment—to hire very bright, motivated people and to trust them to grow into their positions.

A second characteristic that distinguishes entrepreneurs who have made the transition of large organizations is their enthusiasm for problem solving and decision making. They get greater enjoyment from tackling managerial challenges than from tackling marketing or production challenges. This enthusiasm for "improving the business" is the mark of a well-rounded manager, not of a bold inventor. And it suggests that as far as business success is concerned, *it is far more important to be an entrepreneurial manager with a marginal product than to be an entrepreneurial inventor with only marginal management skills.*

The third distinguishing characteristic of entrepreneurs who become enthusiastic managers of large, complex organizations is a philosophic vision of the future. This vision goes far beyond the dream of a successful product or service, and it has little to do with money. These leaders want to show the world how to manage things better, how to motivate people better, how to revolutionize an industry, or even how to achieve some religious or social purpose. These entrepreneurs have something to prove. Their ideals are much larger than the perceived potential market of their original product or service, and their visions are bright enough to lead the company through difficult times.

Business owners who do not share or develop these three traits will predictably reach a point when they ask themselves, "Why can't I find someone to run the day-to-day operations, manage people, deal with organizational issues? Why can't I find someone to do this so I can spend my time doing what I'm good at, and what I really like to do?"

Thus begins the search for a general manager: a surrogate who will make the managerial leap the owners themselves are unwilling to make. Ideally, this person would already be working in the company. He or she would be trusted by the owner and would be knowledgeable about the business and its needs. But this alternative is rarely available. Typically, no managers have been trained to cross functional boundaries and assume other managerial roles. Most top-level managers have simply risen through the ranks in a single area—for example, from street sales to sales management to marketing—and have never performed such alternate duties as personnel or plant management. Therefore, no one manager has the breadth of experience necessary to oversee the entire company.

Even if such cross training has occurred and well-rounded managers are in place, owners are often reluctant to promote them. They fear that recognizing one top lieutenant over the rest would demoralize other senior managers. They also know their employees' weaknesses from their years of working together. They think of all the things these employees cannot do. And then they think, longingly, of finding the perfect candidate from the outside.

But this attitude also paves the way for disappointment. The owner's expectations may be quite high, but the amount of cooperation that such an outsider gets from other senior managers may be quite low. Loyal vice-presidents are not pleased to have a new layer of management between them and their owner/friend. Business owners themselves have little experience filling this role and delegating responsibility. They have hired a general manager because they wanted freedom from organizational demands; instead, they find themselves faced with a new set of demands. First, they must spend time managing the general manager. Second, they become more clearly responsible for the specific new activities they undertake. The result, more often than not, is failure. The new general manager is fired, and the owner sadly returns to his or her old post. He or she may then launch a second outside search or may now look within the company for a replacement.

The fact that the pool of internal candidates is not particularly promising sparks the realization that the company must develop more general managers from within. That means giving present managers more authority. In this manner do business owners, now typically in their fifties, finally acknowledge that they must "let go" of the business in order to give employees room to develop. They are helped in this realization by a growing desire to leave daily duties behind, as well as by the growing need of successors to assume responsibility. The central question for the owner now becomes, "How far should I pull away from my business?"

But once again, the owner is in for disappointment. The forces propelling him or her toward this question usually push him too far for too long. He takes a four-month vacation in Florida, saying that he is going into "semiretirement." Or he establishes his office "downtown." But unless he has laid the proper groundwork for his departure, the organization will feel a sudden void. Typically, the owner gives too little guidance to the person who takes his place; just as typically, he expresses great dissatisfaction with his replacement's performance when he returns. Having thoroughly disrupted the company, he may then decide to take back his old job on a permanent basis.

Leadership Style

Despite these and other common mistakes, business owners who stay with their companies over the years also learn valuable lessons that increase their effectiveness. These influence their leadership style, that is, the manner in which they deal with the company's middle and upper managers.

One lesson an owner learns, for example, is that ambiguity has many advantages. Effective chief executive officers "make an art of imprecision and vagueness in their announced goals," notes one expert on the behavior of such officers (Quinn, 1980, p. 98). At the same time, they know very well where they want the organization to go. Such vagueness has several benefits for business owners. Ambiguity gives them the freedom not to be nailed down. It allows them to avoid detailed challenges from subordinates: there is, simply, nothing tangible to challenge. It permits all employees to think that their jobs are the most important ones, and it also keeps people from forming alliances on a particular issue that would make new ideas difficult to implement (Isenberg, 1984). (Fortunately for entrepreneurs, this skill at maintaining ambiguity comes easily. Entrepreneurs, according to Schere, 1982, thrive on ambiguity. It is one of the few empirically proven personality characteristics typical of this group.)

A second lesson owners learn is that it is often best to allow decisions to "make themselves with time." Sometimes, the need to make a decision simply goes away. Some decisions are better not ever made, and some decisions are better made later as new information develops. The advantage of being patient is obvious: Owners can let certain critical issues lose their sharp edges.

Valuable as both these lessons are, however, they do carry a price. The disadvantage of using these tactics—ambiguity and taking time to make decisions—is that they give the impression that the business owner is in doubt about the direction of the company. This is troubling to the managers who work for him or her. It is especially troubling because it is in such sharp contrast to the decisiveness of the early days, when the owner's goals were clearer and decisions more immediate. Managers conclude, in many cases erroneously, that the company lacks direction.

Business Owner's Motivations

During the owner's twenty to thirty years at the top, his sources of motivation will change. Success, age, and a maturing family all work together to engineer a shift in the forces that drive him. Early on, for example, the owner is fully involved in his business idea. He wants only to be proved right. Much later, when that need has been satisfied, he is instead motivated by a desire to contribute to society, to ensure family security, and to leave a legacy of generosity.

Such a shift has powerful implications for the family business. Its owner may wish to devote an increasing amount of time, energy, and even money to social, cultural, or professional associations within the industry. In addition, the owner may increasingly want to treat all his offspring equally and give each of them more and more chances to achieve success. Stability and family fairness become critical goals. This means, for example, that he may grant all siblings the title of vice-president whether their contributions merit the title or not. It means he may refuse a nonfamily manager a promotion for fear his offspring would perceive it as a shift in power or authority. In his heart, the business owner may hope that such actions will make up for the many years of inattention to his family—the years that he devoted to the survival and success of the business.

As the business owner concentrates more and more on leaving behind a legacy of generosity and fairness, he also grows more conservative. We may define *conservatism* as a preference for the status quo, resistance to change, disposition toward moderation and caution—in short, as aversion to risk. Studies (Sturdivant, Ginter, and Sawyer, 1985) show that such conservative values in managers are linked to a desire for order, stability, and reduction of conflict. These values develop in mature business owners for a number of reasons. For one, the path to success of a small business is usually erratic, with numerous temporary victories and setbacks along the way (Birch and MacCracken, 1981). Owners thus seek to establish cash or other liquid reserves to temper these natural, predictable risks. The idea of using these reserves to experiment with a new product or acquire a second manufacturing line becomes anathema.

Business owners also know it takes luck to succeed. They know the stories of successful entrepreneurs who have failed at one time or another and who attribute much of their eventual success to good fortune. They are unwilling to tempt fate by trying their luck again, and again, and again. This unwillingness is intensified by the realization that time is no longer on their side. In the past, they could put all their energies back on the line to salvage a troubled situation. Confidence in their skills to do so remains. But as they near retirement, they come to fear that they will simply not have the time to recoup lost gains. All this makes business owners far less likely to take risks. It also makes them far more likely to emphasize peace, predictability, and assured profitability within their businesses.

As a result, even money changes its meaning for the business owner, and he now wants to spend it in different ways. In early stages, money is the scarce resource needed to build the business. It is an impersonal commodity. As the business begins to succeed, money becomes a measure of success and a symbol of power. Later in the owner's life cycle, money takes on additional values. It assures personal freedom, it buys influence, it allows him to be generous to society and to his family, and it provides personal security. Money is now chiefly a personal commodity.

All these are understandable—at times, even desirable—developments. But such values in top managers empirically result in lower earnings and less equity growth (Sturdivant, Ginter, and Sawyer, 1985). They deprive the business of new opportunities. Therefore, they are contrary to the long-term welfare of the business. They are usually not consistent with business needs, especially if strategic revolution and fresh leadership are required, and they thus become barriers to a healthy future.

Implications for Owner-Manager

In his managerial capabilities, his leadership style, and his personal motivations, then, the business owner changes significantly over the years. Sadly, that typically has one result: by the time he has reached maturity, his desires and the needs of the business are no longer in harmony. He desires stability and the status quo; the business needs change. He yearns to spend time away from the company; the company needs him more than ever. He wants to spend more money on his comfort and the comfort of his family; the business too needs capital. Owners who have set perpetuation of their company as a serious goal must resolve this divergence between their needs and those of the company. They may do so by several means:

Keep Organization's Aspirations High. High standards for employee performance and corporate growth will stretch the managers' capabilities and generate organizational energy, even when the business owner himself has become satisfied with his station in life. Firm goals for continued growth are important. The owner must hold managers accountable for reaching those goals, even in the face of a declining market. That forces management to consider new or different avenues of growth. Generally, when expectations exceed results, the business will seek new challenges and new forms of investment.

Hire Outside Consultants or Directors. When the company and its owners become complacent, these advisers can help the organization focus on fresh potential in the market and give it new, more exciting visions of the future. They can also lobby for and help develop new standards of performance.

Continue to Experiment Strategically. Managers must constantly try out new products or new ways of manufacturing; they must think of different customer segments they might serve with current lines. Strategic experiments are ideas meant to improve the company's position or to test new directions of growth. They need not be revolutionary or expensive. What is important is to keep the spirit of inquiry and change alive.

Retire from Company Gradually. The business owner who wants to hire a general manager must distinguish his eagerness to relinquish day-to-day decision making from the need to provide room for managers to develop. He should pull away only for brief stretches, keeping in close touch with his customers and with his employees. The key to developing managers is not to simply leave them alone. Rather, it is a matter of the number and kind of decisions that the owner refers to them, as well as how much he coaches and counsels them and how enthusiastically he supports their programs.

Share Decisions. The business owner must attempt to preserve personal control yet allow others to participate in decision making. He must grant managers the freedom to govern day-to-day operations, while preserving his own right to make important strategic decisions carefully and slowly. This will alleviate managers' frustration over the apparent ambiguity and lack of corporate direction that they perceive.

Various Demands for Capital

Early in the life of the business, the owner typically reinvests all funds in the business. Excellent long-term returns seem possible. As a result, the business consumes all available capital. It demands all the money the family can spare. Only the prospect of eventual payoff makes this sacrifice acceptable.

As the business begins to prosper, however, excess cash becomes available. That money is often first used to reduce debt in the business. It is then used to reward the family for its years of sacrifice with an improved standard of living and to meet the family's perceived needs: security for one's spouse, funds for retirement, inheritances for offspring, and so on. Such family spending continues as the business matures. Meanwhile, nonfamily financial needs are growing too. Loyal and longtime employees seem to deserve higher salaries or bonuses. Estate taxes, someday due, are rising as the company's profits increase. Other investments such as stocks and bonds appear alluring. All this competes with the need for more business capital to fund new strategies. Owners perceive the apparent shortage of cash as a stumbling block to new corporate ventures. And so it will be, unless steps are taken to free up capital. Hence, let us look at the various demands on the family "treasury" and then at some possible solutions.

Family Needs. First, there is the usual need to provide lifetime security for the business owner's spouse. In past generations, these spouses were typically wives; just as typically, they were not financially well versed. Consequently, their business-owner husbands wished to accumulate a safe, liquid nest egg that would guarantee their spouses a secure, comfortable life. This desire was built on the assumption that their wives would outlive them by ten to twenty years. It was also based on the notion that their wives should not be financially dependent on their children. This situation continues for many business owners into the present day, with the result that many set aside large sums of cash for their spouses. They handle dependent children who are unable to provide for themselves in the same manner.

Second, the business owner seeks to assure his own standard of living through the retirement years. Very often, he has not funded pension plans and savings accounts sufficiently to provide a secure retirement from these sources alone. Consequently, he either continues to draw down his salary or arranges to receive a consulting fee from the business he founded. He justifies this expense by reasoning that he was underpaid in the past and so deserves continued compensation now.

Third, the business owner with some children in the business and some not seeks to provide fairly for all of them in the event of his death. He wants to make sure that no one thinks that he or she was cheated or feels less valued than the others. Thus he seeks to leave everyone a substantial financial legacy.

Fourth, the family may have to deal with the financial consequences of divorce. In such a case, the financial demands upon the divorced party may exceed his or her cash savings. Frequently, the company's stock may be pledged as collateral for a loan to meet those demands. And where will the money to pay off the loan come from? From a raise in salary. Once again, business capital is sacrificed to the needs of the family.

Nonfamily Demands. In addition to these family and personal financial needs, there are several other significant kinds of demands for capital. Financial security for old, loyal employees, for example, often seems paramount to the business owner in later years. Often these employees did not have pension plans in the early part of their careers; the business simply did not have or could not afford them. Therefore, the business owner is usually willing to pay out generous salaries or "consulting fees" to these employees. These payments are for past considerations, and they decrease the funds available for future strategic investments.

Estate and inheritance taxes in a private company are another demand. They can cost up to half the value of the business. The business owner must pay such taxes because the government considers his personal estate and his business one and the same; thus, when the business changes hands from parent to child, a tax is owed and eventually paid for by the business itself. It is a tax that public companies, whose ownership can trade hands without encumbrance, do not have to bear.

As if the financial drain from employees and taxes was not enough, business owners often feel the need to withdraw money from the business for other kinds of investments. They label this move diversification, reasoning that they should spread their capital risk beyond a single investment and hoping that they will make even more money with a new venture. Sometimes diversification takes such subtle forms as buying the real estate under the business for personal tax purposes. At other times, it is as straightforward as investing in a portfolio of stocks, bonds, tax shelters, and the like. Ironically, few of these investments are likely to earn as high a return as the business itself. Reinvesting money in the vehicle one knows—the family business—is very likely safer than investing in unfamiliar ventures. Moreover, investments outside the business must return a premium over reinvestment in the business in order to cover the substantial corporate and personal income taxes paid as funds are withdrawn from the business.

Implications for the Business's Future Needs. At the same time as all these nonbusiness demands are growing, business needs for capital are growing too. Most industries that reach maturity today are capital intensive because of the new technologies required. A business needs investment just to stay even; it needs even more if it is to make the leap toward regeneration. At this point, then, a conflict has developed between the family and the business. The business needs money for strategic renewal; the family needs money for security and comfort. Yet the money for each must come from the same source; and, given the increasing familial priorities of the aging business owner, the family is likely to win out. Unfortunately, however, that choice will slowly deprive the business of needed funds.

It seems a vicious circle. And indeed, satisfying the twin financial needs of family and business is one of the greatest challenges to the owner of a private company. Creating a business so strong that it can readily support the needs of both family and business is one solution, of course. But most owners will have to make certain choices in an effort to minimize the constraints that stem from competing capital demands. They will probably choose one of the two following solutions:

First, members of the older generation may finance their retirement and other family needs through personal savings. This avoids the need to withdraw funds from the business at the very moment when the business needs that money for new strategies. It suggests several supporting tactics, such as instilling modest financial expectations and teaching the importance of frugality. High levels of personal savings will be encouraged. The family will be taught to sacrifice for the sake of business continuity. This probably means that not all family members will be equally provided for; stock ownership will be preserved for family members active in the business. The inheritance and lifestyle of the others will be more limited.

Second, the business may take on debt. Relatively large amounts of debt can serve one of two purposes. The business can go into debt in order to finance new strategic developments. Or the debt may be used to buy out the previous generation of stockholders to help them finance their estate plans and personal retirement needs. Debt used to retire the ownership of parent generations and pass control to successors within the family can be accurately described as a leveraged buyout between the generations. Leveraged buyouts are a purchasing technique that allows a company to be acquired through use of borrowed funds. The initial loan is secured with the company's assets, an action that "leverages up" the company's capitalization. The greater the leverage, of course, the greater the risk to the company, its shareholders, and creditors.

Such a technique has several advantages, however. Besides providing liquidity to the parents, it eases the leadership transition. A leveraged buyout also puts the burden of risk chiefly on the new generation of management—a burden that may increase its sense of responsibility and commitment. That is healthy for the offspring in a family business, especially since only those really interested in the business will be willing to assume such risk. Offspring with less resolve, or less to offer the business, may not want to be included in the deal. Admittedly, some businesses may not be able to afford the debt levels required for a leveraged buyout. They may supplement the transaction with cash paid out by life insurance policies upon the death of the owner. Insurance policy premiums, of course, must be taken from business resources. But their benefit as a source of cash may outweigh that disadvantage.

In summary, then, if neither the family nor the business is wealthy enough to readily support both units, family members must make a choice. They must give priority either to meeting the financial needs of the business or to sharing the inheritance equally among themselves. The price of the former is the family's life-style. The price of the latter is the health of the business. Whatever the decision, it is essential for the entire family to understand the situation well enough to appreciate the trade-offs. Everyone in the family needs to understand what the business can afford and what the business needs for a successful future.

Family Desire for Harmony

A final challenge to the future health of the business may lie in the family's desire to avoid conflict in the interests of familial harmony. While in many ways this is a laudable goal, conflict and healthy competition among family members may in fact be important to the growth of the company. Business thrives on competition: it is a stimulating, vigorous force that prompts people to come up with better ways of doing things. Stifling it in the name of family unity does the company a disservice, for it tends to also stifle the development of fresh ideas.

Typically, this is not a problem for the family in the early years of a business. The excitement and demands of the business help pull everyone together. They take pride in their burgeoning enterprise and their new accomplishments, and their

objectives are clear. But as the business matures, more challenges develop. As we have seen, its product or service may
change. The organization grows and ages. The owner's motivations shift, and financial demands increase. Family members begin to run their own territories. One takes responsibility for
marketing; another, for production. Each competes for business
resources to improve his or her own area. Members also begin to
develop different dreams—not only for their own futures but
for the company's as well. They may want to expand in different geographical areas or add different product lines. One believes the business deserves a capital infusion; another wants to
postpone it a year or two. The unity that permeated the business in its early years often disappears.

These differences of opinion over the company's direction—a natural part of any dynamic business—are sharpened in
a family business. Elsewhere employees might feel free to argue
and debate. In the family-owned company, however, peers are
often siblings and bosses are also fathers. Home seems an exten-
sion of the business, and vice versa. As a result, instead of debating the pros and cons of ideas—perhaps even risking some family
members' departure from the business—individuals often remain silent so as not to offend other family members. Even
grumbling is discouraged. It is seen as disruptive to family relationships and is therefore "forbidden" along with debate.

But the cost of maintaining family harmony is high: new
ideas and appropriate challenges to the status quo are repressed.
Family businesses thus develop a noncompetitive spirit. They lose
the healthy tension needed for innovation and change and begin
to experience the unhealthy kind of tension that stems from
limiting individual expression. Such tension is often heightened
by spouses, who have heard only complaints from their husbands or wives and are often all too willing to take sides. Family
members should realize that to renew a business and to prepare
it for the future requires uncomfortable changes, mistakes, and
management debate. They should thus consider the following
techniques that may help achieve family harmony while maintaining a healthy business tension.

First, family members can be kept as separate as possible in the business. This minimizes the opportunity for interpersonal conflict among family members. Owners should encourage the natural inclination of individuals to develop different territories. Sometimes they can do this by placing family members in different plants or sales offices or by assigning them to different business units or product lines.

Next, the family should be educated as to what the business needs. In-laws and the business owner's spouse can help to contribute to family harmony instead of disrupting it. But they will need information about the financial and strategic situation of the company to do so. Such education subtly but effectively communicates to family members who is contributing most to the future. It emphasizes just how valuable family resolve and commitment are, and it provides spouses with all sides of the story.

Lastly, owners should create a climate that favors change. At work, they can foster debate and encourage the expression of new ideas. Formal commitment to strategic review and strategic experimentation helps set the stage for these activities.

Summary

We have presented a number of barriers to the long-term health of the family business in this chapter. These barriers include changes in the nature of the business, the character of the organization, the motivations of the owner-manager, family financial expectations, and family goals. These forces can easily result in a business that is resistant to change and an owner who is harvesting the business to satisfy family needs at a time when the need for reinvestment is most keen. Thus, the needs of the business and of the family come into conflict. This contrasts sharply to the early days, when the needs of one were consistent with those of the other.

In such conflicting circumstances, the preferences of people tend to take precedence over the more abstract, impersonal, and unemotional needs of the business. Our data suggest that as a result, business maturity often leads to decline instead of re-newal. We proposed a number of business principles to over-come these problems and revitalize the company:

For the Business

- Adjust business strategies to evolving market needs
- Reinvest actively in the business
- Create and plan new business strategies for the future

For the Organization

- Establish formal management systems
- Delegate authority
- Hire new people
- Prepare a successor

For the Business Owner

- Keep the organization's aspirations high
- Hire outside consultants or establish a board of outside di-rectors
- Relinquish business gradually
- Continue to experiment strategically
- Share decisions

For Family Financial Demands

- Encourage personal savings and frugality
- Put the business in debt

For Family Harmony

- Give family members their own business territories
- Educate the family as to what the business needs
- Create a climate that favors change

Success in business hinges on the development of new strategic opportunities and new management processes. The de-velopment and implementation of these strategies require a good deal of careful analysis, advance planning, and organiza-tional growth. Some successful entrepreneurs and business founders accomplish these objectives themselves, developing their own skills or bringing in a general manager; others leave them wholly or in part to the next generation. This latter technique can be particularly effective. One study (Hershon, 1975) of 35 family businesses concluded that business perpetuation is more successful when each generation of the family implements increasing "professionalization" of the management process and new business strategies. Our own research into 200 businesses suggests similiar conclusions.

THREE

Ensuring Family Interest
in Leading the Business

A family business owner's greatest resource is his or her family. Its members provide the company with employees, ideas, new blood; they also give the owner good reasons to work hard and achieve success. They are a reason for making the business last. Yet raising children who will be truly interested in the future of the business, preparing them for leadership, and selecting one as president are not easy tasks. They raise difficult issues that are further complicated by the fact that family members play multiple roles. They are father, mother, sister, brother, as well as boss, owner, employee. The dual obligations of such roles often clash. A business owner who is pleased to pay and promote employees on merit, for example, suddenly finds that this leads to favoring one child over another. And that is forbidden in the parental role.

The very nature of business often seems to contradict the nature of the family. Families tend to be emotional; businesses are objective. Families are protective of their members; businesses, much less so. Families grant acceptance unconditionally. Businesses grant it according to one's contribution. These and other conflicts can generate a good deal of ambiguity and stress for family members (Hollander, 1983). This, in turn, causes problems that may significantly affect the business.

The process of resolving these conflicts must be established long before the children arrive in the business. It must begin in the home: in the lessons the children are taught, in the way the family conducts itself. It continues with the philosophies that govern the children's entry into the business and their preparation for leadership roles. It expands with proper management of siblings' relationships and of the way in which power is shifted from one generation to the next. Families find that considering these challenges ahead of time increases the chances of solving them to everyone's satisfaction. Their solutions generally rest on the fundamental beliefs that the family and the business can learn to work well together as a unit and that the family's contribution will strengthen the business enterprise instead of weaken it.

Synergies Between Family and Business

As we have noted, the nature of business often seems at odds with the nature of families. And yet well-managed businesses and healthy families do share many positive, constructive traits. They make decisions by consensus. They function smoothly under the standards of teamwork and loyalty. Overriding goals, set by leaders, shape their use of time and financial resources. These shared characteristics should not be surprising, since families and businesses are both also social units. Both are based on commitment to a group ideal (be it the selling of products or the creation of a home). They work especially well when their members assume individual responsibility and offer one another mutual support. And they are each led by figures of authority who set the tone for the entire group.

Such common traits put parents with a business in an excellent position. Because some business and family principles are so similar, parents can work to teach their children the very qualities that will help them in business and simultaneously make the family run more smoothly. Good financial management, for example—*sacrificing* from current profit or consumption in order to *save,* then *investing* money at some degree of *risk* for *future rewards*—can be encouraged with investment experiences, saving from allowances, and discussing ways to finance such family projects as vacations and education (Danco, 1981). Learning to abide by the rules of a group is another excellent basic lesson, and so is learning to adapt smoothly to change.

Even specific business skills, such as marketing, competition, learning, and leadership, can be encouraged. Fund-raising activities such as selling Girl Scout cookies teach marketing techniques. Sports instill a competitive spirit. School activities, home reading sessions, and trips can highlight the importance of learning. Roles in school clubs and activities encourage leadership and management skills, as do responsibility for household tasks and being included in major family decisions. Approaching these routine childhood activities with a larger purpose in mind—bringing the children into the company, should they wish to come—will enhance the natural fit between family and business.

Welcoming Family Members to the Business

Generally, perpetuating the business is a goal everyone in the family shares. The vast majority of parents who own a business want to pass it on to their offspring for reasons we highlighted in Chapter One. Similarly, a study by Birely (1985) indicates that the majority of college students with the option to enter a family business eventually plan to do so. The fact that many traditional professions such as medicine and law do not offer the opportunities they once did makes the family business look even more attractive to these students. In addition, a certain glamour has come to surround entrepreneurship and self-employment.

Yet none of this guarantees that the next generation will actually enter the company. There are many obstacles to be overcome, including the ambivalent feelings of parents. For alongside the desire to hand on the business, parents also fear that a child will never have a chance to be her own person if she enters the business. They worry about family conflicts; they are concerned that hiring their children will drive away loyal managers. Offspring also see drawbacks to entering the family business. They may have trouble with their parents or with siblings. They fear they will fail in full view of the whole family. They worry that peers will think they took "the easy way out" to get a job.

Such ambivalence creates an atmosphere in which missteps magnify fears and may ultimately ruin the chances for succession. If parents fail to actually communicate their desire to have their children in the business, for example, it is easy for those children to assume they are unwanted. They back away from the business into another career. Parental grumbling about business problems—poor help, fickle customers, unpredictable suppliers—can also discourage children.

These problems may be compounded by vague "rules" for entering the family business. Such rules, often unspoken and developed subconsciously by the business owner, emerge when an overt action demands a response. For example, many family offspring assume it is better to get experience outside the business before they join the family firm. Yet many parent-owners silently develop the "rule" that if a child is to join the company, he or she must do so immediately after college. This direct—and hidden—contradiction is revealed only when the child tries to enter the business some years after graduation. Similar misunderstandings occur in other situations: when a child tries to return to the business after leaving it, for instance, or if he tries to join without first getting a college degree. Any of these situations can cause the parent and child to go their separate ways.

Parents who wish to bring children successfully into the business might consider these steps:

First, make it clear to children that they are welcome to join the company. This can be done gently, without imposing any obligation. Key ideas to convey here are (1) the child is welcome, (2) his or her participation in the business is voluntary, and (3) the decision will be supported no matter what the choice. Granting offspring the freedom to take the business or leave it—to make up their own minds, without obligation—is important. Without that freedom, offspring who do enter the business are not likely to perform up to their full capabilities. They will rarely possess the drive and enthusiasm necessary for success in business.

Second, project the business as a special, exciting place. Parents who wish their children to join their business need to express why they like the work and the industry. At home, they should discuss the joys, accomplishments, and fulfillments of work. At work, they may introduce the young ones to the office or offer part-time jobs to school-aged children. This kind of encouragement will make careers in the business look more attractive to children.

Finally, make "rules" for participation early and enforce them fairly. The rules themselves are relatively unimportant. They may be rigid, such as requiring that children possess a degree in business or first hold an outside job, or they may be flexible, allowing children entry no matter what their preparation. The key to success is establishing the rules clearly, then communicating and applying them fairly to everyone. These rules act as a verbal contract between parent and child. They are best established before the offspring are of age to enter the family business because then they will not appear to be after-the-fact rationalizations.

Such verbal contracts lie at the heart of a family business. They are as important as written contracts, and their terms should be handled in the same way. If the rules change, everyone needs to be told what the new rules are, as well as why the old ones were changed. They should also understand what the new rules mean to *them* and to their individual circumstances. Surprise or betrayal in this regard may undermine confidence in the entire family business enterprise. Key rules should cover the following:

- When and under what circumstances children are welcome to enter the business (including how much education and previous experience will be required of them and whether they must fill a vacant post or one created for them)
- When the possibility of entry has been foreclosed (at age thirty? forty? never?)
- Whether reentry is possible after voluntary or involuntary exit (due to child rearing, attendance at graduate school, an argument with other family members, and so on)
- Whether part-time work is permitted
- Whether in-laws are welcome to join the company and, if so, in what capacities

Entering the Company

Once it is clear that the business will be a family business for the next generation—in other words, once the invitation to join the company has been issued and accepted—two immediate questions need attention. How should the offsprings' entry into the business be structured? And what is the best way to groom them for the tasks of general management and ownership?

Earlier, we described the roles that the next generation will play in the business: developing new strategies, adding formal management systems, and building a new management team. Their training should prepare them to meet these needs, as well as their own personal goals. In that light we make several suggestions that might form the basis for the rules of entry:

- Ask successors to gain experience outside the family business
- Provide those entering the business with a specific job that the organization clearly needs
- Appoint a mentor—someone other than a parent—for the early teaching and evaluating of a successor's performance

All these will provide the opportunity for both generations to test their ability to work together in the family business. Once these tests have been passed—and the senior family management team is firmly in place—successors' training may continue with a formal development plan. (We will discuss that plan more fully in Chapter Eight.)

Gain Outside Work Experience. This has many advantages for both the business and the individual. Successors might therefore consider seeking a job in another company immediately after college graduation. They should stay long enough to receive one or more promotions, work for several bosses, and reach a point of sufficient responsibility to implement their own ideas on a particular project. This development may take anywhere from three to five years. What the job actually entails is not critical. Any professional skill—in sales, production, market research, or personnel—will impart abilities useful to the family company. Similarly, whether the job is in the same industry as the family business or a different one is not important. There are benefits on either side: experience in a company in the same industry, for example, makes the lessons and ideas learned more readily applicable. But experience outside the industry broadens perspectives and provides new ways of thinking about business problems.

What *is* important is joining a company somewhat larger than the family business—a company whose size the business seeks to attain. Then, outside tenure will prepare the successor to guide the family business into a future that is more complex and challenging than the present. The overall benefits of such outside experience to successors include: learning their market value as measured by salary, establishing a professional identity apart from the family business, making "youthful" mistakes away from the watchful eyes of the family and future colleagues, developing expertise and self-assurance, knowing they have been evaluated and/or promoted exclusively on their own merits, and finding out that the grass is not always greener in other businesses.

Outside work experience also benefits the business. Typically, potential successors learn various management systems and practices that may be of use in the family company. They meet talented people who may later be important contacts or even candidates for employment in the family business. They are also exposed to different markets, different types of competitors, and different strategies. These experiences broaden their view of the world and better enable them to identify new business opportunities. All in all, gaining experience outside the business is one of the strongest recommendations that can be made for successors. In all of our interviews, no one who worked outside the family business regretted doing so. Many who did not wished that they had (Zaslow, 1986).

Assume a Specific Job Position. Once the offspring have returned to the business, they will need appropriate training positions. Line positions in sales or field service or operations positions that ultimately lead to supervisory management work well in this regard; staff positions or "assistant to the president" posts work less well because they frequently do not offer clear responsibility and accountability. Whatever the job, however, it should be one the organization needs, not one that is invented to provide the owner's son or daughter with a job. Later, successors should earn some organizational autonomy of their own by opening up a new territory, starting a new store, or running a plant. Such projects help develop managerial talent. They also serve to keep siblings apart and therefore to dampen potential rivalry. Projects on which offspring work together as a team are still necessary, however. That is the only setting that will reveal and develop their future family leadership skills—an important prelude to selecting a successor.

Work with a Mentor. A well-chosen mentor, that is, a senior manager outside the family who has broad business experience, can teach young adults much of what they need to know to run a business. Ideally, the mentor would also be the business owner's complement: a key manager who is deeply trusted and is responsible for core business activities outside the owner's direct purview. The owner may handle sales and marketing, for example; his or her complement may be in production or finance. Typically, these alternate activities will be ones that do not particularly interest the business owner. That is desirable because the trainee will then learn dimensions of the business that the owner will more readily share, and he or she will therefore be less likely to compete with the owner for the same business territory. Since the mentor is a trusted, senior manager needed by the owner, the mentor's job security is also assured. That is a necessary condition if he or she is to be an effective teacher.

Through the mentor relationship, offspring will learn how to manage people and time, as well as gain valuable business principles. Such teaching usually occurs over a period of three to five years. After that, however, the mentor and protégé relation tends to lose its effectiveness, and the latter may begin to feel that he or she has ideas on how to do things better. When signs of trouble appear, it is time to give the protégé a new and different job challenge.

Selecting a Successor

These activities will provide excellent preparation of the senior family management team—the offspring who will provide continuing leadership for the company. Usually (though not always) one son or daughter must be selected from this team to succeed the company president.

This selection is a watershed event, a moment that should mark the joyful passage of the business from one generation to the next. Yet it is a choice many families find difficult. Concerns can be so intense, in fact, that many families avoid the issue of succession entirely (Lansberg, 1985). The businesses of these families tend to grow increasingly leaderless, unless one successor takes control through a revolution of some sort. That puts the business through painful organizational turbulence. Alternatively, it may be sold or closed. To avoid these developments, succession should be planned. Key issues for families to consider include:

- How to select one successor from among several siblings?
- What is the appropriate timing for selecting a successor?
- What effect will this change in leadership have on the current owner and president, and how can he best handle the change?

Methods of Selection

Families have several alternatives at their disposal. They may (1) create a fixed rule, such as "the oldest child will be president"; (2) select the best candidate from the group; or (3) develop an interim, nonfamily leader. We will explore the pros and cons of each alternative.

Creating a Fixed Rule. Traditionally, families who *are* willing to choose a successor make the decision according to some long-standing rule, such as "the oldest child" or "the first-born son" or "the best-educated child" will be the next president. As we noted earlier, such rules are not always expressed clearly. Often they emerge only under the accord of tradition or the pressure of crisis, remaining implicit up to the moment of truth. However, when they are stated plainly and well in advance of the time they will actually be applied, they eliminate much of the agonizing indecision surrounding succession. Typically they also force a family to concentrate leadership in the hands of one manager—an effective principle, as we saw in our study of 200 manufacturers cited in Chapter One.

Clear rules are an advantage in that they end delay and indecision. They also allow the family time to adjust to the new leader. However, mechanically applied rules may not result in selection of the "best" candidate. Arbitrary rules can also create conflict.

Selecting the "Best" Candidate. In another approach, family offspring select their leader by allowing him or her to surface naturally during various group assignments. Such assignments may concern affairs outside the established family business—for example, the start-up of a new venture. The final endorsement may be made by the owner or by a board of directors after observing how the offspring work together. Family shareholders might also hold a formal election; this is an approach particularly appealing to large families. Leadership traits on which to base such a decision include reliability, a stable character, and the ability to develop consensus within the family and to effectively lead a group as a team. Determining who is the "best" candidate may also depend on the future course of the business, not just on leadership talent.

The advantage of this approach is that the family feels it has chosen the best person for the job yet has also granted everyone a chance. Time has revealed which candidate is most qualified for the business strategy pursued. However, unhealthy competition may develop among siblings, and family members may bog down in the difficulties of making a decision.

Selecting an Interim Leader. For some family businesses, selecting a successor who is *not* a member of the family is an excellent, albeit temporary, solution. This works especially well in situations where the offspring are clearly too young to assume the presidency. A nonfamily successor provides a buffer between generations that may be as much as thirty years apart. One study (Blotnick, 1984) even suggests that family businesses with such "buffer management" between generations are actually much more profitable than those in which family leaders immediately succeed one another. This study of nearly 600 family businesses showed that those companies with "buffer management" were roughly twice as profitable as those that simply passed from older to younger generations of the family.

"Buffer management" gives time for family members to mature. It also allows an entrepreneurial leader to vent his natural dissatisfaction with any successor on an outsider rather than on his own offspring (O'Toole, 1984). However, a qualified nonfamily successor may not exist in the organization.

Timing the Announcement

Families agonize over whether a successor should be announced sooner (when the offspring are still under thirty years of age) or later (when they are already past forty and the owner's retirement is imminent). Often, they end up postponing the announcement until the issue is forced by illness or the threatened departure of the successor. While every family must make its own determination of the "right time," families that announce sooner rather than later receive several benefits. Thus, early announcement often reassures employees who are not members of the family. Once the successor is known, they are no longer uncertain about the future destiny of the business and who will run it. This is particularly valuable knowledge in these days of rampant mergers and acquisitions, since employees know more and more people who have been fired by the new ownership of acquired firms. Suppliers and customers are reassured for the same reason. Family continuity is intended and planned.

Family members and the successor also benefit by early announcement. True, there may be some disappointed siblings, but time is on everyone's side. Everyone has a chance to adjust to the news and time to plan their personal careers and roles. There is time for the family to find opportunities for those who were disappointed, and there is also more time for family members to learn to work together in new relationships.

Early determination of a successor is thus the preferred option. Still, this determination should follow inauguration of family and business planning. Such planning helps put business needs and family goals into focus, thus paving the way for selecting future strategy. Selecting a successor or successors to implement that strategy can then be considered and discussed in a less emotional context.

Attitude of Owner

The single most important factor in the success of any transition is the business owner. He or she sets the tone for the rest of the company; he or she has the power to make the shift rough or smooth. Yet more often than not, the business owner has difficulty in retiring gracefully. In fact, many simply cannot bring themselves to give up their companies. And therein lies trouble for many attempted successions.

There is, for example, the phenomenon of "semiretirement," in which the owner heads south—or to Europe, or California, or wherever he or she has yearned to be—for three to five months each year before again assuming the president's post for the remaining seven to nine months. Another version of this is the "return of the parent," in which the owner decides to return to the business after some years of unfulfilling retirement. He or she finds many reasons to justify this return. They may range from accusing the son or daughter of doing a terrible job to filling in for a key employee who has left the business. Any excuse is sufficient.

This desire to return to active work is not unique to family business owners. A recent study found that 61 percent of retired senior executives (none of whom owned their own firm) returned to active work within eighteen months of their retirement ("Back to Work," 1985). What *is* unique to family business owners is the devastating effect of their indecision on their companies. Working under different bosses at different times—and facing the likelihood that one will contradict the other—is very confusing to employees. Lack of clear leadership encourages fears that the business may eventually be sold. That, in turn, prompts employees to become shortsighted and passive. They waste valuable business time speculating about the fate of the company. They also lose their commitment to building the business, for they are no longer sure that a future is there to build.

The return of the owner is especially tough on successors. It disrupts successors' ability to take charge of the business. They begin to take fewer chances. They are no longer as willing to make changes. And always, they are in the shadow of the parent and owner. These problems are so severe that "letting go" by the older generation was identified as the number one problem by successors, according to one study of father-son relationships in family businesses (Davis, 1982).

A smooth transition in power seems to require, first of all, that owners plan for an active, fulfilling retirement. Owners who wish to pass the company on smoothly to their offspring need to seriously consider ways in which they can free themselves from their companies. Some may choose to travel, devote time to hobbies, or serve as consultants to other businesses. Others will wish to aid the company in some way— perhaps run a branch in Florida, handle relations with long-established customers, or even write a history of the business. In many ways this will be a responsibility shared by the successor, who needs to make sure that there are attractive alternatives available to the parent who is handing on the presidency.

It is also very helpful to set a final retirement date when the successor will be named. This also requires that a date and arrangement for final transfer of voting stock be set, a recommendation supported by a recent study (Berenbein, 1984) of twenty large family businesses. The actual shift of power and authority from one president to the next should take five to seven years, which means that the successor must be named well in advance of the outgoing generation's retirement date.

Finally, owners should relinquish control publicly and while still in full command of their abilities. According to Berenbein's study, successful successions are characterized by owners' willingness to make a public commitment to retire. They accompany this change in leadership with a statement that sets forth the company's formal objectives and strategies and clarifies any other shifts in responsibility. The statement is jointly prepared with the successor and tendered to the entire company.

Managing Sibling Relationships

As he transfers the company to his offspring—indeed, in the course of his entire family business life—the business owner must deal with relations among siblings. These are shaped by many factors, including the order of birth of children. Each sibling will struggle to outshine the other, perhaps nowhere more vigorously than in a family business. Competition there is likely to be sharpened further by the business owner's need to ultimately select one child as his or her successor.

As we have noted, competitive tension is often healthy for a business. Siblings who are striving for the presidency, for example, will work hard to turn in excellent, individual job performances. Yet if this effort becomes a rough-and-tumble battle —complete with efforts to derail other siblings—it will have negative effects upon the company. Unfortunately, this sort of unhealthy competition is often unintentionally reinforced by siblings' husbands and wives. Even well-meaning spouses are usually ill equipped to play their roles in the family business. Often they do not understand the business or the industry it is in. What information they do have generally comes from their mates, who typically relate only the problems of the business. As a result, spouses get a slanted view of the company and the world in which it operates.

This picture may grow even more lopsided if life-styles vary among siblings. A larger house or fancier car, for example, is easily interpreted either as favoritism ("proof" that one sibling earns more than another) or as a sign of reckless spending. Those with fewer creature comforts assume that their spouses are being treated unfairly or that other siblings are somehow exploiting the expense account. Additionally, outside interests on the part of any one sibling may prompt others to conclude that he or she is less committed to the business. All this can lead to spousal complaints and, in the worst of cases, spousal feuding. Angry feelings can spread throughout the family, widening the gap between siblings and often prompting some to seek higher salaries from the business. As a result, in-laws are frequently blamed, even if they are innocent, for pulling the family and, consequently, the business, apart.

In successful family businesses, both siblings and the parent-owners work to make sibling rivalry positive rather than negative in effect. They use such techniques as (1) determining a general and well-publicized philosophy to govern salaries and promotions, (2) assigning siblings separate positions within the company, and (3) developing a code of conduct that will govern siblings' behavior among themselves.

Rationalize Salaries and Promotions. Several approaches are available to the business owner here. One is that traditional business principles will apply: Salaries will be based on merit and position, and one sibling will eventually be allowed to assume the presidency. This approach puts the business first. While competitive salary schedules encourage good work performance, they may also produce family conflicts.

A second philosophy puts the family first. Here, the opposite risk comes to the fore: business performance is sacrificed for the sake of family harmony. All siblings' incomes are equal. All difficult decisions are made by consensus. The "president" may actually be a team of siblings: Their job is to see that consensus is reached rather than to make final decisions.

The choice here often depends on the size of the business and the stage of its development. In a family business made up of a few brothers and sisters who all work together in the business and share ownership equally, a "family first" attitude may make more sense. In this case, the success of the business depends on sibling teamwork, which would be encouraged by equal pay and leadership responsibilities. But in a wealthy third- or fourth-generation business made up of several cousins or numerous nonfamily managers of various ages, perhaps a "business first" attitude is more appropriate. Such a business requires a company hierarchy, with pay based on position and skill. This system rewards performance on the basis of merit and thus encourages excellent work. And, because of the dispersed ownership structure and highly professional nature of the business, this approach is not likely to create dissension.

In any case, owners should consider the benefits of openly publicizing income levels among all family members. This minimizes the opportunity for spouses and in-laws to draw incorrect conclusions from expensive life-styles. It also says clearly that family members depend on one another for their mutual success, financial and otherwise.

Assign Separate Positions. Until the moment that one is named president, siblings should not be required to report to another if at all possible. Each should also have his or her own area or project within the company, from a special project to a full division. If they perform well and are praised for their efforts, they will feel they are making valuable contributions to the business. That softens the sting of watching one sibling gain a higher title. Eventually, such "niching" may pave the way for corporate spin-offs to individual sons and daughters.

Develop a Code of Conduct. By this code, siblings agree to act in a manner conducive to a healthy business. The code lays down rules on how to work together and avoid serious rifts. Examples are "We will agree to agree. . . . We will not judge each other. . . . We will assume that each has discretionary time to do with as they want. . . . We will respect each other. . . . We will not take any money out of the business except as salary and formal benefits." Issues that siblings may consider for the code include:

- Keeping in-laws and spouses up-to-date on the business
- Publicly recognizing the various strengths of each sibling
- Giving time and attention to spouses' areas of interest, whether these be cultural, sporting, or other
- Spending "friendship" time with other siblings and making considered efforts to keep open lines of communication with them

Some of these ideas were developed during a 1983 conference on siblings in the family business at Loyola University of Chicago (Ward, 1986b). There, siblings noted that managing healthy sibling relationships required conscious effort in attending to each other's needs and in addressing relationships among spouses and in-laws.

Managing the Transition

The transition period—the time between the day the successor is named and the day he or she actually takes over as owner and president—can be extremely stressful. About two-thirds of the companies who take this course of action manage to see it through (Davis, 1982). One-third, however, fall by the wayside. The successor quits or is dismissed; the business is sold.

Much of this turmoil stems not only from the fact that one sibling has finally been "elevated" above the rest but from the parent-owner's difficulty in sharing control with the entire senior family management team. Frequently this leads to such complaints on the part of successors as "My ideas aren't tried," "I have responsibility without authority," or "My role is not clear." Owners often have their own share of complaints. They believe that the successors are running the business poorly. Or they feel that the new managers are not listening to their advice and that they are unwilling to learn. Such complaints are signs that a transition is in trouble. Solving them requires (1) sharing decisions, (2) accommodating differences in values and desires, and (3) planning the shift of power from one generation to the next.

Sharing Decisions. As we noted earlier, the ability to share decisions is first learned at home. Never is this skill more important than when one generation attempts to shift control of the company another. Sharing decisions is an excellent teaching device. It allows the outgoing generation a chance to impart its business philosophies and gives the incoming generation a chance to learn what leadership is like.

To be sure, it is not an easy skill to learn. Asking for a reaction to a decision that has already been made, for example, only creates the illusion that decisions are being shared. The spirit of shared decision making means sincerely seeking the successor's opinion on key issues, listening to his or her answers, and factoring that assessment into a final decision. It means making every effort to understand the other person's point of view. It means communicating the final decision to all concerned and, if that decision goes counter to the successor's own judgment, explaining why it was made. Only through such discussions can the successor learn the business and begin to help shape the future.

Accommodating Value Differences. To be sure, business owners and successors who take this course of action will often find themselves on opposite sides of an argument. Many factors can cause such conflict. But we would suggest that the underlying cause is always a difference in values. Take an argument about whether to install up-to-date manufacturing equipment, for example. It may not be so much an argument about technology as about the value of change versus the value of consistency. The young may argue for change, the old for the status quo. The underlying distinctions in values will prevent them from ever seeing eye-to-eye, because it is difficult to agree on a course of action when opponents cannot even agree on the fundamentals that underscore it and, worse, begin to argue about personalities. Such discussions can easily deteriorate into shouting matches, and the original objective, to decide whether or not to install new equipment, is forgotten.

This notion of differing values contradicts what most families believe, namely, that members share the same values simply because they *are* a family. Sometimes this is the case. But far more often, it is not. Values vary among members of the same family for several reasons. For one, people are unique individuals. Some are aggressive, others are cautious. Some like to talk, others prefer action. These personality traits will shape the belief systems of their owners, encouraging natural distinctions within any one family. The period in which an individual came to maturity also influences his or her values. Children who grew up in the sixties will tend to value social change and liberal mores; those who came of age in the forties will lean to more conservative views.

Most important of all, values develop as people pass through stages of their lives (Levinson, 1978). As a result, parents and their offspring will tend to differ significantly simply because of the difference in their ages. This can lead to predictable patterns, as proposed by a recent study (Davis, 1982) at Harvard University of 200 father-son business teams. Davis found that sons between the ages of seventeen and twenty-five longed for their own identity. They wanted to break with tradition; they also wanted to break with their parents. Between twenty-seven and thirty-three years of age, they eagerly explored career choices and development. They sought a role model to help guide those choices; in many cases, the father became the model. After that stage, they again typically sought independence and had stormy relationships with their mentors. They yearned for recognition and sought out risks.

Fathers, meanwhile, when between forty to fifty years of age, had been working on the big picture themselves. Their goal was to expand their businesses. They wanted to centralize power in their own persons. Between the ages of fifty and sixty, however, they began to emphasize business and family philosophies. They grew less competitive, they wanted to teach, they were more tolerant of differences. Past sixty to sixty-five years, they struggled to make sense of life. They became very conservative and did not want to relinquish responsibility. They placed great emphasis on loyalty and stability.

Conflict and agreement between parent and offspring, then, can often be explained by their respective stages in life, which are some twenty-five years apart. Such differences show up in various ways in the business itself. They shape choices of business goals, personal goals, risk preference or aversion, theories of motivation, and philosophies of learning. Value differences can also show up in family decisions that shape business strategies and siblings' work relationships. In the family these values influence such choices as (1) how much money the family needs for security, (2) to what degree family differences should be openly discussed and tolerated, and (3) how close family relationships should be.

All this might be a simple intellectual exercise were it not for the fact that, as we have noted, opposing value systems often create nearly insoluble arguments. Understanding that there is no absolute right or wrong in most business decisions is often one step toward a solution. Understanding that values will vary in the same family is another. This understanding encourages tolerance, growth, and learning, the hallmarks of a fast-paced, upbeat organization. Understanding *why* they vary will also help families work in harmony with developmental stages. The Harvard study, for example, suggests that successors who are nearing thirty when their fathers are in their fifties will likely work together well as a team. The converse is often true when the successor is in his early twenties or in his forties. At these critical junctures, it may be better for the successor to work outside the business or to create autonomous business interests. Both sides can then do it "their way."

Readers who wish to discuss some of the different values at work within their own families and businesses may turn to Appendix A. They will find, however, that the most valuable tool of all is developing common understanding, that is, developing the same assumptions about the world in which the business operates. As we have seen, this does not happen naturally. It requires strategic planning to build common understanding and identify fundamental assumptions. The planning process also helps structure family and business relationships in a way that will allow them to accommodate the value differences that are bound to remain.

Summary

The business and the family undertake similar activities, from setting goals to sharing decisions. This creates a certain synergy between the two units, and it makes possible a framework in which the lessons of one can serve the aims of the other. On this belief rest the elements of planning the family's participation in the business:

On Family Lessons

- Learn to develop explicit family rules rather than rely on individual assumptions about the proper course of action
- Adapt to change
- Encourage activities that teach financial management, marketing, leadership, and competition

On Welcoming the Family to the Business

- Communicate the invitation
- Project the business as an exciting place
- Make rules for participation

On Entering the Business

- Get outside experience
- Fill a needed job
- Work with a mentor

On Selecting a Successor

- Determine the governing philosophy
- Decide the right timing
- Shape owner's attitudes (plan an enjoyable retirement)

On Managing Sibling Relationships

- Decide how to treat salaries and promotions
- Assign separate roles
- Set philosophy on equality
- Establish code of conduct

On Managing the Transition

- Share decisions
- Accommodate value differences
- Begin strategic planning

Such planning will help families face the key challenges of working together in a business: (1) attracting the interest of capable offspring, (2) preparing them for the business, (2) selecting a successor, (4) assuring good sibling and in-law relationships, and (5) managing the transition from one generation to another.

FOUR

Assessing the Firm's
Financial and
Market Situation

As we have just seen, the foundation for future leadership of the business begins in the home. But the foundation for its growth lies in a financial and market analysis of the business. A complete analysis will reveal much more than the state of sales and profit. It will show whether a company is gaining or losing market share, using cash efficiently or inefficiently, and increasing or decreasing its productivity. It will even uncover whether the family is reinvesting sufficiently in the business to help ensure a vital future or whether it is primarily financing personal needs at the expense of the company.

As we noted in Chapter Two, natural forces at work upon the family business encourage the latter kind of activity. Sadly, many successful families are unaware of its damaging effect. Most assume that all is well if profit is strong and sales are rising. They think they can afford high levels of personal spending. And yet successful businesses absolutely require a certain amount of reinvestment if they are to continue to grow. Families that do not make the commitment to reinvest and instead spend the company's profit in other ways run the risk of milking the business. They set in motion forces that silently weaken the business, often in ways that will not show up at the bottom line for years. At that point, it may be too late to reinvest.

In this chapter, we will explain the analyses a business manager can perform to assess what is actually going on in his or her company. We will also discuss the rules of thumb to guide reinvestment and, what is even more important, the pro-

cedures for determining whether the business still merits revitalization. These analyses include (1) a financial analysis that as-
sesses the internal fiscal health of the business and (2) a market
and competitive analysis that will reveal how the company's
product and service shape up against competitors. Together,
they will indicate whether the business is currently decaying
and/or compromising its future.

The assessments of current and future decay are quite
distinct. A business that is already decaying looks unhealthy
right now; by contrast, a business that is compromising its future may not show signs of decline until much later. In fact, the
latter may often look quite healthy. Sales may be growing rapidly, so may profit. The analyses are thus intended to uncover
trouble signs that indicate future decay—signs that develop
when "excess" money is taken out of the business for purposes
other than reinvestment and that are often hidden beneath an
apparently promising trend.

The financial analysis and the market analysis, then, will
each be divided into two parts: (1) a set of assessments to determine whether the business is already decaying and (2) a set
of assessments to determine whether the business is compromising its future. A case analysis of "What's Happening, Inc.," included as Appendix B, methodically illustrates how to perform
the necessary financial calculations. Overall, the barometers of
current decay include declining profitability, declining productivity, inefficient use of cash, and declining competitive strengths.
Barometers that indicate a company is compromising its future
include a declining number of strategic experiments; declining
reinvestment in marketing, research, equipment, and training;
declining market value of the company; and declining market
share.

When the calculations have been completed, three critical
questions will have been answered:

1. How well are we actually doing now?
2. What does our future hold if no new strategies are under-
    taken?
3. What kind of planning do we need to do?

This chapter will primarily address the first two questions. Answering them will lay the groundwork for Chapter Five, which will identify the kinds of planning that businesses should undertake.

Financial Analysis

The barometers of business health that we have just listed are usually difficult to find in standard accounting and information systems. Uncovering them requires a variety of calculations, ranging from figuring the relative profitability of the business to determining its sustainable growth rate. Once the resulting ratios have been tracked over time, important trends can be identified and interpreted. The process is not complex, and the insights gained will provide a solid groundwork for later planning.

It is worthwhile to share these insights with the owner's family and key managers. Everyone then learns to interpret the financial history of the business in the same way. They all know, for example, what happened two years ago to increase sales or decrease labor costs. Everyone also begins to use a common language and to agree on the definition of such terms as *return on investment* or *market share*. All watch key business issues surface at the same time, becoming aware, for instance, that productivity is declining or that reinvestment rates are dangerously low. This focuses the attention of managers and the family on the business itself—on data and facts—and puts the emphasis on objectivity and rational analysis. Personal conflicts and personal agendas are then more likely to be put aside.

Using financial statements in this manner will be new to many family business owners. That is partly because many regard financial statements as a necessary evil required by the Internal Revenue Service. The statements are generally construed to represent past history that has little relevance to the present and even less to the future. Some accountants and financial advisers contribute to this interpretation. They do not organize the statements to highlight important financial ratios, nor do they take the time to analyze the statements for the business owner. Using financial statements to make the following calcu-

lations will clearly put the company in a new light for both
business owners and their financial advisers. If sales and profit
in the business are already slipping, these calculations will help
pinpoint *why*. They will also quantify just how serious the
problems are.

Barometers of Current Decay

Most owners describe their businesses as "profitable,"
"increasingly profitable," or "decreasingly profitable." Yet they
typically draw their conclusions only from their financial statement's bottom line or from net income. Many are not aware of
more meaningful measures. As a result, they do not know just
how profitable (or unprofitable) their companies really are.

Return on Investment (ROI). As a true measure of profitability, this ratio is much more valuable than net income. This
ratio indicates what percent the owner earns on the money he
or she has invested in the business. Accepted wisdom suggests
that the higher the ROI the better, but this is not always the
case, as we shall see later.

Return on investment is figured by dividing net assets
into total operating income, as shown in Table 6. So calculated,

Table 6. Calculation of ROI.

$$\text{ROI} = \text{Operating income}^a \div \text{Net assets}^b$$

Note: Measure only the income, expenses, assets, and liabilities required to run the actual business; ignore other activities reflected on the
books. Deduct only a reasonable market value salary for family members.
Other "bonuses" are really a return for ownership, not for work efforts.

[a]Operating income is income before taxes, interest income, and
extraordinary family expenses.

[b]Net assets are total assets, excluding cash and marketable securities, less current liabilities.

ROI provides a basis of comparison with the returns of other investments such as money market funds or stocks. It can also
show how profitable the company is in comparison to other
businesses: Figure 2, for example, illustrates the distribution of

Figure 2. Average ROIs of Business Units Differ Widely.

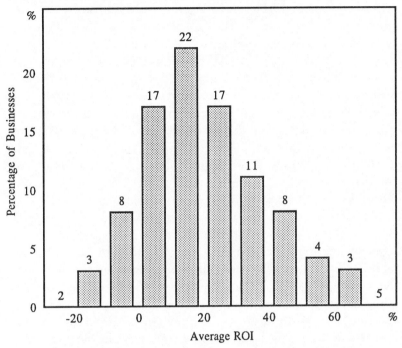

Note: Earnings are before interest charges and taxes; investment is working capital plus fixed capital at book value.
Source: Gale (1984).

ROIs for more than 2,000 public and private businesses. The average return is about 20 percent. That may sound high, compared to other investment vehicles. But such a return reflects the cost of money (currently between 9 percent and 12 percent), the owner's own sweat equity, and his willingness to take risks. Other ROI performance comparisons are available in such business magazines as *Forbes, Fortune,* and *Business Week,* as well as in the industry analyses of the *Robert Morris Report.*

Tracked over time, ROI shows what is happening to the profitability of the business. Whether the ratio is actually increasing or decreasing, however, is not as important as *why* it is doing so. An ROI might slump simply because low ROIs have become characteristic of a particular industry. In such situations, there is little an owner can do to increase return. ROI may rise either because its owner is running the business more efficiently or because he is failing to invest in projects that will encourage future growth. The former is probably a sign of success; the latter, a sign of failure.

"Real" Profitability. An owner's return on investment is a good measure of profitability. Yet if this understanding of profitability is based on a financial statement that has not been adjusted for inflation, an owner can get a skewed assessment. For a precise picture of the performance of the business, statements must be corrected for the impact of inflation on both price and cost levels. Profitability calculated on this basis may often reveal a lower level of "real" profitability, much to the business owner's surprise. Thus, many businesses have actually, in absolute dollars, benefited from inflation. They have unwittingly created "artificial" profits by raising prices to keep pace with posted increases in inflation (as measured by cost increases in raw materials and labor). They have done this even though the company's total costs, including such expenses as rent and administrative salaries, may not have risen as quickly as prices changed. As a result, profit margins widen, even though the business may be growing less price competitive in the market.

If a business were to raise its prices by exactly the same percentage as its costs increase, net profit dollars might still rise artificially, because the percentage increases would be calculated from different basis points, as illustrated in Table 7. Companies that are not aware of this effect may be more satisfied with their results than the facts of the case warrant. This is particularly dangerous when, unknown to its owners, a business is actually decaying, that is, losing profitability.

Cash Flow. The core of many business problems is revealed in an analysis of cash flow. Analyzing cash flow reveals the origin of money in a business—whether bank borrowing, price increases, or real sales—as well as its ultimate use. Business owners and their accountants can determine cash flow by comparing this year's balance sheet to last year's and asking a few questions of themselves. Did inventories increase or decrease? Have receivables gone up or down? Are payables and debt higher or lower? Such comparisons reveal whether managers are using

Table 7. Artificial Profit Increases.

Before 10% Inflation		After 10% Inflation	
Sales	$100	Sales	$110
Costs	90	Costs	99
Profit	$ 10	Profit	$ 11

Note: The extra $1 (or 10%) increase of profit is a product of pricing strategy, not necessarily the result of running the business more efficiently.

cash to build a better business or simply to fund the status quo. For example, if receivables rose along with sales and inventory held steady, this would indicate that cash is financing increasing sales for new customers. That is good. But if receivables and sales declined while inventory rose, that is bad. Cash is tied up in hard goods and is not being used efficiently.

Owners should also ask themselves if cash has been used to finance programs with future benefits (such as new equipment or research projects) or merely to reduce debt (a conservative measure that often has no real merit except providing owners with peace of mind). Additionally, they might ask whether receivables and inventories are rising due to sales growth or simple lack of managerial discipline. Signs of the latter include allowing customers to delay payment or manufacturing lines to produce more goods than sales warrant.

Productivity. Productivity is a measure of how much value a business produces, relative to the number of its employees. A highly productive business, obviously, turns out a large number of products with few people, given a particular level of automation. An unproductive business is the converse. It uses more people to produce less value. Most companies measure productivity by calculating sales dollars per employee, tracking over time. They figure that if the number goes up, the business is growing more productive; if the number declines, then the opposite is true.

Calculating productivity this way is better than not doing it at all. But the formula is flawed, partly because it does not require that sales dollars be adjusted for inflation. Nor does it show whether any effort has been made to improve the value of the product to the customer by providing extra services or adding new features. Either strategy may require more employees. In that case, what owners really need to know is whether their investment in personnel is paying off. Perhaps the added labor *has* added profitability. But perhaps it has instead eroded the company's productivity and thus lessened its potential profitability.

To determine the worth of an investment, we recommend another method of calculating productivity: one that will examine the *real value added* to the company, over time, per employee (Gale, 1979). Value added refers to the entire contribution a business makes to enhance the raw materials it purchases from others. This contribution includes labor, packaging, distribution, and marketing image, among others. (For a service business, there may be virtually no outside purchases; for a distribution or retail business, outside purchases may total 60 to 80 percent of revenues.) Added value can be calculated by taking inflation-adjusted sales figures and subtracting from them the inflation-adjusted price of raw materials and outside purchases required to make those sales. Then, to calculate productivity, divide the added value by the number of employees. This reveals how much "real value" (after inflation) each employee has truly created for the business. It is the best measure a manager can have for measuring the company's productivity. Over time, of course, a company wants to see this figure rise.

In a second method, which centers more directly on the efficiency of operations, productivity is measured by the rate of change in the company's overhead. Overhead includes not only general and administrative office expenses but also individual labor costs in manufacturing/operations (shipping, receiving, supervision, quality control, industrial engineering, and so on). By dividing indirect labor costs by direct labor costs within the manufacturing area and following the resulting percentage over time, one can track the ratio of these costs. An increasing percentage of indirect labor costs indicates increasing overhead relative to productive labor.

Using a similar method, one can divide general and administrative expenses by sales. An increasing percentage over time means that office costs are rising without proportionate support by sales. Again, that usually indicates a business that is growing less productive, although owners often rationalize such expenditures with the argument that certain increases in overhead—better information systems, better financial reporting, and so on—will also increase productivity. If that argument is to carry any weight, however, owners should subsequently record reductions in other expense categories at least equivalent to the increase in overhead costs. Such an actual management audit will indicate whether the desired economies were in fact achieved.

Sustainable Growth Rate. The growth of any business is often sustained by debt, which provides cash for projects that will encourage sales. Just how much debt a company should carry is, of course, an emotional subject about which people have strong opinions. The issue of how fast a business *can* grow —and how fast a family *wants* it to grow—can also spark heated debate among family members. Undertaking the following kind of analysis, which reveals how rapidly a company can grow without taking on proportionately more debt, is one way to add some objectivity to the issue. It puts in perspective both the profitability of the business and its tolerance for risk.

This tolerance for risk is called the sustainable growth rate (SGR). Managers can calculate it by dividing the aftertax, postdividend net income by the amount of equity the owners have in the business. The resulting percentage will indicate how much sales can increase annually without increasing the corresponding percentage of the assets of the business that are financed by debt. Most business owners will be pleasantly surprised by this ratio. They will probably be able to take on more debt than they had expected and thus will be able to fund projects to help the company grow faster than they had thought feasible. In fact, annual sales growth could reach as much as 30 percent in many businesses without increasing the proportion of debt. Other businesses, however, may discover that their level of profit does not allow much growth at all, perhaps 5 percent or less. These businesses will need to increase their debt load more rapidly to finance new projects or work harder to increase profitability if they are to grow.

Public companies escape this trap by selling stock in order

to raise funds. That option is not open to family businesses that wish to keep their stock closely held. As a result, businesses that want to continue to grow may have to take on a certain level of debt.

Barometers of Future Problems

The previous analyses will reveal any soft spots that are harming the company's *current* fiscal health. If they exist, sales and profit are probably already on the decline. Taking immediate steps to eliminate them is essential.

A thorough analysis must go one step further, however. For other kinds of soft spots, which are often hidden, can seriously damage the company's *future* fiscal health. They can be present even though sales and profit look robust; ironically, many of them may even be created by the business owner's desire to improve profit through conservation of capital. Such owners reduce debt. They buy no new equipment. They run no experimental programs that could expand the company's markets. Such tactics do increase net income now, but they lead to almost inevitable slumps later.

Alternatively, soft spots may occur because of the desire of business owners to improve the standard of living of their families. If profit is good, for instance, they may use that capital for family bonuses, a year-end vacation trip for all family members, or hefty salary increases. The result is the same as above: without reinvestment in the business itself, profit is likely to slump in the years ahead. Our assumption, of course, is that money spent on the business will help to secure a brighter future and that money invested outside the business will erode its prospects. As we have noted, families can sometimes engage in the latter unwittingly. That critical mistake is usually based on a belief that the business produces enough profit to cover all its needs, as well as the family's.

Hence, this second half of the financial analysis examines the sums that the family is either plowing back into the business or spending on other things such as debt reduction and family bonuses. Specific calculations include figuring the rate of reinvestment of the business, its strategic expenditures, and its market value. We will begin by discussing several ways to figure the rate of reinvestment. We can do this by examining ownership returns versus business investment, the family business annuity, the debt-to-equity ratio, the capital budget, depreciation of fixed assets, and strategic experiments.

Ownership Returns Versus Business Investment. One way to calculate whether the family is absorbing too much cash at the expense of the business is to figure family salaries and perquisites as a percentage of the total sum available for future business opportunities. That sum is typically measured by net income before taxes; therefore, to figure the percentage, simply divide family salaries plus perquisites by that sum. Family salaries and perquisites should usually be no more than 33 to 50 percent of operating income for mid-sized companies with more than twenty employees.

Over time, this percentage should decline even if more family members enter the business or family members begin to earn legitimate raises. Such a decline would indicate that net income is increasing relative to the income of the owner and the owner's family. That, in turn, would free up more cash to invest in the business. An increasing payout percentage of ownership signals the converse: more and more money is flowing out of the business into family pockets. That is an ominous sign if the family wishes to rejuvenate the company for the next generation.

Family Business Annuity. Another way to determine whether the family is taking out "too much" is to calculate what we may call the "family business annuity." This calculation clearly reveals how dependent the family is on the business for its current standard of living.

To make this calculation, first note the approximate worth of the business on the open market, that is, what it would bring tomorrow in clear cash if it were sold. Let us say $2 million is the rough estimate; that figure, then, is the "endowment." Now consider what return the family could earn on that same $2 million if it were safely invested in stocks or bonds. Let us say that return is 10 percent. That means the "earning power" of the business asset is potentially 10 percent times $2 million, or about $200,000 per year. That is the perpetual "annuity." Any more than that sum, flowing out to the family in the form of salaries, bonuses, and perquisites in excess of the replacement salaries of family management, means the business is slowly being devalued. Any less than that (with the rest invested back in the business) means the family is instead building the value of the business and, consequently, the benefits available to future family generations. Table 8 shows an example of this calculation.

Table 8. Calculating Family Business Annuity.

Endowment	Approximate cash sale value of business	$2 million
Annuity	Risk-free return on endowment if invested elsewhere (say 10%)	$200,000
Family Withdrawals	Cost of all family salaries, perquisites, and bonuses	$350,000
Replacement Cost of Salaries	Market value of family-held jobs	$120,000
Return on Ownership	Family withdrawals less replacement cost	$230,000
Excess or Reinvestment	Return to Ownership less "annuity"	$ 30,000

Note: The family is withdrawing more capital than the sum of their replacement salaries plus their annuity. This analysis assumes the family would take other jobs at their replacement costs if the business were sold. If family members do not obtain jobs outside the family business, their dependence on devaluing the business for the purpose of salary will become ever greater.

The fictitious sale is a good device to figure this particular calculation. In the real world, however, a sale is unlikely to occur if the family's draw is greater than the annuity value of the business. Under such circumstances, the owner really cannot afford to sell. Accustomed to spending more than the business is truly worth, he has trapped himself in a negative spiral of consuming business capital. This makes it increasingly difficult to increase the profitability of the business or to build a stronger business for the future. Families that wish to avoid this trap might consider one rough rule of thumb: annually take out no more than 10 percent of the market value of the business for salaries, perquisites, and dividends. That keeps "investment" in the family in proper relation to investment in the business.

Debt-to-Equity Ratio. Most owners of family businesses are eager to pay off debt. This gives them a sense of security and safety. Yet paying down debt means taking cash from operations—cash that could have gone into new product development, additional employees, or some other program to brighten the future of the business. To calculate the ratio of debt to equity, divide the amount of debt by the owner's investment in the business. (A healthy range for this ratio is 33 percent to 100 percent for most businesses.) Tempting as it may be to reduce that ratio, we suggest that businesses resist. Keeping the debt-equity structure constant keeps funds free for future investment.

Capital Budget. Another useful indicator of commitment to the future is the size of the company's capital budget or its annual expenditures for new assets. This budget should be much greater than the cash savings that result from depreciation expense (the amount written off for tax purposes each year). Most businesses should have a capital budget one and a half to two times more than annual depreciation in order for the business simply to maintain its current level of fixed assets, let alone improve that level. If capital spending is less than that, inflation is effectively depreciating the company's future, since the replacement values of assets usually increase much faster than annual depreciation.

Depreciation of Fixed Assets. Another useful indication of business reinvestment is the degree to which fixed assets (plant and equipment) have been depreciated. If they are *more* than half depreciated, the company's past reinvestment rate for the future is lower than average. If they are *less* than half depreciated, the business has newer assets than the average business.

Strategic Experiments. Still another way to discern the rate of reinvestment in the business is to count the number of strategic experiments underway. These include any new projects that have as their goal improving the profitability or competitive position of the business. These projects might involve a new product, an experimental distribution route, use of a substitute material in production, or an effort to sell to a new type of customer. Such experiments do not have to be risky or expensive. What is important is that they allow the company to explore new ways of doing business. At least one such project should be underway at all times. This is the best available indicator that the future prospects of the business are bright.

Strategic Expenditures. Trends in strategic expenditures—money spent on marketing, research and development, employee training, and newer fixed assets—are an excellent indicator of commitment to future business growth. These trends can be calculated by translating each category on the income statement and balance sheet into a percent of sales. Marketing expenditures, for example, may be 4.3 percent of sales. Managers should plot these expenses for several years running and note the resulting trends. If the business is not spending aggressively on the future, these ratios—marketing to sales, research and development to sales, training and development to sales, and equipment to sales—will decline. But if the business is increasing its investment in the future, the ratios will rise.

At the same time, a rise in strategic expenditures will lower another ratio we spoke of earlier: return on investment (ROI). Given our interpretation of financial ratios, a rising ROI would be bad for business. That contradicts accepted wisdom, which says that every company should seek high returns through a program of capital conservation, tight fiscal controls, and efficient operations.

We would recommend that companies learn to live with a low return on investment and rely on other indicators to determine how well they are performing. This sort of thinking is not new: the Japanese, for example, keep their ROIs much lower than ours—as much as 50 percent lower—and their debt levels much higher—often twice as high as those of American companies. This reflects a high level of current investment for purposes of building a stronger business future (Kotler, Fahey, and Jatusripitak, 1985). But the ROI must be low for the right reasons, of course. If a company's ROI is low because its money is being reinvested into strategic projects for future benefit, that is appropriate. If it is low because the money has been dissipated through slowing productivity, poor working capital discipline, and increasing overhead, the company is in trouble. Two calculations can help us make the distinction here:

The market value of the company should tell the true story. If the market value of the company is increasing, then— regardless of the level of current ROIs—the general investing community has sized up the company's future as increasingly attractive. But if the market value of the company is not increasing, observers believe the converse is true. For this reason, periodic appraisals of the business should be carried out.

The previous method has its drawbacks, however. Market values are fickle, and valuation methodologies yield approximate figures at best. Another tool to help assess the business is the strategic budget. The strategic budget includes all expenditures made for future benefit at current expense to ROI. Large, growing strategic budgets are proof that a business is committed to its future.

Business analysts can calculate the strategic budget of a company by deducting the dollars targeted for future payoff from the financial statements. These dollars would include expenses for marketing, new product development, employee training, or added technology but not expenses for replacement projects such as patching a leaky roof or replacing a truck. The adjusted statement would then reflect only those expenditures required to maintain the status quo. The ROI, calculated on the basis of this statement, should be very high; and in the years ahead it should become higher yet. Such a trend would reflect efficiency, tight controls, and managerial discipline. Using this adjusted ROI as a guide, a business can manage itself for future profit as well as for a maximized current ROI. This adjusted ROI will have only internal meaning, of course. It will not be useful in comparing the business to other companies or in negotiating a bank loan. Yet as an internal indicator, it has immense significance. It is demonstrable evidence that the company is committed to the future. As such, it foreshadows future profits and an increase in the overall market value of the company.

Market and Competitive Analysis

Just as a financial analysis provides valuable clues to what the future holds, so too does a market and competitive analysis. Its calculations assess how well the company is performing against its competitors. Improving this performance, of course, is the ultimate aim of reinvestment; a company wants to use its funds to initiate projects that will attract customers, beat competitors, and increase market share. This investment cycle is illustrated in Figure 3.

Figure 3. Strategic Investment Cycle.

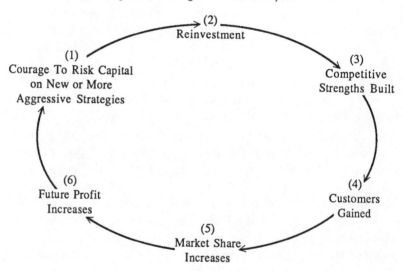

We have divided market analysis into two parts. In the first part, we will assess whether the company is compromising its future. To do this, we will measure changes in market share (specifically, this requires measuring how well or poorly competitors are doing, how many accounts the company has gained or lost, the degree to which it participates in fast-growing segments, and the rate of growth of customers and suppliers). In the second part, we will assess whether the company is already decaying, and here we will examine the company's relative competitive strengths: relative price, relative quality, relative rate of new product introduction, relative sales effort, relative promotional effort, and relative breadth of product line.

Assessing Future Prospects

We will begin this section with a discussion of one of the most crucial market barometers, as well as of ways to measure it.

Market Share. Many managers are satisfied if sales and profit are growing. They feel that is measure enough of business health. Yet those interested in a more insightful analysis will wish to study what *creates* strong sales and profit. They will track those indicators as closely as they do the bottom line. In this regard, sizable market share is one of the most important factors in creating a high level of profitability (Buzzell, Gale, and Sultan, 1975). Sizable share has many, many benefits: it increases employees' pride in their company, it enhances the company's market reputation, it eases access to distribution channels, and, obviously, it provides many economies of scale.

Furthermore, if a company's market share is not only sizable but is increasing, owners may expect higher profits in the future, since it proves that customers are increasingly happy with the company's products. By contrast, if sales are not growing as fast as the market or as fast as competitors' sales, then the company is probably in trouble—its market share is declining. Unless customers are increasingly pleased with the company's products and willing to buy more and more of them, the company will eventually lose market share and, thus, will suffer a decline in profitability.

Market share, then, is a critical indicator of business strength. But calculating market share is often difficult. In theory, measurement should be easy. One should only have to compare the sales of one company to the total sales of the entire market. Yet few businesses know the size of that "total market." Even large corporations that spend a good deal of money to ascertain such numbers must resign themselves to estimates; smaller companies without such financial resources must resort to even further guesswork. Making matters worse, the industries to which family businesses belong are typically fragmented, they include scores of competitors, and they have no trade associations to monitor sales. Still, several excellent measures of market share are available to the astute manager. They require only a good eye and an analytical mind.

How Competitors Are Doing. First, owners can monitor the growth of major competitors. While they will not learn the actual results achieved by other companies, observable signs such as the number of employees (count cars in the parking lot), raw materials purchased (talk to suppliers), or recent renovations are all good clues. The company growing the fastest is likely gaining the most market share.

Gained and Lost Accounts. Second, owners can examine the quality of gained and lost accounts. Listing the names separately is often helpful. They can then look at their respective lists and ask themselves, "If I had it to do over, which list would I concentrate on? Would I prefer to keep the accounts I gained? Or do I really want the ones I lost?" If they are pleased with the customers they gained, they are probably gaining market share. If they would rather have the ones they lost, however, they are probably losing share. Businesses work hard to develop new customers to replace lost ones, but what is most revealing is the trend in the quality of the accounts: Do they have more potential for growth, profit, and successful long-term relationships?

Participation in Fast-Growing Segments. Still another approach is to identify the fastest-growing segments of the market and to try to ascertain whether the company is in the thick of these new developments. A few questions asked of colleagues or suppliers will provide clues to markets that will be good for the long haul. A company should be growing at least as fast as anyone else in these segments, since they hold out the most promise. Riding such successes will help an alert company increase its market share, especially since many of its competitors will never expand into new segments; they are more likely to continue selling only to that segment of the market they have traditionally served.

Growth of Customers and Suppliers. Finally, business

owners who want to measure their market share can look at the growth of their major customers and suppliers. If their suppliers or customers are growing faster than the owner's business, then it is likely that some competitors are also getting the business. If the owners' companies appear to be growing the fastest, then they can rest more easily.

Assessing Relative Competitive Strengths

Knowing how to measure market share is one thing. Knowing what actually causes share to fluctuate—in other words, what causes customers to buy more or less of a company's product—is another. Customer preferences are strongly influenced by a number of variables, ranging from the price and quality of a particular product to special company promotions, such as new product campaigns. Those variables that attract the most customers can be collectively described as a company's *relative competitive strengths.*

All these require a certain degree of reinvestment, which we have already described how to monitor. Tracking the variables themselves, however, provides an even more valuable analysis of a company's health. Often these variables signal the future direction of a company's market share long before that share itself turns up or down, and they indicate a company's current condition as well. As a result, the entire management team should monitor and discuss these programs.

Of the six relative competitive strengths, *price* is usually the marketing variable that managers concentrate on in any battle for market share. Sadly, however, it ranks dead last among all the factors that contribute to long-term growth in market share. Price cuts can be copied too quickly to have any lasting effect. As a result, it is a transitory way to gain market share. Price cutting usually results in a large loss for everyone.

Price is important only in relation to *quality,* which is the most important cause of changes in market share. A product's *quality* describes everything the customer associates with that item *except* price; a company's overall *quality position* refers to its ranking against competitors according to the customer's own intangible yardstick. Phrased another way, quality indicates why customers prefer one product over another. In most industries, customers rely on much more than the physical traits of the product for this assessment, though such traits do typically account for 40 to 60 percent of their preference (Thompson, DeSouza, and Gale, 1985). Other characteristics they seek include support services (just-in-time delivery, good owners' manuals), the "right image," a professional sales relationship, ease of ordering, and so on.

Such characteristics can be difficult to measure. Yet the quality position they establish is the number one barometer of the future market share of a business. If a company's quality position is superior to that of competitors, it has the choice of either keeping prices competitive and thus gaining customers or charging a premium price and using the resulting profit to fund more growth.

To measure quality, owners should ask themselves and their managers this question: What percentage of any 100 people in our markets would say our company's products and services are clearly superior to those of our key competitors? What percent would say we are clearly inferior? What percent would say we are all about equal? (Companies that wish to confirm their estimates may consider hiring local college students or market research firms to perform more formal studies.) For example, if 30 percent say the company is superior, 10 percent say it is inferior, and 60 percent say it is about equal on everything but price, that company's relative quality index is plus 20 (30 less 10, or the subtraction of the inferior percentage from the superior). The index should be tracked over time to determine how well the company is serving the market compared to its competitors. A rising index, of course, foreshadows future increases in share and profit. A declining index should send an urgent message to managers to take steps to reverse the trend.

This index is a valuable tool. But its greatest value lies not so much in the percentage it yields but in the learning that results from making the calculations. By asking what customers really want, a management team can bring the company's products that much closer to truly satisfying market needs, and, ultimately, it can increase market share. Reaching agreement on such a subjective issue also helps the team develop cohesiveness and shared business goals. This automatically puts them ahead of managers who do not take the time to ask such questions and compare answers. If managers can offer the customer more quality and more value in addition to a good price, then they have created a company that can truly gain share. For it is the *price-quality relationship* that obtains share (not price alone). This means offering the same product at a lower price or a better product at equivalent prices.

Such strategies are powerful. Yet they work only until other companies begin to copy them. That means a company must include other tactics in any long-term plan to gain market share. Determining whether such programs are in place within the company gives a good indication of what lies ahead for it. The *rate of new product introduction,* for example, as measured by the percentage of sales drawn from new items over the last three years, is a very meaningful barometer. Once this percentage has been determined, it should be compared to the estimated percentage of the company's competitors. If the company's percentage is larger than that of its competitors, it will likely gain market share in the years ahead. If the converse is true, the company is likely to lose share instead.

Other measures of relative competitive strength are *relative sales force effort, relative promotional effort,* and *relative breadth of product line.* Additional spending on each of these usually results in increased market share. If two competitors have similar market shares, for example, but one spends 6 percent of sales on advertising and the other only 4 percent, the former will likely gain the advantage. While it is difficult to determine the amount of money spent by competitors in these areas, reasonable estimates may be made. For example, comparisons can be made on sales force compensation, media dollars placed, number of catalogue pages, frequency of coupon use, width of store shelf facings, and so on. When aggressive expenditures on sales, promotion, and products are implemented intelligently, market share gains can be expected. The trick is to avoid imitation by competitors and to ensure that the sales and profit gained are indeed worth the marketing dollars spent.

Summary

The future strength of a family business depends on continued financial investment in it. The longer family members want the business to live and the more prosperity they want to enjoy in the years ahead, the higher their rate of reinvestment must be. Yet, as we discussed in Chapter Two, the converse is often the reality. The longer business owners live, the lower their reinvestment rates are likely to be. They typically choose instead to take out money to satisfy their own needs, as well as those of their families and other constituencies. Unfortunately, many owners, especially those with profitable businesses, are unaware that they are making the family comfortable at the expense of the business. Signs that indicate that a business owner is funding the present at the expense of the future include:

- Declining profitability
- Declining productivity
- Inefficient use of cash
- Decline in competitive strength
- Declining number of strategic experiments
- Declining reinvestment in marketing, equipment, research, and training
- Declining market value of the company
- Declining market share

All these are the early warning signs that a family is harvesting or milking its business. For some families, that tactic may be desirable. Perhaps a family has concluded that the future of the business is dim or even hopeless for reasons beyond its control. If that is the case and the family still wants to find a long-term, prosperous role for itself in business, the family *should* harvest profit and seek out other business ventures in which to invest. But if the family has concluded that the business is a satisfactory investment, harvesting profit will not take ıt where it wants to go. Harvesting clearly compromises the future vitality of the family business.

    None of these issues can be decided easily. They require a certain amount of study, forethought, and planning in the formal sense of the word. Planning provides a process by which family members and managers can together decide whether to reinvest in or harvest a company.

FIVE

Developing a Strategic Plan
for the Business

The term *strategic planning* refers to the process of developing a business strategy. Strategic planning provides a systematic way of asking key business questions and is designed to create insights into the company and the environment in which it operates. Such an inquiry challenges past business practices and opens the way for choosing new alternatives. The result should be a well-prepared *strategic plan* that spells out specific steps to better satisfy customers, increase profit, and revitalize the company for the next generation. To accomplish these goals, the plan sets forth the chosen mission of the business, the direction of future growth, and various programs to achieve that growth. It thus indicates ways in which the business can compete more effectively.

Strategic planning is practiced by most large, successful companies, as well as by a handful of smaller concerns. Their approach is similar to the process we will recommend here for the family business, with one critical distinction. Here, we recommend preparation of a family strategic plan—right alongside the business plan—to spell out the long-term personal and professional goals for family members and clarify the "family structure" suitable for accomplishing those goals. In its ultimate choice of strategy, the business plan must reflect these considerations. In fact, the selection of a final strategic direction depends on the family's vision of the future.

All this represents a special challenge for the family business. For it means that the business and family plans are absolutely interdependent. The business plan requires the family to

98

determine the extent of its commitment to the company; but that commitment, in turn, depends on the prospects for the business that the planning process reveals. The business plan seeks to choose the best of several alternative strategies; but, again, that choice must reflect such considerations as the interests of offspring and the family's attitudes toward investment.

This intricate overlay of family and business plans *requires* that the family not separate strategic business planning from family planning. They must undertake both in a connected and simultaneous way. There is no single path to follow in order to accomplish this. It may take several years for the plans to fully interconnect and for the goals of each to become fully harmonious. But the principle remains clear. Planning for the future of the business and for the future of the family cannot be too far apart, either in emphasis or timing (see Figure 4).

In this chapter we will concentrate on the *business plan*

Figure 4. Interdependence of Family and Business Planning.

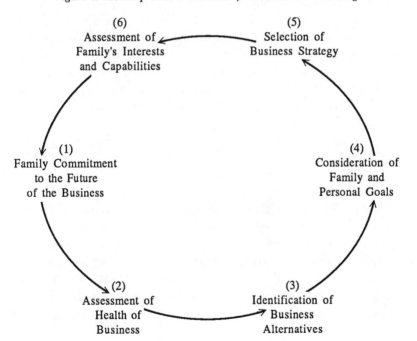

that the company's managers, including both family and non-family members, should prepare. Its documents will include (1) a preliminary statement of family commitment, (2) a business mission statement, and (3) a business strategic plan. In Chapter Six, we will discuss the preparation of a *family plan.* Then, in Chapter Seven, we will show how these two plans interact to lay the foundation for the managers' final selection of a business strategy. Ultimately, such a strategy should (1) lift the company onto a new level of sales and profit, (2) revitalize the company as it moves from one business life cycle to another, and (3) provide a healthy, growing company for the next generation to manage. Preparing such a plan will not only keep healthy businesses healthy but will reinvigorate any company that has somehow become stagnant over the years.

Family Commitment

Because of the interconnection between business and family planning, a family could take up the planning process at nearly any point. It could first take up family issues and determine whether the children are or are not interested in running the company. Or it could take up business issues first, asking accountants to analyze the health of the business and managers to examine its markets. We would suggest, however, that for a family business the ideal starting point is the family itself. Specifically, we suggest that the family first establish its commitment to the future of the business and to planning as a way of securing that future.

This commitment may be secured at a family meeting. If the children are young, participants might not extend beyond a husband and wife; if the youngsters are older and part of an extended family, the meeting might include the entire clan. The discussion should determine whether the family is willing to make a general commitment to the business. It should also attempt to determine the depth of that commitment: whether the family is willing, for example, to sacrifice certain material gains in order to invest money back in the business. Other matters for discussion might include the time it takes to build a business, the family's willingness to work together, and the leadership capabilities that offspring possess.

If family members reach consensus, managers can write a preliminary statement of commitment that says, in effect, "We are fundamentally interested in the long-term future of this business. We want this business to last forever. And we will do what it takes to accomplish that!" The wording does not have to be elaborate. A sentence is all that is required at this stage: "XYZ Corporation will remain a family business" or "Our family is dedicated to the long-term success of this business" are both quite adequate. Once the initial agreement of the family is secured, the rest of the planning process will flow from it. If the offspring are very young, subsequent planning is likely to focus almost exclusively on business issues. The goals that emerge will very likely be those of the business owner alone. As family successors become available, however, family considerations will become more and more important. The planning process will reflect that shift.

The family's statement of commitment provides a good opening sentence for the announcement to employees that the planning process is about to begin. Many owners, to be sure, may wish to keep the planning process private until they are ready to share its results. Yet making the process public has untold benefits. Employees in a family business, for instance, *expect* to see family considerations affect the direction of the business. They watch for signals as to the owning family's plans and openly speculate about what is happening in family discussions. As a result, they waste valuable business time discussing these questions among themselves.

Of course, it is not entirely idle gossip. Employees are naturally concerned about their own careers and about what would happen if the business were to be sold. But it creates a good deal of idle time from a business standpoint. Family members, whether they are employed in the business or not, are not exempt from these worries. They too are eager to learn about the owner's plans. A statement of commitment, made publicly, reassures employees and family members alike. It allows them all to go on with the business at hand: developing the best possible family business.

Strategic Planning Defined

The basic planning process we propose here is applicable to all businesses. Integrating the results of the process with *family* strategy, which we treat in the next two chapters, tailors this approach to family businesses, however. We recommend discussing the business plan first because business topics are less emotionally charged than family issues. Discussing such topics also helps family members in management begin to assess their assumptions, values, and goals. In the end, however, it will be the family strategy that shapes the thrust of the business plan.

Budgeting and Long-Range Planning. The terms *budgeting, long-range planning, strategic planning,* and *strategic management* are often used interchangeably. Each has a particular meaning, however. Budgeting, for example, involves setting business goals for the coming year; developing a one-year budget for sales, costs, profits, and cash; identifying what tasks are necessary to fulfill budgeted expectations; and identifying whose job it is to complete those tasks. It is an essential step in the business planning process. As a result, businesses should have working budgets in place before undertaking other planning efforts. Most businesses require two to three years to successfully integrate the budgeting process into their other management processes. They begin it at a fairly predictable point in their evolution, that is, in the early stages of growth when they need to ensure themselves of sufficient cash flow and begin to delegate management tasks.

Once a business has grown accustomed to budgeting, it needs an even more sophisticated tool to ensure that it does not come up short on financial, physical, or human resources. Then the company is ready to undertake *long-range planning.* Long-range planning recognizes that the achievement of future sales, profits, and cash flow will require certain preparations in the near term, such as building a new plant or expanding the sales force. The results of long-range planning include budgets that cover the next *three to five years*; reasonable goals for sales, profits, and cash over that period; and the assignment of tasks this year that will make it possible to reach those goals later.

To successfully complete long-range planning, the business must consider potential threats and opportunities in the external environment (such as shortages of raw materials, rising interest rates, and so on). The business must also determine what its growth goals demand of the present. Reaching the goals may require building a new warehouse, training new salespeople, or replacing a soon-to-retire key executive. Funds must be provided for these projects now, even though the payoff may not come until several years later.

For obvious reasons, none of these plans can be worked out in a short afternoon conference meeting. Indeed, long-range planning often requires several daylong meetings, which are sometimes held during once-a-year "retreats," at a hotel or resort and attended by top managers. Typically, businesses pursue this kind of long-range planning for several years before embarking on *strategic planning*. But that is not always the case. Some companies simply include long-range planning as one portion of strategic planning. These companies graduate directly from budgeting to strategic planning.

Strategic Planning. Unlike its more simplistic predecessors, strategic planning does not assume that business growth will automatically occur. Instead, strategic planning assumes that growth will occur only if specific steps are taken to encourage it. The purpose of the planning process is, of course, to determine what steps are necessary. This awakening to the need for planning emerges at a predictable point in the company's evolution, usually when one of several circumstances occur:

- The market stops growing, competition heats up, and the business seeks to protect historic growth rates
- New competitors (discount stores, direct mail or private label competitors, foreign competitors, and so on) enter the industry with new ideas on how to compete
- The industry's technology changes dramatically

- The size of the business reaches 200 to 300 employees and/ or some of its units require more delegation of key decisions, better development of management talent, and improved responses to competitive change

Readers will notice that these are the same forces that propel a business toward regeneration, as discussed in Chapter One. Consequently, strategic planning often becomes attractive as a tool to achieve such revitalization. It is also a way of solving the problem of developing successors in mature businesses.

Strategic planning is distinct from *strategic management* in that the latter generally makes its appearance after the business has pursued formal strategic planning for several years. At that point strategic planning has become ingrained in the management process. Its questions have become an integral part of how managers think. They perpetually challenge basic assumptions, pursue new market information, experiment with new ideas, seek new opportunities, and work hard not only to do their own jobs but to train their people for the future. When this sort of strategic thinking becomes second nature to managers, the firm is *practicing strategic management.* At that point, all parts of the planning process have been integrated into the management process.

Research suggests, however, that only a very few businesses reach this advanced stage of strategic development (Gluck, Kaufman, and Walleck, 1980). In this book, therefore, we will concentrate on strategic planning. We will assume that readers are already budgeting within their companies and may have begun a little long-range planning as well.

Results of Strategic Planning. Strategic planning recognizes that a business has the power to shape its future direction. It also appreciates, however, that outside forces, especially competitive forces, can alter that direction. Strategic planning thus defines what kind of company its owners envision, as well as what owners must do to achieve their goals. Specifically, strategic planning addresses three issues:

1. *Where* do we want to compete—in what markets?
2. *How* can we compete effectively in those markets?

3. How aggressively do we want to *reinvest* our corporate and family resources?

These questions can be answered through a step-by-step process of inquiry, which we will outline in the next section. Answering the questions *where to compete* and *how to compete* will provide insights into the marketing and operating strategies necessary for competitive success. Exploring the question *how aggressively to reinvest* will suggest the direction of growth and the broad goals that are most appropriate for the future of the business. When the inquiry is complete—a process that can take one or more years—managers will have the raw material to produce two documents that will outline the company's future: (1) the strategic plan and (2) the mission statement.

As illustrated in Table 9, the strategic plan has five sections: (1) Business Goals, (II) Business Programs, (III) Business Policies, (IV) Departmental Plans, and (V) Strategic Plan Responsibilities. The full plan summarizes the managers' marketing

Table 9. Strategic Plan Outline

I. Business Goals
   A. Financial goals
      1. Growth goals
      2. Profit margin goals
      3. Asset turnover goals
   B. Market share goals
      1. Build or hold or harvest
      2. Rate of change
   C. Investment goals
      1. Reinvestment goals
      2. Risk goals
II. Business Programs
   A. How to respond to strategic issues
      1. Build stronger competitive advantages
      2. Counter competitors' efforts
      3. Adapt to changing industry and market
      4. Adapt to changing environment (for example, technology and demographics)
      5. Develop a key business competence
      6. Overcome strategic weakness
   B. How to achieve strategic goals
      1. Reduce costs

(continued on next page)

Table 9. Strategic Plan Outline, Cont'd.

---

    2.   Increase asset use
    3.   Improve pricing
    4.   Improve productivity
    5.   Develop technology
    6.   Improve quality
    7.   Improve service
    8.   Penetrate current customers
    9.   Expand product line
    10. Acquire new customers
    11. Enter new markets
III. Business Policies
    A.   Products and services policies
        1.   Breadth of line
        2.   Quality, branding, and packaging
        3.   Service
    B.   Market policies
        1.   Geography
        2.   Segments and priorities
        3.   Types of customers
    C.   Channel policies
        1.   Types of channels
        2.   Extent of coverage
    D.   Pricing/credit/terms
    E.   Promotion policies
        1.   Choice of forms (that is, direct mail or media, and so on)
        2.   Levels of expenditure
    F.   Product line development policies
        1.   Rate of new development
        2.   Developed internally or copied or acquired
    G.   Market development policies
        1.   Rate of market expansion
        2.   Goals and tactics for market development
    H.   Operations and manufacturing policies
        1.   Degree of vertical integration
        2.   Level of capacity utilization
        3.   Use of capital vs. labor
        4.   Union status and relations
        5.   Choice of and terms for suppliers
        6.   Location of facilities
    I.   Organization policies
        1.   Degree of decentralization
        2.   Form of organization (for example, functional or profit center)
        3.   Character of organization culture
    J.   Administration policies
        1.   Information developed and shared

Table 9. Strategic Plan Outline, Cont'd.

		2.	Reward system
		3.	Review and control system
		4.	Planning system
		5.	Hiring and training system
	K.	Financing policies	
		1.	Sources of debt
		2.	Uses of excess resources
		3.	Balance of debt vs. equity
IV.	Departmental Plans		
	A.	Departmental objectives	
	B.	Departmental goals	
	C.	Departmental budgets	
V.	Strategic Plan Responsibilities		
	A.	Key tasks	
	B.	Responsible manager	
	C.	Resources needs	
	D.	Dates of accomplishment	
	E.	Form of review and feedback	

analysis and then spells out its competitive implications in terms of specific financial goals and business programs. Managers will be able to write this plan after answering the inquiries in Chapters Five and Seven and after considering the Family Plan outlined in Chapter Six. (A sample plan is included in Appendix D.)

The mission statement, which defines the future vision of the business, is a distillation of the entire strategic plan. This statement is not just a simple sentence that describes what the company makes or what service it provides. Rather, the mission statement reflects specific decisions that the company has made about its products, strategies, and goals, as shown here:

• Choice of products/services, markets, and geographies
• Choice of priorities among market segments and business units
• Choice of growth direction for future
• Choice of "generic" strategy (that is, competing on price or differentiation or specialization)
• Choice of competitive advantage
• Choice of key business competence(s) or strength(s)

- Choice of goals for the future
- Choice of management style
- Responsibility to various constituents: customers, suppliers, employees, stockholders, and community

One such statement from an English glassmaking company, for example, describes the company as "a worldwide, diversified, innovative, high-technology glass company dominantly positioned in flat glass in selected developing countries and the British Empire, operating in a highly decentralized mode, with strong centralized creative planning, developing a new professionalism in its management and in its employee-human relationships, intending to grow at 15 percent per year with pretax returns on investment at least in the upper one-third of the industry worldwide" (Quinn, 1980, p. 180).

Such a statement is clearly more effective than one that merely says, "We are a glass company." Properly done, the mission statement becomes not a string of hoped-for attributes but a solid summary of strengths and goals, as determined by the strategic planning process. The formulation of this mission statement and its companion strategic plan may seem like a formidable task. Yet it is the natural outgrowth of management meetings concerning the plan. We have already noted that the ideal starting point for the planning process is a meeting of family members at which their commitment to the family business is secured. We suggest the process continue with a series of meetings among top managers, the outcome of which will be the documents we have just described.

Format. Many formats are available for these strategic planning meetings. We recommend an annual calendar of twelve half-day meetings, each scheduled to pursue a particular topic as outlined in Table 10. Meetings should be held monthly to allow time for both preparation and assimilation. Half-day meetings are recommended because the sessions can become quite intense. Meetings should be spaced a month or more apart to allow time for processing information and developing ideas that will later be useful. These strategic planning sessions should take place, if possible, away from the company. This prevents inter-

Table 10. Sample Twelve-Month Strategic Planning Calendar.

Preliminary Preparation (January)
1.   Analyze past performance to develop issues and performance goals.

Where to Compete? (February through April)
2.   Define market segments, their relative attractiveness and importance to the company.
3.   Determine customers' desires and company's capability (relative to competition) to serve them.
4.   Identify competitors and analyze their strategies.

How to Compete? (May)
5.   Identify strategic alternatives for growth and profitability.

How Aggressively To Reinvest? (June and July)
6.   Analyze external opportunities and threats; outline programs to respond.
7.   Identify company's strengths and weaknesses; outline programs to respond.

Finalizing Plans (August through November)
8.   Set preliminary goals, keys to success, and business policies.
9.   Refine marketing and operating strategies.
10. Determine final goals and policies.
11. Develop departmental plans for strategic action.

Conclusion (December)
12. Discuss mission statement proposed by chief executive based on preceding analysis and planning.

---

ruptions, which can be fatal to productivity and creativity. It also underscores the importance of planning in the eyes of top management. Productive meetings are also aided by good facilitation. This includes written agendas, recording of minutes, orderly discussion, controlled debate over controversial subjects, and specific follow-up activities (including assignment of tasks and "to-do lists").

Some businesses prefer to run these sessions themselves, with only a book such as the one you are now reading for a guide. Others, especially those without anyone on their staffs with experience in strategic planning, use consultants to help facilitate this process. Fees for such a service customarily range from $5,000 to $20,000 for the year. Under certain circumstances this is also an excellent role for an educated, mature successor. It will provide him or her with a tremendous opportunity not only to learn the business but to gain the respect of the management team.

Participants. As a rule, those who participate in the strategic planning process are those who report directly to the chief executive. Depending on the size and structure of the business, others may also be included, either on a regular basis or from time to time. The regular planning group should be limited to between five and eight people. Alternatively, some owners may wish to include family members who are working for the business but who have not yet reached the level of senior management. If it is clear that a particular family member *will* be a top manager within the next three to five years, much can be gained by including him or her.

Larger companies with several lines of businesses have special considerations concerning the composition of the planning group. Each major business unit might have its own planning group, carry out its own planning process, and issue its own final written plan. In such cases top managers must make two decisions: (1) whether to begin planning at the top management level (before the business units begin their planning) or at a decentralized level (before top managers begin theirs), and (2) whether to begin planning as an "experiment" in one business unit or simultaneously in all units. These decisions depend on the needs and culture of the individual business. Generally, however, planning is best done on a decentralized, experimental basis. That approach tends to elicit broad support for the planning process, which is critical to its success.

All companies, large or small, may find value in occasionally consulting experts on particular topics in the planning process. Persons knowledgeable in such areas as technology, government regulation, or customer needs can open up the group's thinking beyond customary boundaries. Inviting members of the board of directors to planning meetings is also useful. As observers, they can help the company critique the planning process and evaluate the strategic plans that result. And in so doing, the board members themselves will learn a good deal about the business and its organization.

All family business owners must make a strong effort in these planning sessions to encourage challenges. They should openly question their own assumptions, actively solicit the opinions of others, and create an atmosphere in which managers can mutually explore options and share perspectives. This will encourage key managers and family members to challenge the president's practices when they see good reason to do so. That is fundamental to successful strategic planning. Owners will also need to overcome their natural reluctance to share financial statements and results. Lack of access to financial performance greatly lessens the ability of top managers to take a comprehensive view of the business. And, obviously, they need to know the actual amount of money available for future projects.

The Questions of Strategic Planning

There are many formats available to help a company formulate a mission statement and its companion strategic plan (Aaker, 1984; Steiner, 1969; Rothschild, 1979; Brandt, 1981). In the next section we will propose one that we hope will provide a complete checklist of strategic planning questions.

Specifically, the question *where to compete* includes: What market segments exist for a particular company? What makes a segment generally attractive? Which market segments should be emphasized in the future? What will it take to succeed in these segments? What should the general marketing strategies be for attractive segments? How well is the company now performing in each segment relative to the competition? What market share does the company have in each segment; what share do competitors have? What generally makes for an attractive customer? Who are the most attractive potential customers in the most attractive segments? For these target accounts, what selling strategy is most likely to work?

The questions involved in *how to compete* are: What are the possible sources of competitive strategies? On what does each of our competitors base his strategy? Is there any strategy competitors cannot use? What strategic weapon is the company using? What is the company's sustainable competitive advantage?

The question *how aggressively should we reinvest* includes: How attractive is the general environment in which we operate? How healthy is the industry? How much opportunity is present in the market? How strong is the company itself?

Category One: Where to Compete?

The question *where to compete* involves more than geographical considerations. It involves determining the market segments that are most worth the company's time and effort. The premise of this exercise is that different market segments, each composed of a certain type of customer, have different requirements. Some expect excellent service, others want low prices. Still others put personal attention as a priority. The company cannot satisfy all these requirements in an effort to be "all things to all people." If it tries to do so, it will lose focus and likely lose market share to cannier competitors. Instead, managers must determine the customer groups that their company can best serve. To do this, they must answer a series of detailed questions:

What market segments exist for a particular company?

A market is the world of customers who might buy a company's product. *Segments* are defined by the aggregate differences among these people. Segments can be classified according to many different measures, including:

- Purchase decisions (how different customers decide what to buy, how often they buy, and who makes the ultimate decisions)
- Product-service package (the additional services that customers expect when they buy a product, ranging from prompt delivery to gift wrapping)
- Geography (whether customers are local, regional, national, or international)
- Method of selling (from whom customers buy—retail stores, sales representatives, catalogues, and so on)

By using these and other categories, imaginative managers can come up with a list of market segments. They can then determine which segments require different strategies. Segments that differ according to (1) growth rate, (2) market share that the company already has, and (3) types of competitors will probably require different tactics for penetration.

Managers can sharpen their feel for the segments that the company already serves by doing a market history, which analyzes sales by category (see Table C-1). These histories analyze past sales five ways: by type of product, type of customer, geographical area, top twenty customers, and selling method. Managers who wish to pursue this analysis should list sales dollars, sales units/orders, sales rank, percentage of gross margin, and gross margin rank for each category. By doing this three or more years in a row, managers will be able to see the relative importance of each segment and how much each contributes to profit.

Another way to analyze segments already served by the company is to analyze customers that the company has recently gained or lost. *This is probably the most important and insightful single analysis a manager can make of his or her business.* Here, managers should list the company's top twenty accounts, including the dollars they contribute to sales and profits, for the past three to five years (see Table C-2). They can then determine who has been gained, who has been lost, why, and to whom.

In coming to understand why it is losing customers, a company will also learn how its competitors compete and how their methods differ from its own. As a result, this kind of analysis will clearly pinpoint where a company is competitively weak and also, through the customers it has gained, where it is competitively strong. Managers will discover why the company disappoints some customers and satisfies others. The analysis will also identify its most aggressive competitors.

Managers can conclude the market segment identification process by using the market segment map (see Figure C-1) to analyze how segments differ. This map is probably the best way to describe a company's market segment alternatives and the competitive circumstances of each.

What makes a segment generally attractive?

A segment is generally attractive if it is growing and prof-

itable and offers reasonable odds that a company can outper-
form the competition. Several factors contribute to a segment's
underlying attractiveness. Managers should consider the following factors and identify those most likely to make a segment
attractive within their particular industry:

- Larger size
- Faster growth rate
- Clear indicators of demand
- Less buyer concentration
- Less cyclical and/or seasonal fluctuation
- More buyer profitability
- More buyer sophistication
- More buyer professionalism
- Greater loyalty of buyers to suppliers
- Smaller number and greater concentration of sellers
- Less capability of existing competitors to satisfy needs

*Which market segments should be emphasized in the fu-
ture?*
Managers should rank the segments previously identified
according to the above criteria of "attractiveness." The result
will be a list of segments in a particular industry that hold the
most promise for growth and profit.
What will it take to succeed in these segments?
Success depends on knowing what the customers in these
segments want, that is, on knowing the demands they will place
on a particular industry and company. These desires are based
on a number of characteristics, ranging from materials and price
to production technology and personal relationships. A more
extensive listing is included in Table C-3. Readers can probably
add many characteristics of their own, tailored to their individual industries. Taken together, these characteristics form the
"critical success factors" for a particular business. Performing
the same exercise for each segment identified as attractive for a
particular company will give managers a feel for what is and is
not important to pursue. Listing these factors in order of importance for each segment further refines the analysis.

What should the general marketing strategies be for attractive segments?

In marketing, a company has basically three choices. It can offer one thing to everybody; this is an "undifferentiated" strategy. Or it can use a "differentiated strategy" and offer something special to each segment. Finally, it can offer one thing to one set of customers; this is a "concentrated" strategy. A concentrated strategy focuses on a single customer group and works to give that group precisely what it wants. Managers should determine what kind of strategy their company is now actually using and decide if that is the best approach. After considering what customers want, they should answer the question: For each segment, should the company's strategy be differentiated, undifferentiated, or concentrated?

How well does the company perform in each segment relative to the competition?

Managers should make a list of the company's top three to five competitors in each segment. They can do this by ranking each market player (including their own company) according to the critical success factors listed earlier. *This may be the second most important market analysis that can be made* (see Table C-4). The analysis should reveal some competitors who compete similarly to the company in similar segments, as well as some who compete differently and/or emphasize different segments. Competitors similar to the company are its key competitors—in other words, they are the company's "strategic group." It is against these similar competitors that "improvement strategies" must be developed because they are the ones most vulnerable to competitive attack.

What market share does the company have in each segment? And what shares do competitors have?

Managers should review the list of competitors developed so far, estimating each competitor's market share, strengths, and weaknesses. They must then rank the market segments according to those that are most attractive, namely, those in which the company has the greatest market share and the strongest competitive advantage (see Table C-5 as a summary of this section so far).

What generally makes for an attractive customer?

In answering this question, managers should identify criteria for evaluating preferred customers. These may range from paying on time to keeping sales appointments. Others include:

- Size of the customer's company
- Market share of the customer in its market
- Customer's rate of growth
- Customer's loyalty to suppliers
- Number of sources the customer uses
- Profitability of customer
- Customer's fairness to suppliers
- Customer's stability of need
- Purchasing sophistication and quality expectations of customer

Who are the most attractive potential customers in the most attractive segments?

After considering the range of potential buyers, managers should make a list of names in each of the most attractive segments, keeping the list short. It will be assigned at some point to the company's salespeople, and the more they can concentrate on just a few key accounts (no more than five or ten), the better their chances of securing the business. The potential buyers thus identified become the target account list.

For these target accounts, what selling strategy is most likely to work?

The selling strategy is a plan of attack tailored to a particular customer in a particular segment against a particular competitor. It will reflect the best the company has to offer that particular account. The elements of a good selling strategy for each customer include the following information:

- The critical success factor most important to the customer
- Past sales experience with the customer
- The total businesss potential with the account
- The sales goal sought with the customer
- The competitors already dealing with the customer
- The advantages and disadvantages the company has relative to each competitor dealing with the customer

- The best "sales pitch" the business can make to the account
- The salesperson best suited to approach the customer
- The expected sales cycle, including the number and frequency of sales calls anticipated to secure samples and/or quotes and/or the order

Clear selling strategies for each customer are especially useful for members of family businesses who are expected to somehow "learn the business" through sales. Often they are left to fend for themselves; and, as part of the outside sales force, they may come to feel detached from the family. Thus, setting clear sales goals and targets will clarify expectations and aid in the coaching process. Actively involving such family members in determination of the selling strategy can also help them greatly.

The upshot of this planning stage is that managers will have developed a list of the company's different *market segments* and ranked them in *order of attractiveness* or priority to the company. They will have identified the *critical success factors* for each segment. They will know the *key competitors* and also know the company's *competitive position* in the segment. They will have clarified the company's key *selling advantage* against those competitors in a way that should improve its position in the future and enable it to attract new customers. Finally, they will have identified the *target accounts* and worked out the *selling strategy* needed to win over those accounts and allocate their sales force resources. The conclusion of all these determinations forms the marketing strategy elements of the company's overall strategic plan.

Managers will now be ready to turn to the second category of analysis: how best to compete in the market segments of choice, given their company's relative competitive strengths and weaknesses.

Category Two: How to Compete

All business owners want to beat the competition. To do so, they must be able to offer a product or service that is significantly better, cheaper, or otherwise more attractive to the

customer. They must, in short, make their products (and therefore their companies) *different* from those of their competitors.
Determining that difference—in a way that builds on the company's natural and cultivated strengths—is the heart of strategic
planning. It is the essence of knowing *how to compete,* that is,
of crafting a competitive advantage for a particular company
that will withstand all challenges. A competitive advantage that
can withstand all competitive challenges is the company's *sustainable competitive advantage.* The company should eagerly reinvest to strengthen this most important advantage.

What are possible sources of competitive strategies?

Competitive strategies should be based on a unique cost
or service advantage that is difficult for other competitors to
copy or even recognize. Raw materials may be a strong point;
for example, a company may simply have a cheaper source of
steel or silver than competitors. A more efficient process for designing and manufacturing a product is another possible advantage. Again, a company may be able to produce at a level of
technical excellence unmatched in the industry, or it may have
a similarly high level of skill in distribution, promotion, or marketing.

A company can add significantly to the value of its product in the eyes of the customer by skillfully using one or more
of these tools. A strategy based on one of them that makes the
company distinct from competitors and attracts customers in a
profitable manner that the competitor cannot copy or attack is
a truly creative and successful strategy.

On what does each competitor base his strategy?

Managers should determine what competitors do with the
"weapons" just identified, estimate what it costs them to do it,
and determine why they do it that way.

Is there any strategy that competitors cannot use?

As we have noted, real success comes from doing something competitors cannot or will not do. For example, if a competitor sells nonbranded products through independent distributors, he will not be able to benefit much from advertising. A
successful counterstrategy in such a case would be a strong advertising campaign, emphasizing the good name and service that
the company can provide.

What strategic weapon is the company using? Are there weapons it cannot use? Are there any additional ones it might use?

This applies the previous logic of competing, wherein competitors cannot effectively respond to or determine how the company is vulnerable and how to limit the vulnerability.

What is the company's sustainable competitive advantage?

The previous questions should have illuminated the variables that set a company apart from competitors. The unique characteristics that emerge will form the core of the company's *competitive advantage.* The *sustainable* competitive advantage is that which makes the edge last over time—in other words, that which will keep competitors from matching or copying a strategy. To pinpoint a company's sustainable competitive advantage, managers should not look to the desires of their customers but should instead examine crucial aspects of their own company—for example, the sums spent on research and development or the time spent on developing a top marketing team. Such expenditures greatly increase the chances of long-term success.

These sustainable competitive advantages vary widely. For example, one competitor's capital-intensive mass production and automated scheduling systems may allow it to be the low-cost producer. Another competitor may have established a good joint venture with a software programming house—a venture that allows him to do custom programming for customer service applications in different industries. Advantages may also be more general: brighter employees attracted by high salaries, for example, tend to create a better company. A low-paid pool of employees makes a company less costly to run. A small plant with the latest equipment is likely to give a company flexibility. A large plant with adequate equipment will probably make for cheaper production runs.

Ultimately, the advantage of each competitor will fall into these "better" or "cheaper" categories. By matching these advantages with the factors that make for success in a particular market segment, a company is on its way to working out a sound strategic plan. Pinpointing these elements also provides early clues as to whether a company is worth reinvestment. If what a company has to offer matches what the market wants, that company will be well worth the additional investment. If the converse is true, owners should perhaps put their money to work elsewhere.

Companies whose capabilities allow them to do things "better" will choose a "differentiated" generic strategy; those whose capabilities allow them to do things "cheaper" will pursue a "low-cost" generic strategy. Some businesses, of course, will be able to identify capabilities that allow them to do things both better and cheaper for a particular type of customer; they will follow a generic "focus" strategy (Porter, 1980). A focus strategy recognizes that specializing in only one type of customer can offer opportunities to not only serve the customer better but also more cheaply. Selling paint only to contractors, for example, can allow the company to serve particular needs of contractors—such as the size of containers—as well as keep costs down through such tactics as avoiding the media advertising necessary for paint companies who also sell to retail consumers.

Once the basis for success has been determined, managers need to outline the policies or programs necessary to maintain and extend the company's competitive advantages. Relevant policies that should be addressed include:

- pricing
- promotion
- selling
- distribution
- customer service
- product development
- market development
- research and development
- manufacturing/operations
- financing
- administration

If, for example, the business has identified its competitive advantage as that of a low-cost, mass manufacturer, appropriate policies may include (1) offering the lowest prices in the marketplace on its high-volume products, (2) developing new products that utilize the equipment already in place or permit the purchase of more automated machinery, (3) selling to the largest customers in the market, (4) distributing its products in full truckloads, and (5) investing aggressively in research and development engineering that will reduce the material content cost of its products. Such a collection of policies would consistently reinforce the competitive advantage—and generic strategy —that this low-cost, mass manufacturer has determined for itself. The development of programs to implement the firm's competitive advantage has the added benefit of identifying action plans for individual key managers. Many family businesses desperately need job descriptions that clearly specify roles and responsibilities. Such descriptions greatly lessen conflict among managers, and they also promote enthusiasm for the business.

By this point in the strategic planning analysis, managers should have gained many insights into their company. They have defined their market, determined what potential customers want, analyzed competitors' ability to meet these desires, evaluated market segments, examined the potential strategic weapons within the industry, and considered what competitive advantages are available to them. Most importantly, they have decided what the company can do to sustain its strengths, and they are thus on their way to selecting a final strategy to guide investment decisions. But one major task remains: examining the real overall strength of the company within its political and social environment, its industry, and its market.

Category Three: How Aggressively Should We Reinvest?

Business owners typically depend on personal effort to overcome challenges. As a result, they come to think that the fate of their companies lies completely within their own hands. So they often avoid analyzing objective business factors that will affect the future. Both elements are important, of course. A business owner does have a critical influence on his company. But if, for example, Congress were to pass a law requiring companies like his to purchase $3 million worth of safety equipment over the next two years, he might be better off not investing any more time or energy in that line of business.

There are in fact numerous factors that influence the question of whether or not to reinvest in a business. Before business owners decide to implement a new strategy, therefore, they should ask the following questions:

1. How attractive is the environment?
2. How healthy is the industry?
3. How worthwhile is the market?
4. How strong is the company itself?

The more positive the answers to these questions, the more aggressive business owners can be. A very attractive external environment and a very strong business, for example, make possible a very aggressive approach—one that would exploit the marketing strategy already identified. An unattractive environment, coupled with a strong business, indicates instead that managers should seek new market opportunities. A weak business, operating in an attractive environment, suggests the need for strategies to develop new business capabilities. A weak business in a weak environment points in the direction of divestiture.

Resolving these questions—and settling the issue of how aggressively to reinvest in the future—is one of the most fundamental (and difficult) tasks for those involved in a family business. As we will discuss in Chapter Seven, family businesses tend to underassess the potential of their companies. This can lead to family discord, especially between conservative and risk-taking members of the family. Approaching these questions in a professional manner focuses the family on business assumptions, instead of on differences in personal philosophies. It will also begin to reveal the family's true commitment to the future of the business (see Figure 5 for major alternative directions).

How attractive is the environment?

Managers should examine economic, demographic, and technological trends, social currents, and political and legal developments and should then ask, What is the impact of these trends and developments on demand? On key customers? What

Figure 5. How Business Situation Dictates Strategy.

Very Attractive	Very Aggressive Market Exploitation Strategies	Moderately Aggressive Business Development Strategies
Evaluation of External Situation (Environment, Industry, and Market)		
Very Unattractive	Moderately Aggressive New Market Strategies	Very Unaggressive Strategies

Very
Strong   Very
                                 Weak
            Evaluation of
       Company's Relative Strength

is their likely effect on the market, competitors, the industry, and the company? The result of this analysis will be identification of the three to five environmental trends that create the greatest opportunities and/or threats to a business. It will in fact be revealing to see whether the trends appear to produce more opportunities or more threats. It may be worthwhile to develop task forces to deal with the most important trends. For example, a task force might be assigned to explore alternatives to dramatically escalating insurance costs.

How healthy is the industry?

The health of any given industry can usually be forecast by recognizing the trend of profit margins and sales growth rates as the industry's product life cycle evolves. For example, young, emerging industries are usually less price competitive and more profitable than older ones. Mature and declining industries offer less opportunity and usually face stiffer competition.

The task for managers is forecasting where any particular

industry will be at any given time. Clues to market maturity and price competition—and, therefore, industry profitability—may be found in the power that suppliers and buyers have over companies. The degree of rivalry among competitors, as well as the degree of difficulty that *new* companies have in entering the market, is also a clue. Such factors shape the industry and have significant impact on the choice of strategy for a company (Porter, 1980). They are further elaborated in Table C-6.

One of the keys to planning, then, is to know how much of the company's profitability (or lack thereof) is due to industry pressures that are beyond managers' immediate control, as well as what forces are actually shaping the future of the industry. The more favorable these industry circumstances and trends, the more bullish a company would be in its choice of strategies and in its reinvestment philosophy. The more unfavorable the conditions, the more conservative it would be in the future. Recognizing that much of a company's profitability is related to external industry factors has special value in a family business. Very frequently the firm's profitability is attributed purely to "good" or "bad" management. This can cause tension in a family, especially between members of different generations. Such tension can be significantly eased by the simple realization that other important factors may be at work in any given situation.

How much opportunity is there in the market?

Managers may differ in their opinions of how strong a market is and how many opportunities are available in it. Factors to consider include the market's potential volume, its diversity, and its growth rate. Other factors are listed in Table C-7. Ultimately, if the disagreement is too great, it may be necessary to call upon a market research firm to separate opinions from facts. Generally, the more opportunity a market promises, the more eager a company will be to invest. The optimum situation would be a growing market with specific opportunities for an individual company in certain segments. If the market lacks opportunity, the company should consider strategies that would open up other, more attractive markets.

After evaluating the environment, industry, and market

assumptions, management should be able to come to a conclusion about the attractiveness of their situation. It is highly important that they reach agreement on the choice of future strategies and the rate of business reinvestment.

How strong is the company?

Earlier questions designed to pinpoint the company's competitive advantages provide important clues for determining how strong a company is. Managers will also know in some rough way whether their company has a big or small chunk of the market. Still, there are some specific questions they can ask that will create fresh insights into their company's relative strength. While asking managers about the strengths and weaknesses of their business often elicits only broad, positive statements (Stevenson, 1976), asking this question in the following, more specific ways may help to suggest plans for improving weaknesses and exploiting strengths:

First, what are our functional strengths and weaknesses? Are we strong in marketing, weak in purchasing; strong in operations, weak in data processing? What strengths and weaknesses do we note when we consider our skills, talents, and resources? A checklist, included as Table C-8, may prove helpful in answering these questions.

Second, what can we learn about our strengths and weaknesses by comparing the discrepancy between our past goals and our actual achievements? Do we always fall short of our goals? Or do we usually exceed them? In what ways do we exceed them or fall short? Why?

Third, what have we done that we are most proud of? Served customers well? Gained new accounts? Improved quality? And what can we learn from these achievements?

Fourth, what can we learn about our strengths and weaknesses by examining our most profitable and least profitable accounts? Analyzing our most profitable customers should reveal our relative strengths, while examining our least profitable customers should expose some of our weaknesses.

Fifth, what can we learn about our strengths and weaknesses by looking at our employees? What is their typical education and background? How long do they on average stay with the company? Do we tend to lose our worst employees, our good ones, or our best ones? Does the company fire many employees? (Determining the kinds of employees that we hire, keep, fire, and lose will tell us much about our strengths and weaknesses in recruiting, management development, and compensation policies. So will analyzing where they go and where they came from.)

Sixth, are our current advantages strong? Are they sustainable?

Seventh, are our competitors' current advantages strong? Are they sustainable?

Eighth, do we have a strong and/or growing market share, or do we have a small and/or declining market share?

Finally, do we search out opportunities to create new advantages? These inquiries into relative business strength and weakness should build consensus on how strong the company's managers believe it to be. The stronger they think its position, the more willing they will be to choose aggressive strategies and high reinvestment rates.

We intentionally focused on business strengths and weaknesses last because doing so earlier in the strategic planning process, as many planning methodologies recommend, is risky for a family business. At that point, many family members are not yet ready to hear criticisms from other members. Objectivity and a business focus for the future have not yet been established. By the end of the planning process, however, consensus has almost always been achieved on important issues. Then, planning programs are more likely to reflect a shared vision of the future rather than differences in management styles.

At this point in the strategic planning process, managers have done enough to make an informed, preliminary decision about the company's prospects. They have pinpointed the market segments that show promise. They have decided how their company can best penetrate those segments. And they have assessed whether any weaknesses in the environment, industry, market, or company itself will stand in the way of implementing those plans. As a result, the strategic "data base" or set of business assumptions is complete. Managers can now tentatively finish most of the Business Programs (section II) of the Strategic Plan Outline. They should also know what Business Goals are feasible (section I) and what Business Policies (section III) are appropriate for the current business evaluation.

However, managers do not yet know the family's objectives. As a result, they still cannot make a final determination on how aggressively to reinvest in the company and in what direction. The emphasis of the plan will later be adjusted to reflect family issues, as we will discuss in Chapter Six. In Chapter Seven, we will then show how managers can combine the results of family and business planning to make final determinations concerning strategy and reinvestment and thus select a strategic direction for the company's future. When that strategy is clear, managers may then set about determining the Departmental Plans (section IV) and the Strategic Plan Responsibilities (section V). Tasks for the plan's implementation are delegated to specific individuals.

Summary

For many family businesses, developing a strategic plan has substantial value. First, it begins to establish the future direction of the business. Second, for those family businesses that have become stagnant over the years, strategic planning discussions can revitalize operations. They are fun, they motivate people, and they create hope.

The process of developing strategy begins with the family's statement of commitment to the business. It continues with a series of management meetings among those who report directly to the chief executive officer. Over a period of months or even years these managers will systematically study the business and the markets it serves, according to a specially formulated series of questions. They will then be able to draw up a preliminary assessment of the prospects of the business.

Meanwhile, the family, too, must explore its options. Its decisions will significantly affect the future of the business. Families that are experiencing conflict often find these meetings to be much more therapeutic than traditional processes or organizational consultation. Strategic planning is therefore useful as a special brand of counseling, especially since it occurs in a setting far more acceptable to most business owners than does traditional counseling.

When the family and business inquiries are complete, managers should be able to write a mission statement for the company as well as a business plan. These documents set forth specific goals for the business and ways to achieve them.

 SIX

Planning the Family's Role in the Company's Future

In a family business, the family takes on a special significance. It acts as a source of employees. It draws upon company resources. Its members even act as sounding boards and providers of new ideas. The personal goals of these people therefore critically affect the direction of the company. They are the single most important influence upon the business plan outlined in the last chapter.

Because of this, many successful business families find it useful to develop a strategic plan for the family and the family's role in the business. Such "family planning" allows the family to identify the goals of those involved. It formalizes the family's commitment to the company's future, and it helps shape the vision of that future, both for the business and the family.

Such a plan requires (1) preparing a family mission statement that will detail *why* the family is committed to perpetuating the business, (2) working out a family "vision" or conceptual model that will outline how the family sees itself and its business in the years ahead, (3) developing key programs that will provide a systematic approach to such family activities as making decisions and resolving conflict, and (4) establishing objectives that specify steps for accomplishing the goals that the family has set. Such materials may take a variety of forms, ranging from an open family letter to formal statements. Whatever their format, the preparation of these documents is a demanding process. It requires each family member to freely discuss his or her plans. It frequently requires that at least one person spend many hours coordinating the plan's development,

129

researching the experiences of others, and analyzing the plan's financial implications. The effort can be so time consuming that leaders of some family businesses have taken a year-long sabbatical to accomplish the task.

Many family leaders, however, feel that these planning formalities interfere with what should be a natural process. A family should simply *happen*, they feel. They resist the idea of formal family planning because it is time consuming, it seems to involve too many unknowns, and it may invite trouble by initiating discussions of sensitive topics. Our research suggests, however, that many successful families work hard to explicitly plan their direction. Developing a plan provides an opportunity to discuss family goals and business opportunities, and it aids in formulating the family philosophy. Lastly, when the plan is complete, it can serve as a guide to all the family's efforts and decisions.

We believe that most families have inherent strengths that will help them carry out this planning process. Most families, for example, have learned over the years how to resolve conflicts. They have persevered through difficulties. They have developed members who are able to act as peacemakers and who know how to listen to others and keep a discussion constructive. They have leaders experienced at mending the disagreements that will inevitably arise. Almost all families also share strong emotional bonds—formed during childhood—that encourage cohesiveness and the pursuit of common goals. Extending these bonds to the family business will strengthen and ease the planning process. Families also understand the need for sacrifice to help build a better future. Think, for instance, of the amount of emotional effort and money that parents "invest" in rearing their children.

Moreover, families adapt well to change. Despite the stresses to which it is now exposed, the family unit remains one of the most flexible structures we know. It can accommodate birth and death, changing values and changing times. As a result, families often find that the kinds of changes encouraged by the planning process are easier to handle than they had thought they would be.

To be sure, families with serious emotional problems will find it difficult to focus on the planning process and have productive meetings. But what we propose in this chapter is for "normal" families—families that possess listening skills, the ability to resolve conflicts, the flexibility to adapt to change, and bonds of affection (Walsh, 1982). These families may have disputes and disagreements. Their members may have different needs, roles, and expectations. But these differences are normal, part of the inherent challenge in running a family business. And for such families, the planning method proposed in this chapter can be invaluable.

Family Meetings

The starting point of family business planning is the family meeting. This is the mechanism through which most plans are made and the forum in which the family's future hopes and ideals are developed. Gaining consensus and opening discussion on critical family business issues are its valuable by-products. Moreover, formal planning is not the only purpose these meetings can serve. They can also help settle disputes and increase family members' awareness of the history of the business. They provide a vehicle to communicate any topic of general concern. As a result, they make a vital contribution to keeping a family business healthy.

Long before formal planning is undertaken, these meetings may be used to help educate and govern the family through discussion of such topics as the nature of the company, the kinds of leadership skills it needs, conditions for coming into the family business, decision making, and resolving disputes. Casual conversation on these and other subjects can provide a solid foundation for later, formal family planning. Their nature depends greatly on when they begin in the family's history.

Evolution of Family Meetings. Some families hold meetings when the children are young, typically discussing family matters only. They talk about the assignment of chores or household rules. Parents hear the complaints of children; children hear the complaints of parents. They then learn to resolve

conflicts through discussion. Family psychologists who recommend this approach (Adler, 1970; Dreikurs and Saltz, 1964)
argue that it teaches family members each other's logic and personal goals. The family also learns to conduct well-run meetings; it learns the importance of starting on time, listening carefully, and following up on results. Such habits lay the groundwork for sharing business decisions, an important element in
perpetuating family businesses.

Families that begin to meet when their offspring are teen-
agers and thus old enough to work in the business have different
agendas. They tend to discuss the history and the nature of the
business. In these conversations, owners may comment on pride
in the family's heritage and achievements. They may highlight
the fact that the behavior of individual family members affects
the family's community standing. And, like the meetings with
younger children, these meetings establish a valuable forum for
the mutual exchange of views and values. At this stage of the
family's development, planning is seldom a topic. Meetings are
usually casual, perhaps held over the dinner table or on a family
vacation.

As offspring become adults, however, the nature and purpose of these meetings often change. Now the "children" are
likely to begin actively considering careers in the family business. As a result, owners who had never before considered holding a family meeting may now convene one for the first time.
But they may be uncertain as to who should attend these meetings, who should lead them, what the agenda should be, what
format should be followed, and how often meetings should be
held.

Who Should Attend. Two schools of thought govern the
question of who should attend family meetings. One group says
that only those who are adults and blood relatives should come.
The reasoning here is that sensitive family matters should have
only a limited audience because it is then easier to maintain
confidentiality. The other group says that *all* family members, including young teen-agers and spouses, should be welcome. This
group reasons that since the family business affects these people
—and vice versa—they should be included.

We subscribe to the latter school. We think that all family members should attend family meetings for several reasons, including the fact that in-laws will inevitably hear the results of the meetings from their spouses. Far better for them to gain their information firsthand! Attending meetings also helps acculturate them to the family's traditions and processes and acquaints them with the "larger vision" of the family and the business. We also believe that both teen-agers and spouses can make valuable contributions by providing fresh perspectives. And if the mood of the meeting is right, they may begin to articulate their own intentions regarding the business. That is information vital to family planning. For many families, however, the issue of who attends these meetings will settle itself over time.

Who Should Conduct. Readers may assume that the natural leader of these meetings is the owner of the business. Yet family meetings provide the perfect opportunity to broaden the leadership base. As a result, the job of organizing and conducting the meeting should rotate among different members. This trains potential successors in leadership skills. It offers older family members the opportunity to recognize which offspring might later lead the business. And it creates an awareness that the leader of the family and the leader of the business do not necessarily have to be one and the same person.

Format. The frequency and setting for family meetings vary widely. Some families, for example, meet regularly, even weekly, for discussion over supper, Sunday dinner, or Saturday morning coffee. Others meet once a year in a formal setting with formal presentations; the Newhouse family of newspaper and publishing fame, for example, gathers all seventy-six descendants once a year over Thanksgiving dinner (Machalaba, 1982). Another family spends the first three days of a two-week vacation at a modest villa discussing family business; another meets as a family immediately after its quarterly board of directors' meeting. Still another large multigeneration family meets twice a year—once at a formal dinner at a family member's home, preceded by a meeting, and once at an informal recreational picnic, also preceded by a meeting.

Agenda. At least once a year, the family should review the company's performance and plans, assess the family's own plan, and update personal activities and goals. Some families use these meetings to develop committees, elect members to various positions, and share information about financial investments. The agenda of one active family's annual meeting is given here (real names are not used):

1. Family history update by Uncle Pete Sass: slide presentation of Sass family's contribution to community activities and charitable causes
2. Review annual corporate financial results, goals, and *plans* for next year
3. Family development session: "How To Be More Effective Listeners" by Professor Steven Sloane
4. Review family activities for past year: stock club, family newsletter, and family office for bookkeeping and insurance records
5. Elect officers of Descendants' Club
6. Cocktails and dinner
7. Special recognition ceremonies for Linda Sass—high school yearbook editor, and for Bob Sass, Jr.—college graduation

In addition to these regular functions, meetings can also serve some very specific purposes. Some families, for example, hold two-tier meetings: one for the whole family and one for the next generation alone. This system helps the incoming management or ownership team develop its own leadership and relationships. It also encourages self-sufficiency. Following is a list of activities at one such "cousins' club" meeting:

- Review family's code of conduct
- Discuss dreams for the business
- Circulate published family business articles
- Discuss extracurricular interests
- Plan corporate social event
- Plan individual social events

Development of the Family Strategic Plan is also a specific purpose for family meetings; in fact, working out that plan is their most significant purpose. It thus requires a formal agenda and approach.

Planning Agenda

When a family is ready to discuss strategic planning, children are often in their twenties and thirties, parents in their fifties. At this point, families will ordinarily be in the habit of holding meetings of some sort. For purposes of the following discussion, however, we will assume that the family is meeting formally for the first time. We will also assume that the extended family's knowledge of the company and of one another's plans is sketchy. Such circumstances call for certain preliminaries before the start of planning itself. The planning process we are about to describe can take anywhere from one to five years, depending on the pace at which the family chooses to proceed. The documents it will cover are shown below. (A complete example of a Family Strategic Plan is included as Appendix E.)

1. Family Mission Statement
    A.   Commitment to business and family continuity
    B.   Reasons for commitment
    C.   Values and philosophies underscoring commitment
2. Family Vision: Conceptual Model for the Future
3. Family Programs
    A.   To govern and make decisions
    B.   To resolve conflict
    C.   To relate to each other—code of conduct
    D.   To educate the family
    E.   To ensure family unity
4. Family Objectives

The first meeting should center on the history of the family and the business: who founded the business, why, which family members joined and when. Here, the eldest family members have a chance to share special stories. So do other family members who have taken key roles in the company's development. Photographs, scrapbooks, business mementos, and product catalogues may all be part of the presentation.

In the second meeting, the focus should be on "business." Family members should be given an overview of the company's financial history, complete with charts of sales and profit. Accompanying the charts should be some indication of how profitable the business is relative to other companies in its industry. An explanation of where profits actually went—into securities, for example, or for new equipment—is also very important. So is some description of the company's overall strategy: where it competes, how it competes, and in what direction it is headed. Here, presentations by nonfamily managers that outline key issues facing the business can be valuable additions. For these first meetings, it is important to leave almost unlimited time for questions, no matter how naive some of them may be.

At the third meeting, the family begins to lay the groundwork for the writing of its mission statement. This groundwork is twofold. It should include a discussion of the pros and cons of perpetuating the business. It should also cover the critical issues the family will face, should it decide to take up the challenge of carrying on the business.

Perceived benefits of the business will vary widely from member to member. One may see it as a source of jobs; another, as simply a source of pride and achievement. Some may view the business as nothing but a drain on family energy and resources. Whatever the opinions, the key purpose of the discussion is to address the question, Why should the family work to perpetuate the business into the future? The answer to this question will later form the basis for the first section of the mission statement.

The balance of the meeting will identify the critical issues that the family foresees, should members decide to keep the company in the family. These issues might include: How should it pick the next president? What happens if a family member proves to be a weak manager? What if a family member gets a divorce? The possible issues are outlined in Table 11. The intent of the discussion is not to solve all these potential problems—at least, not at the moment—but merely to develop some understanding of the challenges ahead. This will encourage conversation on these difficult topics.

Certain techniques can facilitate such discussion. Some families, for example, bring in a family business expert to outline the issues. This removes the burden from any one family member; it also encourages the asking of questions. Other families attend business seminars that highlight such topics. León Danco's semiannual seminar at his Center for Family Business in Cleveland introduces more than 100 families a year to the problems of succession; so too do workshops by trade associations and the Young President's Organization. Some families even put together their own seminars, inviting other local families that own companies to present ideas and solutions at a panel discussion or business round table. As in the case of the outside consultant, such seminars depersonalize the topic. They also make plain the comforting fact that many families confront the same challenges.

Whatever the means—meetings, consultants, seminars, family business panels—the main goal of the third meeting is to provide the whole family with a sober recognition of the issues and effort required to be successful and to set forth some of the reasons why members feel it will be worthwhile to perpetuate the company. The goal is also to open up a broad range of topics and concerns around which family members may begin to develop philosophies and principles. These, in turn, will begin to shape the family's overall strategic plan.

Family Mission

We will assume that the third meeting revealed a broad base of support for continuing the company. Now is the time to prepare a mission statement that will describe in detail the family's commitment to the business. This statement will explain *why* the family is committed to perpetuating the business, and

Table 11. Critical Issues for Family's Future.

Succession

- How do we assure our parents of lifelong financial security?
- What nonbusiness interests will keep the parents fulfilled during retirement?
- How do we pick the next president?
- When does the presidential transition take place?
- How do we decide that?
- How do we evaluate the next president's performance and consider his replacement?

Participation

- How do we decide which family members can join the family business?
- What preparation, if any, is required?
- How do we determine titles and authority?
- What if a family member employee doesn't work out?
- What if a family member chooses to leave the business?
- Do we permit spouses or other nonblood relatives to work full or part time in the business?
- Do we allow the next generation's children to enter the business?
- Under what circumstances?

Compensation and Ownership

- How do we evaluate and pay family members?
- Who participates how much in the financial growth or future of the business?
- Who can own stock in the business?
- What returns and rewards do shareholders get?

Harmony

- How do we deal with conflicts between generations?
- How do we deal with sibling conflict?
- How do we teach in-laws the business and also our family traditions?
- Who will lead the family activities and customs into the next generation?
- How do we make future family decisions?

Responsibility

- How do we help family members in financial and/or career need?
- What responsibilities does one family member have to the other?
- What if there is a divorce?
- What if a family member breaks the law or acts in a seriously irresponsible way?
- How much financial information do we share with whom?
- How do we protect the contributions of good, nonfamily employees?
- How do we support family members' new business venture ideas?
- How do we cope with public visibility and the public's expectations of successful families?
- What responsibility do we have to the community?

---

it will also specify the central values of the family. Such statements might also include (1) a summary of family priorities, (2) a list of the strengths that the family can contribute to the business, and (3) an outline of what the business needs from the family. An excerpt of one such mission statement is shown below. (Real names are not used.)

> We seek to achieve growth and prosperity, extending beyond the present generation, through our business. . . . We are committed to providing opportunities for descendants of Richard C. and Iris Carlson . . . and their families to (1) obtain a firsthand understanding of the risks and rewards of American business ownership, (2) gain insight into the value of Christian principles in business, (3) experience the sacrifices and rewards of family members closely working together toward common objectives, and (4) maximize the quality of life for their families and future generations.
>
> To encourage all descendants of the founders and their family members to develop and apply their specialized talents to the business and to compensate them according to their contribution.
>
> To provide an ownership opportunity to all direct descendants of the founders while they are full-time participants in the business.
>
> To foster a spirit of belonging as "extended family" to nonfamily employees as well, by sharing appreciation, rewards, and benefits that will maximize a mutually prosperous and enriching long-term relationship.

Such a statement may be developed in several ways. One way is for each family member to prepare in advance his or her personal beliefs on the pros and cons of perpetuating the family business. These would be presented aloud at the fourth meeting, then drafted as a formal summary. Alternatively, each member might begin with a statement of his future goals and career hopes and make clear whether or not they involve the business. These individual statements can then be shaped into a family consensus statement.

A third approach is for the family to recall certain of the critical issues, or questions, presented at the third meeting. These might include:

- Which family members will be welcome in the business?
- What qualifications must they have?
- What compensation do they deserve?
- What titles should they be given?
- How should ownership be distributed?
- What returns does ownership deserve?
- Who has what leadership responsibilities?
- How are business decisions to be made?
- What role should the leaders of the business play in the community?

Once the issues are again on the table for discussion, various members may propose "family philosophies" to serve as guidelines for resolving them. These philosophies—call them propositions—can then be developed and distributed among family members for acceptance, revision, or rejection. One family member should draft a proposed family mission statement for continued discussion at the next meeting. The following is a list of such propositions from one family:

1. We believe that the best business is an ethical business based on Christian principles.
2. We place a high value on doing things together rather than "doing your own thing."
3. To perpetuate the rights of future ownership and participation to *all* descendants of the founders.
4. To offer rewards from the family business to those who are actively managing and participating in the family business and not to pay dividends to any possible passive owners.
5. To continue to try to maximize the quality of life of the shareholders now and in the future.

6. To encourage all direct descendants of the founders and their mates and their children to participate in the family business.

7. To utilize the talents of each family member to increase the power of the business.

8. If an opportunity or an idea is a good idea for one of us, it's better for all of us—therefore, let's share business opportunities collectively.

9. We have a responsibility to fulfill, in every way possible, the entrepreneurial instincts and needs of individual family members.

10. Whoever is running the business should be in control of the business.

11. We recognize that entrepreneurship is a part of our family blood and tradition, and we need to encourage and support entrepreneurship and entrepreneurial ideas within our family business. We believe we should encourage and offer advice to family members to pursue independent business interests.

12. Foremost, we should provide every family member the opportunity to fulfill their interests and capabilities. First of all, within our family business, and second of all, to their own independent business interests.

13. We wish not to have in-laws or nondirect descendants have ownership of stock.

14. We prefer that ownership and its rights be continued in proportion to the current relationships of immediate family ownership. We believe that the rewards should be in proportion to contribution to the business. We believe it to be possible to return stock for cash through buy-sell agreements within the family.

15. We want to allow people to return to an equity position, even if they've given it up or left or not come into the business for a long period of time.

16. If anyone were ever to own some passive ownership, it should appreciate in value, not in relationship to the business but in relationship to the purchasing power of the dollar.

These form the basis of the family mission statement. For example, this family clearly wanted to include as many family members as possible in the business (see propositions 3, 4, and 6). Hence, the mission statement emphasized that *all* family members would receive the opportunity for ownership.

Typically, these propositions will cluster around an answer to the basic question: "Whose interests should come first—those of the business or those of the family?" The resolution of this issue will shape a consistent response to matters such as business participation, ownership distribution, and compensation. It will also present a philosophy that can be communicated throughout the family and that family members can understand when anticipating difficult family business decisions such as how to handle an undisciplined family member employee. The family profiled above, for example, decided to offer rewards from the family business only to active managers and to make those rewards proportionate to their business contributions (see propositions 4 and 14). These propositions indicate that the family is willing to put the concerns of the business before those of the family. The family is willing to risk personal conflict over unequal incomes because it thinks that a competitive salary schedule will provide an incentive for good business performance.

Any family has three basic choices for its philosophical orientation. Some, such as our sample family, may choose "business first." They choose to support what will be best for the company, including its customers, employees, and shareholders. They select sound business principles to govern such matters as compensation, hiring, and titles. They reason that such principles are fair and thus constitute excellent criteria by which to make the tough decisions that will affect the entire family. They are willing to abide by these principles *even if* they lead to unequal treatment of family members or, ultimately, to selling the business.

Others take another perspective. They believe that the family's happiness and sense of togetherness should come before everything else. Their decisions will favor family equality and unity, even if they come at some expense to the company's future. The practical result of this philosophy is that differences in the quality and degree of family members' contributions to the business will not be recognized. Such families will allow everyone to enter the business and will pay everyone equally. It is unlikely that a family member would ever be fired. The family believes these principles are important, even if they cause financial harm to the company.

There is a third philosophy, which seeks a balance between these "business first" and "family first" attitudes. This philosophy holds that any decision must provide for *both* the satisfaction of the family and the economic health of the business. Only under such conditions can a company stay in the family well into the future. Only a good compromise will win the enthusiasm of the family and support for the business. Family members who hold this view believe that abusing the needs of either family or business will damage the future. We describe this philosophy as one that promotes the "family enterprise." It implies a long-term commitment to the future of the business and the family and requires the family to creatively resolve conflicts between the two interests.

As we have noted, the choice of the family's philosophy helps resolve the very decisions most likely to arouse conflict. While every family must decide what is best for it, we propose that special consideration be given to the "family enterprise" doctrine. Table 12, which outlines ways to resolve difficult family business decisions, details how different business philosophies affect decisions common to all family businesses. When deciding who will and who will not be allowed to enter the family business, for instance, families would select only those offspring who could actually contribute to the business. But the family would also work diligently to make certain that others had suitable career opportunities outside the business. On monetary matters—compensation, dividends, and stock ownership—the family would work to keep personal financial expectations in line with business reality. But the family would also work to share the benefits of business success with all family members.

Balancing both the family and business goals in such sit-

Table 12. Family Philosophy's Impact on Business Decisions.

Business Decision	Business First	Family First	Family Enterprise First
Entry Rules	For specific job, if qualified	All welcome	Opportunities will be developed for all individuals in or out of the business, depending on family business needs
Compensation	As job description warrants	Equal pay for all members of same generation	Acceptable family standard of living assured for everyone
Stock Ownership	According to business philosophy (that is, all to chief executive or distributed according to contribution or possibly among nonfamily employees)	Equal by branch of family	Equal values for all—some in business stock, others in passive investments or entrepreneurial opportunities
Dividends	None	Stable, fair return to capital	Variable, modest return to capital
Titles and Authority	Based on merit in a business hierarchy honoring the principle of each person having only one boss	Equal titles for all members of same generation and role in decision making for all shareholders	Equal roles for all those with high degree of competence
Governance	Board of outside directors	Broad family consensus	Representative family council
Role in Community	Leadership	Voluntary	Active according to family needs and individual interests

uations requires compromise, extra effort, extra planning, and extra communication. However, this approach not only preserves the integrity of the business but also serves the individual needs and interests of the family's members. Once the family mission statement has been developed, the next step is selection of a conceptual model, or so-called family vision. Preparing it will allow the family to discuss its future.

The Family's Future Vision

The eight models described below are all constructs of what a family could become five to twenty years from now. Each has its pros and cons, and each has particular implications for the family's business. A list of these models should be passed around the family prior to the meeting at which they will be discussed. Family members should select the one that most closely matches what they would like the family, and the business, to become. The ensuing discussion should reveal each family member's personal hopes for his or her future, as well as his or her hopes for the business.

As a result of this exercise, a mental vision of the business—and the family—will develop. Many believe it is just such a vision that determines what will eventually be accomplished and that motivates people to achieve their goals. The models' clear labels also broaden understanding and facilitate communication by giving family members short, specific taglines for concepts that they may not have hitherto clearly articulated.

Few families will accept two of these models—the "royalty family" and "the anarchy family"—as ideals for the future. Ironically, however, these models are very descriptive of the current situation in many family businesses. Perhaps these families can use one or the other of these models to contrast their present situation with their future aspirations.

Royal Families. These families believe that the right to run the business belongs to the oldest son, who is also usually the first child to enter the business. In addition, such families often believe that only sons belong in the business over the long term and that daughters should seek out other alternatives and commitments. However difficult it may be to justify such a belief many families do, indeed, lean toward the oldest son. Some families also extend the "royalty" principle to the decision of who can enter or share ownership in the business. For these families, only males or first cousins may participate in the business.

This approach is the simplest way to keep the business in the family. It keeps leadership and ownership together, and it is an easy rationale for unequal treatment of offspring. But in today's world, where equal opportunity for women is highly valued, automatically favoring sons over daughters seems Victorian. And if the oldest son is not also the most capable sibling, this approach will be damaging to the business and its employees.

Anarchical Families. In these families, there are no rules to guide future plans. Parents believe that all children should have both an ownership stake and a voice—usually an equal voice—in corporate affairs. They also believe that each child should be master of his or her own destiny. Therefore, offspring may leave and join the company at will. Such a family has no vehicle for resolving conflicts and no policy to guide the growth of the business. Ownership becomes dispersed broadly across the family and is unrelated to roles within the business. All family members have a say, whether they contribute to the business or not.

Using such an approach, the family does not have to face the difficulties of planning, but it also loses its ability to shape the future. Decisions are made on an ad hoc basis. The "winners" are usually those who outmanipulate other family members.

Laissez-Faire Families. These families allow everyone to do what he or she wants to do. As in the anarchical family, the parents think that every child should be master of his or her fate. But where the anarchical parent leaves open the question of retaining the business, laissez-faire parents foreclose that possibility. They believe so strongly that each child should govern his or her own affairs that they plan to sell the business at some point. They will give the money from the sale of the company to their offspring in equal shares to do with as they will. "We have set a wonderful example for our children," such parents might say to themselves. "We have shown them what it takes to build a successful business, and if they want to repeat our success in a business of their own, fine. But it is up to them. Our children should take the money and do what with it what they want."

In a laissez-faire family, the business never becomes the source of family conflicts. At the same time, the family will eventually lose the business.

Social Democratic Families. Parents who believe in social democracy think that all their children should be given equal opportunities and equal shares of all family resources. For example, those who choose to enter the business or qualify to enter the business should share equally in its ownership. They should make decisions in the business as equal partners and share equal titles. Those who are not in the business receive assets of equal value—in real estate, life insurance, stocks, and so on.

The family practicing social democracy makes every effort to share everything evenly, even if that means dividing up the business so that each member can have an equal portion. As a result, they split their wealth equally among their children: one business unit to each, perhaps, or a business unit to one and mutual funds to another. Buy-sell agreements are critical to success in these family businesses. Partnership agreements and buy-sell agreements recognize that shared ownership in a business may not last. In these instances, prearranged rules to help dissolve the partnership if conflict becomes overpowering can help, in the long run, limit the damage to the business and to the family.

Most parents derive emotional satisfaction from treating their children equally. But the social democratic approach may not be feasible financially, and it is hard for many people to run a business as a democracy.

Democratic Capitalist Families. Such families believe that one should get what one works for or deserves. Thus they think that only family members who work in the business should share in its benefits—in proportion to their contribution. Such families hand out rewards and allot ownership on the basis of merit.

Rules are developed to distribute stock in proportion to the success of the business each year or in proportion to salaries earned or years of business service.

Many families of this kind establish a system of rewards that distinguishes between birthright ("blood equity") and actual contributions to the business ("sweat equity"). The calculations required to figure the relative distribution of stock or rewards under the democratic capitalist model are found in Appendix F.

This approach rewards those who contribute to the business and creates a rationale for distributing resources unequally. But it leaves no room for measuring an individual's contribution to the family—"blood equity," so to speak. Moreover, an individual's business merit is difficult to measure. Any method for doing so is partly subjective and so may pave the way to conflict.

Representative Democracy Families. Families holding this philosophy appoint a trustee of some sort to represent the extended family in the business. This trustee may be a bank officer, a family lawyer, an outside board of directors, or even an individual from the family. The trustee, who is sometimes elected, represents all shareholders in voting matters. Equity value is shared among all of them as shareholders or as investors. Such a model helps keep the business in the family, since it prevents any one member from selling his or her shares. Its centralized leadership also helps preserve family harmony. This structure is especially useful to families that seek equal distribution of ownership because the value of the business has greatly increased or because nonbusiness resources are insufficient to spread among family members not in the business.

Representative democracy concentrates leadership in the hands of a few capable people who are experienced at running a business. But the leaders of the business tend to be governed by rules of their own making. Therefore, they might not work for the best interests of the family as a whole.

Pure Capitalist or Entrepreneurial Families. Here, the founder of the business, usually a classic entrepreneur, thinks no one will be able to follow in his or her footsteps. It would be unfair to expect offspring to try, the entrepreneur reasons, and it would also prevent family members from establishing their own identities and achieving business success on their own. Therefore, he or she refuses to select a successor and will eventually sell the business perhaps to employees through an employee stock ownership plan or perhaps to another company.

The entrepreneur is willing to share some of the resulting cash with his or her children. But since he or she believes that one should work for one's reward, the money will be shared only under certain conditions. The entrepreneur thinks that simply handing over the money would probably weaken the children and deaden their spirit. It will be granted instead as seed money for new businesses. The sum of money available thus becomes a venture capital fund, complete with standards for use of the money and instructions on how to apply for it. Until family members petition for money from the fund, it remains there.

This approach has the value of allowing individual family members to start successful entrepreneurial careers, and it may prevent the family from becoming "soft." Unfortunately, however, the original business, along with a good deal of tradition and heritage, passes out of the family's hands.

Utopian Families. A family of this kind believes that its business is a great resource around which to build both an empire and a closer, more vigorous family. Such a family is committed to high ideals and is unafraid of hard work. This spirit takes the shape of a holding company, that is, a corporate conglomerate containing several business enterprises and governed by a family group.

The utopian family recognizes that all businesses have periods of prosperity and decline. Consequently, the family's multiple investments allow its mature and profitable concerns to fund the development of riskier and more experimental endeavors. This portfolio of businesses shares a central staff to provide "economies of scale," as well as a central source of funding. Funds are not used only for business needs, however. The family believes *everyone* in the family should benefit from the business and its resources, whether they work in it or not.

So they develop special perquisites for all to share. These might include office space; access to services such as tax preparation, investment advice, or insurance coverage; educational resources; provisions for helping family members in need; and so on.

The utopian model offers exciting ideals. This system benefits the whole family and simultaneously attends to business needs as they change. But it requires a great deal of hard work and intelligent planning. And only families that already have very successful businesses should consider this model.

Key Influences on Choice of Model

Family members may disagree about which model best suits their family. But coming to understand the forces that underlie such disagreements will make discussion of these models easier. Three elements will likely be present throughout the debate: the size of the family and the business, the values of individual family members, and the traditional values of the family.

Family and Business Circumstances

The size of the family, the size of the business, the number of family members in and out of the business, and the nature of the business itself will all shape the choice of the model or vision. For example, if a small number of offspring are running a mid-sized business in an efficient way, the family might choose a social democratic model, leading to an arrangement of equal partners. If there are numerous offspring in a small business (or offspring with expensive life-styles in a larger business), the result may be the anarchical or royal model, which would effectively "prune the family tree." A family with a large number of offspring working in a big business will probably lean toward the model of democratic or representative capitalism, unless the family also has ambitions to establish a strong, united family dynasty. In that case, the utopian model will hold the most attraction.

Values

Even more influential than physical circumstances will be the individual values of family members. A discussion of key views that influence the preference of a model follows (see Figure 6 for a summary of these views). Although different family analysts use different typologies of family values and behaviors, the approach taken by Olson, Portner, and Lavee (1985) is closest to our own format and measures the degree to which families are flexible and interdependent.

Nature's Will Versus the Master Plan. Many people believe that the future is so unpredictable that planning makes no sense and nature should simply be allowed to take its course. Others believe the future may be influenced through prepared plans. The plan may be rigid or flexible; the important thing is to have one.

Flexibility Versus Rigidity. A flexible family or family leader allows things to evolve. Relationships may change over time, well into the future. A rigid family struggles to prescribe the rules of the game as well as its outcome.

Security Versus Risk. Many family members value security and hate risk. They would like to maintain the business in its present condition and use extra cash to support the family. Others yearn to preserve the spirit of risk taking and experimentation that sparked the business in the first place. They want to create business spin-offs and new opportunities for people.

Equality of Results Versus Equality of Opportunity. Family members who believe in equality of results will bend over backward to give each child the same chance. For instance, they will hire the son who failed to finish high school at nearly the same salary as the one who graduated from business school with honors. In contrast, those who believe in equality of opportunity think that after a certain point individuals should make their own way in the world and deserve no extra help. They will be welcome to share in the business or the family's resources, to be sure, but they must succeed by their own efforts.

Independence Versus Dependence. Families who believe in independence grant each member the freedom to follow his

Figure 6. Effect of Assumptions and Circumstances on Choice of Family Model.

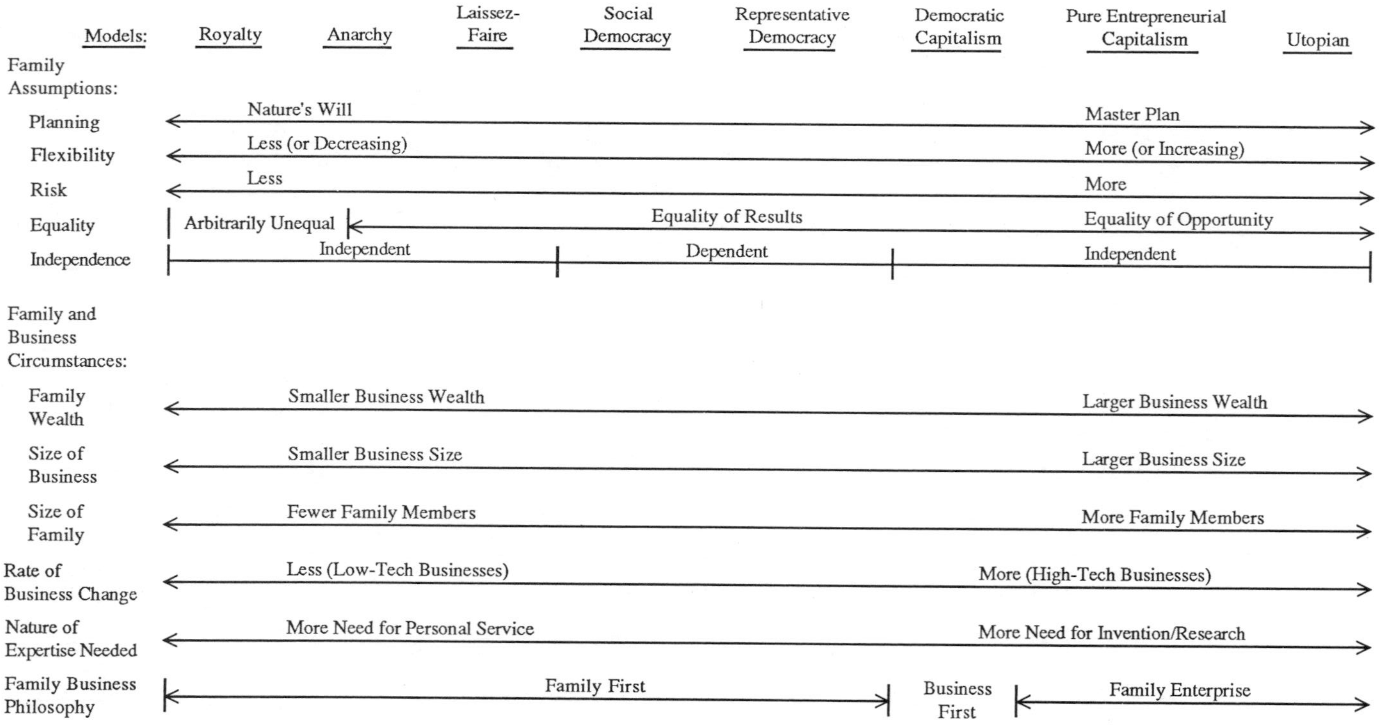

Models:	Royalty	Anarchy	Laissez-Faire	Social Democracy	Representative Democracy	Democratic Capitalism	Pure Entrepreneurial Capitalism	Utopian
Family Assumptions:								
Planning	Nature's Will						Master Plan	
Flexibility	Less (or Decreasing)						More (or Increasing)	
Risk	Less						More	
Equality	Arbitrarily Unequal			Equality of Results			Equality of Opportunity	
Independence		Independent			Dependent		Independent	
Family and Business Circumstances:								
Family Wealth	Smaller Business Wealth						Larger Business Wealth	
Size of Business	Smaller Business Size						Larger Business Size	
Size of Family	Fewer Family Members						More Family Members	
Rate of Business Change	Less (Low-Tech Businesses)						More (High-Tech Businesses)	
Nature of Expertise Needed	More Need for Personal Service						More Need for Invention/Research	
Family Business Philosophy				Family First		Business First	Family Enterprise	

or her own bent, whether that means leaving the family business or running the company's foreign unit. Families who believe in dependence, however, think that geographical separation implies emotional separation and is therefore a bad idea. They also believe that each family member is responsible for the others. In such a world, going your own way is not an option. Everyone's well-being is inextricably linked to everyone else's.

Business First Versus Family First. As we noted earlier, perhaps the best way for a family to summarize its collective value system is to determine whether it will generally put business before family, will favor the family over the business, or will work to generate a solution that meets the needs of both (the family enterprise approach). The model that favors a business first philosophy is democratic capitalism. Four models (royalty, anarchy, laissez faire, and social democracy) all favor a family first philosophy. The family enterprise philosophy would match the entrepreneurial capitalism model or the utopian model. These last two models are appropriate for a family and business of any size. But they become especially attractive when a company's shareholder base expands sufficiently to require a decision on how to share ownership, that is, a decision on whether shares should be divided among family members in *and* out of the business or only among those who are active managers.

For many, circumstances make the choice between family and business self-evident. Thus, if the family is large and the business small, there is usually no room to support family interests at the expense of the business. Business survival is paramount. In the case of a small family and a prosperous business, however, there is little penalty in serving family needs. The business can readily afford it. The choice grows difficult only when the business has modest resources and the family is large enough to spawn conflicting career and financial goals among members. The choice is also difficult in a business of any size when ownership is shared among several relatives, some of whom are active in the business while others are not. In such circumstances, developing a shared vision, or model, is critical (see Table 13).

Table 13. Family First or Business First?

Health and Magnitude of the Business	Number of Family Members in Leadership Generation		
	1 to 2	*3 to 5*	*5 or More*
Weak and small	No debate; business survival first	No debate; business first	No debate; business first
Modest	No problem; family first	*Conflict; resolution critical*	*Conflict; resolution critical*
Large (probably partially publicly held) and significant resources	No problem; family first	*Conflict; resolution critical*	No problem; business first

Note: The vast majority of family businesses are in the *"conflict; resolution critical"* stage due to typical family and business size. Those cases require deliberate planning and effort to develop the family's philosophy and vision.

Traditional Family Values

Each family member will develop his or her own reasons for selecting one family model over another. When all is said and done, however, the reasons are likely to cluster around a dominant set of values. The question that best reveals such overriding family values is, What do family members think holds the family together? Money? Shared ownership? Working together? Family gatherings? Fun and social activities?

The more the family leans to money as the familial "glue," the more dependent, rigid, and security conscious it will become. Its members will probably choose a model such as social democracy or representative democracy. The more family members lean to social activities, however, the more independent they will be. That family will probably choose the utopian model or the democratic capitalism model.

Programs Needed

After formulating a mission statement and selecting a model to shape future decisions, the family can begin to develop the programs necessary to implement its mission and its view of the future. The programs that need to be developed include:

- How to govern and lead the family and make decisions
- How to resolve family conflicts
- How achieve satisfactory relations among family members
- How to educate the family
- How to preserve family unity and harmony

Family Governance, Leadership, and Decision Making

As family businesses grow, they will need to fashion more formal methods for making decisions and selecting leaders. These methods will vary widely among individual families. However, the models previously discussed suggest several possibilities:

Individual Leaders. In many families, the chief executive of the business also serves as the family's chief arbiter. This arrangement is often effective, especially in families with first-generation entrepreneurial firms. Historically, the position of chief family decision maker has been assumed by the father; as a result, the mother has often assumed the implicit and invaluable role of family emotional leader. She works, usually quietly, at the critical tasks of emotional leadership: interpreting the behavior of one family member to another, keeping communications open, making sure that feelings are considered, and planning special family functions.

It is our experience that finding a successor for the emotional leader is even more important to the long-term health of the business than finding a successor for the chief executive. As a result, some families deliberately groom a leader who will cultivate family unity and see that everyone feels appreciated in his or her individual roles. In some cases this is the oldest daughter of the founder of the business; in others, it might be the daughter-in-law of the successor. Occasionally, in large families, the role is taken by a younger sibling of either gender. With more women leading family businesses as chief executives, the pool of applicants for the role of family's emotional leader should expand and will likely include males more often than in the past.

Family Councils and Boards of Directors. As the family expands and matures, the power of individual leaders to hold it together is not always sufficient. The family may then seek other avenues of decision making and leadership. Formal family councils and boards of directors can be effective instruments. These groups may simply offer counsel on tough decisions or be given the power to resolve them.

Family councils are made up exclusively of family members who address family matters. Boards of directors are made up of family members plus outsiders (typically other business owners and executives). While they address only business issues, some of these issues will certainly affect the family. Families that choose to use these devices must decide (1) the issues that these boards or councils will consider, (2) the length of members' terms, and (3) who will serve on these groups. For example, a family may want to ensure representation for different branches of the family or seek to balance representation between those members in the business and those outside the business. In other families, a council or board position is determined by family birth order or role in the business.

Together, these councils, boards, and individual family leaders will likely determine such important matters as family hiring and compensation. However, as families develop collective interests beyond the business—such as investment clubs or shared vacation sites—then these smaller matters, too, may come to be decided in a formal way. Each family needs to find its own method of selecting people to lead these efforts and of reviewing their performance. These methods will vary; our point is that they need conscious attention.

Conflict Resolution

However well developed, the family decision-making process will sometimes lead to serious conflicts. Emotions will run high, and differences will come to seem irreconcilable. At such points, a program for resolving conflicts promptly is absolutely necessary. Otherwise, issues will fester.

A good plan for conflict resolution requires anticipation of sensitive issues, as well as mechanisms that have been agreed upon in advance. Some families actually invest time in learning conflict resolution skills. Others develop mediating mechanisms, such as a family council or board of directors. They defer certain decisions to those groups. Still others employ a professional —perhaps an expert on organizational development, the family lawyer, a family consultant—to guide them through difficult decisions. A certain amount of family meeting time should be spent in discussing the family's methods for resolving predictable future conflicts before these issues become personal. Once the family has some experience in applying its skills and mechanisms, then the lessons and precedents need to be promoted broadly. Such shared history will make future conflict resolution easier for all family members.

Code of Conduct

Family members may find themselves constantly arguing with one another, avoiding one another, or making disrespectful remarks about one another. These are all signs that unhealthy family relationships are developing. In such a case, or to help prevent such a case, the family needs to develop a "code of understanding" or "code of conduct," which would include caveats against arguing with or criticizing another family member in public, passing judgment on the private lives or parenting practices of other family members, spending company money on personal needs without the full knowledge and/or approval of others in the business, and so on. On the positive side, the code would ask that family members always strive for consensus when faced with difficult decisions and, even more important, always treat one another with respect. Such codes are often passed on from one generation to the next, complete with illustrative stories and reasons why a particular rule is valuable. They become essential when siblings are working together in a company. Their value increases as cousins and in-laws also become involved in the family business.

Family Education

For the family to realize its long-term strategic plan, it must understand what is critical for future success and fully understand past family resolves. Some families hold regular educational meetings to discuss these matters. In fact, in many families these educational forums and efforts are begun long before formal family strategic planning. In other cases, they are natural extensions of family strategic planning meetings. These educational meetings include presentations on:

- the history of the business and its current performance and its needs
- the family's future strategic plan and objectives
- ways to help the family work together, including conflict resolution, team building, and community leadership
- the family's history and traditions
- the value of entrepreneurship, investing, saving, and risk taking
- the importance of business success to the family.

Formal programs that cover these issues may include case discussions of successful or unsuccessful family dynasties. They may also include guest speakers from business or from academia, as well as presentations by family elders. Other families address these topics more informally through such vehicles as written family histories, stories, or letters. The informal nature of the latter devices does not mean they are casual, however. In most of the successful multigenerational families we have observed, they are quite premeditated, and they also provide important roles for one or more family members.

Keeping the Family Together

Perpetuating a successful business family is not all business. It allows for fun, too. Enjoying activities together builds rapport, friendship, and ease of communication among family members. All families should spend some recreational time together. It is best to leave business concerns totally out of these occasions, according to the experience of many families. This puts all family members—whether they are in or out of the active management of the firm—on common, equal ground. Many families formalize "fun times" through regular vacations or by purchasing a farm, boat, cottage, or resort condominium for the entire extended family.

The activities needed to implement the family's strategic plan form the family's objectives. These are established after the final review of the family's plan; they include the assignment of responsibilities and the procurement of the resources needed to accomplish them. A family might choose to update everyone's estate plans, for example, establish buy-sell agreements, or set up an outside board. It may form a committee to develop a proposed "code of conduct" or set up enjoyable family outings. Or it may have to iron out differences between two family members or look into tax shelter opportunities for certain members. The possibilities are endless, depending on each family's needs and priorities. Each year the family will probably single out several main objectives to pursue. These objectives should be made known to the entire family, and progress in obtaining them should be carefully monitored at subsequent family meetings.

Summary

It is not by coincidence that most successful families work consciously to overcome the problems inherent in perpetuating a business. Our research suggests that, however casual these families may appear, they deliberately promote such seeming intangibles as commitment, vision, and philosophy. It is these so-called intangibles that provide specific solutions to challenges and that determine how the family interacts with the business. It is these that shape the roles family members play in the company's future.

No one particular philosophy or vision seems best. Many patterns are apparent in various successful family firms. However, three principles do appear across the board: commitment to the future, extensive communication, and conscientious planning. Family meetings are the appropriate vehicle to establish each of these principles. At family meetings, techniques to encourage commitment can cover a wide range, from simple expressions of support to enjoyable family outings. The strategic plan itself rests upon the preparation of (1) a mission statement that outlines why the family is willing to continue the company, (2) a vision of the family's future structure, (3) programs that will maintain a supportive family, and (4) annual objectives that will help the family put its plans into effect.

Ultimately, this strategic plan will mesh with the other plans cited in Chapter One. These include the Estate Plan, Plan for Family Participation in the Business, Business Strategic Plan, and Plan for Successor Development. While all are interwoven and interdependent, it will become clear as the children and business mature that certain plans form the foundation for others. For example, early in the life of the business—and when children are still young—only the Business Strategic Plan seems to matter. But as offspring age, it is the Family Strategic Plan that becomes more critical. Indeed, it is the strategic plan that ultimately shapes all other plans, for it is *that* plan that establishes the vision of the family.

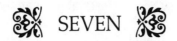

SEVEN

Shaping a Business Strategy That Includes the Family

In a family business, family issues ultimately shape the business strategy. Such issues include: Should family members in the company work together or apart? How much money does the family need from the company? Are older family members confident that their sons and daughters can run the company well? The answers to such questions will be joined to other assessments of the strength of the business and the attractiveness of the industry. These three forces—family, business, and industry, all analyzed by managers and owners during the planning process—will together produce the future strategy for the family business.

Chapter Five outlined the formal planning process for developing the company's strategy, while Chapter Six outlined a formal planning process for the family. In the course of that process, individual members establish their commitment to the company's future, as well as the roles they may play within it. This chapter will illustrate ways to combine the information from both those plans to select the strategic direction for growth in the years ahead. This decision will determine how aggressively the family will reinvest in the current business to fuel growth for the next generation. It will also determine whether the family will channel resources into other opportunities and, if so, into what sort of opportunities.

Note: I am grateful to Dean Joel Goldbar of the Illinois Institute of Technology for his assistance in formulating some of the ideas in this chapter.

161

To help the reader decide what is best for his or her own situation, we will set forth some broad strategic alternatives. We will also suggest what strategies make the most sense in terms of particular family and business circumstances. Finally, we will present some recent trends in business strategy. These new ideas are tailored to the smaller, private family firm, although many will apply to very large family concerns as well.

The actual choice of a business strategy is, and forever will be, more art than science. Truly effective strategies are creative. They go against the grain of past patterns. They combine ideas in a unique way but one well suited to the times. As a result, their development might not follow the predictable, step-by-step process we describe. Strategies are frequently spawned not by corporate officers working in consensus but by the chief executive officer working or dreaming alone; at other times, they develop through the efforts of many managers doing their jobs and reacting to things as they come along. This reality is reflected in the debate currently underway in academia (Mintzberg and Waters, 1985), where some suggest that strategy selection results from deliberate planning and others contend that strategy emerges from unpredictable, trial-and-error efforts. Either way, it is clear that selecting a future strategy will never be as simple as saying, "If A occurs, then B must result."

Regardless of the process, the choice for a family business will necessarily reflect, whether formally or intuitively, considerations such as these:

- The family's commitment to the company's future
- The family's vision of its future structure
- The relative attractiveness of the business environment
- The relative strength of the business

Business Alternatives

We will propose here twenty-two alternatives for managers' consideration. Several may be selected as appropriate possibilities, based on the attractiveness of the environment in which the business operates and the strength of the business itself. These assessments result from the planning process outlined in Chapter Five. The alternatives may then further be narrowed to one or two possibilities, according to what is best for the family as determined by the plans outlined in Chapter Six. This progression is illustrated in Figure 7.

Figure 7. Selecting a Future Strategic Direction.

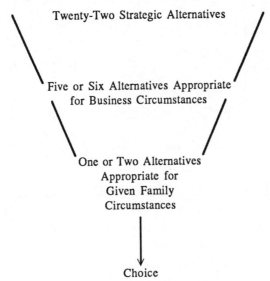

Twenty-Two Strategic Alternatives

Five or Six Alternatives Appropriate
for Business Circumstances

One or Two Alternatives
Appropriate for
Given Family
Circumstances

Choice

The twenty-two alternatives can be considered in six categories (see Figure 8). Specific examples of these categories will follow in Figure 9.

The first and most aggressive group of choices is intended for those who can fully *exploit* the resources of their company. In this situation, managers will have determined that their business is in excellent shape and so is the industry in which it competes. They will want to capitalize on those advantages, aggressively invest more money in the company, and make it grow.

In the second circumstance, the business will appear fairly weak. The industry, however, seems in excellent health. Managers must then come up with some new ideas to significantly improve the company. They must *invest* something, thereby gaining new strength.

In the third category of strategic direction, the business

Figure 8. Categories of Future Strategic Directions.

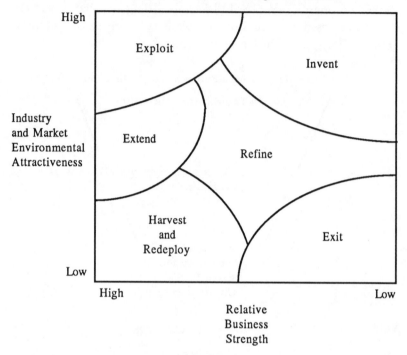

appears strong but the market and industry are mediocre. Managers must *extend* what they are already doing. This will probably entail either marketing current products to new customers or selling new products to current customers.

In the fourth case, both the business and its environment are only mediocre. Hence, managers might merely *refine* their current strategy. They might seek a fresh market niche or copy a competitor's product.

In the fifth category, the business looks strong but the industry looks very weak. Such an assessment should prompt managers to *harvest* the company and *redeploy* financial resources; that is, they should extract funds from the company in order to spend them elsewhere on new opportunities.

The sixth and final category—the weak business in a weak

industry—includes only one option. Managers must *exit,* divesting themselves promptly before the value of the company erodes even further. They must sell the company for as much cash as possible and then seek out new opportunities. The needed business strengths are simply not present.

Within these broad categories are numerous alternatives (see Figure 9). The location of the various alternatives that are portrayed suggests which one might be most appropriate, given a particular assessment of the industry and the firm. For instance, if the industry/market attractiveness is relatively high (say 8 on a scale of 1 to 10) and the company's strength is also relatively high (say, another 8), then the most appropriate strategic direction is the *expansion of the product line.* But *expanding into new markets, forward integration,* or *aggressive marketing* to build share are alternatives that are almost as appropriate.

Exploit Resources of Company

1. Market more aggressively across the entire line of products. Increase promotion. Reduce prices. Expand the sales force. Do whatever it takes to gain more market share and thus dominate the business.

2. Build barriers to entry. Discourage small and potential competitors from realizing profitable opportunities in the market. Such barriers may include threats of lawsuits over patent infringements, long-term contracts with suppliers and customers, changes in product specifications that increase capital requirements for new entrants, or the establishment of a strong brand identity. Do not pursue high prices or other policies that will offend customers or distributors. That only invites new competitors to enter the field.

3. Expand the product line. Broaden coverage of niches so that competitors can see no unfilled opportunities that could ultimately lead to a strong foothold in the market. Offer a broad line of models and services in order to take full advantage of business strengths.

Figure 9. Determining Choice of Strategic Direction.

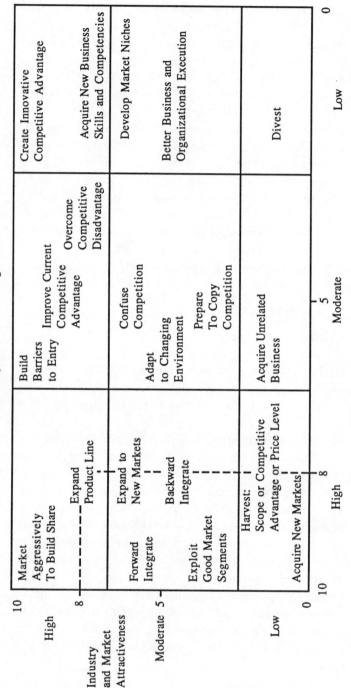

Invent New Strategies

4. Create a new competitive advantage. Find a new way to make, distribute, or promote a product. For example, if everyone else is selling through retail stores, consider catalogue sales. If strong competitors are making standard products, consider specialty products or services. The weak competitive condition of the business requires innovative ideas to take advantage of attractive industry and market circumstances.

5. Improve the company's current competitive advantage. Take its strengths and enhance them. If customers perceive the business as a quality supplier, invest money in strengthening those perceptions; if it has the advantage of being the lower-cost supplier, strengthen that aspect.

6. Overcome the business's competitive disadvantage. If for some reason customers do not prefer the company's product or service, identify the chief relative disadvantage—a weak sales force, an inferior product, a high price—and try to rectify it.

7. Acquire needed skills. Purchase a firm that is strong where the company is weak—one that has more plant capacity, perhaps, or a larger, more effective sales organization. Or hire the people necessary to strengthen the business. The market opportunity is ripe enough to justify the investment. But it is probably too late for the company to build up the needed skills; acquiring them is the better alternative.

Extend Current Approaches

8. Expand into new markets. Take the excellent strengths of the business and pursue new types of customers, enter new territories, or look for new market segments.

9. Forward integrate. Enter customers' business by acquiring some of them or go into competition with them. Note, however, that this is among the riskiest of all strategic directions, as it puts the company into end markets that managers may not understand. It also runs the risk of offending and losing current customers who will resent doing business with a sup-

plier who is also a competitor. This strategy requires tremendous business strength.

10. Backward integrate. Add increased profitability to
the current business by making what the company used to buy.
Assemble what was assembled for it, paint what was painted,
package what was packaged, and so on. Like forward integration, backward integration can be accomplished through acqui-
sition of another company or through internal development.
But it is typically a less risky path than forward integration.

Refine Strategies

11. Confuse the competition. Pursue strategies that keep
competitors off base by unpredictably changing the rules of the
game. This might be a matter of altering the industry's seasonal
pattern of promotional expenditures, offering new credit terms,
or providing a new package of related services, such as training
or computer programs.

12. Adapt to the changing environment. Here, industry
and environmental analysis will have revealed several concerns
—perhaps a shortage of skilled labor, rising insurance costs, or
stiffer governmental regulations. Responding to these threats
and opportunities with new programs or analysis by a task
force will provide the core of the company's strategic direction. Since the business is not particularly strong and the industry is softening, it would probably be better not to spend
money on expensive innovations or pursue aggressive strategies.

13. Seek market niches. The company's weakness will
not allow it to effectively compete in the bulk of the market.
Managers should identify a few market niches (such as local de-
liveries, private label production, a particular customer group,
and so on) that the company can target. These will not be big
enough for larger, stronger competitors, or they may be too demanding for them. As a result, the business will perform in a
relatively sheltered environment. That may help managers gain
sufficient strength to broaden strategy later.

14. Improve execution. In situations where neither the
market nor the business promises exciting new directions, cor-

recting internal weaknesses often becomes the core of future strategy. Such weaknesses, revealed through the planning process, might include unaggressive sales managers, declining plant productivity, or increases in the collection period of receivables.

15. Copy the competition. When a company's market and business strength do not justify speculative investment—and when competitors are obviously pursuing superior ideas—the best strategy may simply be to mimic their products, use similar packaging, provide the same kinds of services, or replicate their pricing and promotion methods.

Harvest Company and Redeploy Funds

16. Exploit good market segments that are faster growing, larger, or have other attractive features. Even mature markets boast pockets of high activity, ranging from discount stores to customers overseas. A strong company can identify these segments and decide to enter them aggressively.

17. Cancel marginal customers and/or products. Let us say that planning reveals a need to maximize the return from the current business in order to redeploy funds into new, more attractive market or business opportunities. Companies may harvest some income by selectively raising prices to discourage less profitable customers. They might also choose to discontinue less profitable products.

18. Stop reinvesting new money in the company's current competitive strengths. Planning may reveal that the business is stronger than the future of the market warrants. If the company is a high-quality operation, it might consider becoming only average in its product or service quality. If it is a low-cost outfit, it should cease to emphasize that advantage and allow the cost of the operation to slowly rise. It could then funnel the freed cash into new market opportunities.

19. Raise prices across the board. Harvest cash from the deteriorating market situation by raising prices on all products and services. Again, the purpose is to funnel the cash into fresh businesses.

20. Diversify into related markets. This strategy applies

a company's current strengths to new but related markets. For example, a bicycle manufacturer might begin making stationary exercise equipment or cross-country skis, perhaps utilizing the same brand identity or distribution system. A seafood distributor might add a line of fresh fruits and vegetables. Market weaknesses require the business to identify new opportunities where it can effectively use its strength.

21. Diversify into unrelated businesses. Managers who choose this route have recognized that while the business itself is fairly strong, related market opportunities are unattractive. Funds are better spent, then, on new types of businesses. A manufacturing concern might move into shopping center development, or a food supplier might begin a retail store.

Divest and Exit

22. Sell the family business. A business without good market opportunities and without the strength to capitalize on new ventures is obviously trapped. It can only erode the family's and the company's capital. As a result, the only logical strategy is to prevent further erosion.

Family Considerations

Several business alternatives have been identified through the business planning process. Family considerations should now further narrow the choice. Some managers will resist this idea, believing that business decisions are best and most cleanly made when one *ignores* the personal interests of the family. But those who subscribe to this school of thought should consider the following: In 1982, we studied twenty family concerns from different industries and different locales. They were asked to assess their companies according to the planning procedures outlined in this book. Managers first determined the relative strength of their company and next explored the attractiveness of their markets. They were then requested to select their *actual* strategy from the aforementioned twenty-two alternatives. (More background on this study is presented in Appendix G.)

Much to their surprise, the majority of business owners discovered that they were undershooting their strategic potential. They were pursuing strategies less ambitious than their own assessments would justify. Many were simply fine tuning past strategies; the actual strength of their companies, meanwhile, suggested that they could use much more aggressive tactics, such as expanding product lines or building market share. In subsequent interviews, owners offered these explanations for the disparity between their strategic potential and their actual strategic choices:

First, they were unsure of the kinds of influences that their families might have upon their businesses. They did not know, for instance, whether all members would want to work together under a single corporate roof or would want to work apart in autonomous units. They did not know whether those in the business would have to provide financially for those outside the business. They did not know whether they, as parents, would need to set aside cash for funding the new ventures of entrepreneurially minded offspring.

Second, they were unsure of the degree of their commitment to the company's future. They were unsure because they had not settled some key issues, ranging from the amount of money available to fund new projects to the amount of talent possessed by potential successors.

As a result of these uncertainties—all related to their families—the owners usually selected cautious, conservative business strategies. They chose this route *despite their confidence in their respective companies.* The influence of the family had overridden almost all business considerations. Such a study illustrates that family considerations shape business judgment, whether their power to do so is formally recognized or not. Under such circumstances, we believe that the most advisable course is to admit their influence and then turn them to the best possible advantage for the company. Otherwise, managers are likely to misunderstand the real forces at work, and that in turn may lead to poor decisions and frustration.

Fundamental Issues. In our study, the owners' explanations for their conservative course revealed an inability to answer three fundamental questions:

1. Should the family create a fragmented business empire that consists of diverse business opportunities for various offspring? Or should family members literally work together under one roof and one corporate entity?
2. Does the family have sufficient confidence in the next generation to go ahead with succession plans? Or does unspoken concern about possible successors encourage a conservative wait-and-see attitude?
3. Does the family have sufficient financial resources to satisfy both family needs and business reinvestment requirements? Or does uncertainty lead it to simply conserve available funds?

These three fundamental, family-based issues will shape the final selection of strategy by business owners. Uncertainty about any of them will increase their conservatism and make them less willing to reinvest in their companies.

Business owners who have undertaken the family planning process outlined in Chapter Six will have resolved two of these questions. Their choice of family model or vision will answer the first; successors' performance throughout the planning process will help supply the answer to the second. The question involving financial resources, however, can only be determined through the separate development of an Estate Plan. This plan assures that there will be sufficient funds for estate taxes and for dependents in case of parental death or disability, while also providing for the retirement of the business owner and spouse. Its preparation helps define what funds are truly available for the business and what funds are needed for family purposes.

Discussions of estate plans are among the most difficult for a family to undertake. Quite often, there are misconceptions about the actual sum of money available—misconceptions that usually stem from owners' reluctance to give accurate figures. Owners may want to preserve cash for unforeseen events, or they may simply not wish to encourage ambitious spending habits in their offspring and so understate their financial strength. Some go on to fuel the illusion by creating a hidden nest egg of funds in nonbusiness assets. As a result, the family makes estate decisions based on faulty or incomplete data or becomes unable to reach a conclusion at all.

Breaking through these uncertainties, of course, is what the strategic planning process is supposed to do. It is meant to encourage honest exchanges and full disclosure. The only way to resolve the problem just outlined, for example, is for the owner to state openly the financial position of the business and the family. How well the family has attended to the family issues—such as family vision or philosophy and family rules on compensation—will determine the business manager's ability to reconcile business strategy choices with family plans. In some families the business planning process brings to the surface some unresolved family issues, such as who has how much interest in business leadership. In such cases the family then must resolve these issues or uncertainties before the company can begin narrowing business strategies to the final choice of direction.

Narrowing the Choices. Let us say, as one example, that two owners agree that their business is strong. They also agree that the industry and market environment is strong. They agree that the company should pursue new products and markets as a result. But let us also say that one owner believes that family members in the business should have autonomy, functioning in geographically separate locations. The other wants to keep the family and its leaders physically close and more dependent on one another. The former owner will make the search for new markets or forward integration his or her strategy of choice. The latter will want to build barriers to the entry of competitors or pursue backward integration. Entry barriers and backward integration allow the company to keep everyone close and interdependent; addressing new markets opens the way to more individual autonomy. Similarly, two owners of a weak business might also choose different strategic directions. The committed owner might seek to acquire a new business, while the less committed owner might consider divestiture the best alternative.

Specific, detailed interactions among these elements are outlined in Table 14. This shows the full range of the twenty-two strategic alternatives as they might be influenced by various assessments of the industry, the business, available family funds,

Table 14. Evaluation of Strategic Direction Alternatives.

	Industry Attractiveness	Business Strength	Funds Available	Commitment Due to Confidence in Succession	Family Vision Structure
1. Market aggressively to build share	+	+	$	+	C
2. Build barriers to entry	+	0	$$	−	C
3. Expand products	+	+	$$	+	C
4. Create new competitive advantage	+	−	$	+	C
5. Improve competitive advantage	+	0	¢	+	C
6. Overcome competitive disadvantage	+	+	$	−	C
7. Acquire new business skills	+	−	$$	+	C
8. Expand markets	0	+	$	+	F
9. Forward integrate	0	+	$$	+	F
10. Backward integrate	0	+	$$	−	F
11. Confuse competition	0	0	¢	−	C
12. Adapt to changing environment	0	0	?	−	C
13. Seek market niches	0	−	¢	−	C
14. Better execution	0	0	¢	−	C
15. Prepare to copy competition	0	0	?	−	C
16. Exploit fast-growth segments	0	+	$	+	C
17. Harvest scope (products/markets)	−	+	¢¢	+	C
18. Harvest competitive advantage	−	+	¢¢	+	C
19. Harvest price	−	+	¢¢	+	C
20. Acquire new markets	−	−	$$	+	C
21. Acquire unrelated business	−	0	$$	+	F
22. Divest	−	−	¢¢	−	N/A

Key:
+ = Strong
0 = Neutral
− = Weak
$$ = Large amount of long-term capital investment needed and available
$ = Some internal cash needed for capital investment and available

¢ = Small amount of cash flow needed and available
¢¢ = Does not require reinvestment of funds
F = Fragmented
C = Concentrated

family confidence in successors, and the future. Alternative 19, for example, suggests a business strategy of raising prices across the board in order to harvest or free up cash for investment in other opportunities. As shown on the chart, this strategy is appropriate if (1) the industry and market environment appears weak, (2) the business appears strong, (3) cash is scarce, (4) the family is willing to assume a fragmented structure, and (5) the family commitment is strong.

Since Table 14 lays out all the possible permutations in chart form, it can serve as a checklist to evaluate the various strategic alternatives as shaped by business and family assumptions. It also clearly illustrates the impact of family assumptions on the final choice of strategy. This exercise will narrow the possible strategies to one or two.

The Final Choice

Truly clever strategies artfully capitalize on unique market insights and the relative competitive strengths that a business enjoys. While we cannot hope to list the unique advantages or opportunities that any one company might possess, we can note some relative competitive strengths that good family businesses often possess by the very nature of the fact that they are family businesses. The following description portrays a family business situation at its best. Clearly, not all businesses reflect these strengths in their operations. For purposes of this discussion we have generally assumed that family businesses are smaller than others in their industry, as well as privately owned, since the vast majority of family firms in this country share these two characteristics. However, well-managed, large, public family businesses may also possess some of the following strengths.

Long-Term Orientation. Family businesses are in business for the long haul. They rarely have outside shareholders to whom they constantly have to justify quarterly performances on sales and earnings. They have no stock market to judge them harshly if they deliberately increase expenses. Instead, they may focus their vision five, ten, fifteen, or even twenty years out. They can afford patience. They are freer to experiment with distant, future markets and wait for the eventual payoff than public companies are. Tax laws encourage such attitudes. Family companies may deduct all they spend on marketing, human resource development, and research. Such deductions are available to all businesses, of course. But public companies are not as eager to take advantage of them, because they are more interested in "saving" the money for earnings. Private companies, in contrast, have a greater motivation to spend the money, minimizing corporate taxes and conserving cash flow in the process.

Flexible Organization. Employees of a large corporation often waste valuable business time engaging in political warfare. The large company pays a double price for this behavior. It loses productivity while the battle is underway. And it often finds it difficult to respond to change because its employees may be more interested in defending their territories than in developing a new product or service. The family business can usually react more quickly to changing circumstances by, for example, adding a new manufacturing line, reassigning responsibility for a new marketing program, or developing a new business unit. It can do this because the power to decide such moves typically lies with just a few people or even one, not with a corporate bureaucracy. The family business head does not have to defend the proposed expense (and subsequent cut in profit) to layers of higher authority. He or she can also more readily gain the commitment of employees to the change.

Quality Motivation. Bigger companies often must seek a standard of excellence through a costly and time-consuming set of personnel and management controls. But small, family companies come naturally by a certain pride in their products or services. It is *their name* on the door. They are inherently motivated not to tarnish it with poor workmanship or service. Such pride is reflected in dozens of ways critical to a successful showing in today's marketplace. Family firms often respond more quickly to customer complaints; employees take such complaints personally, especially when they come from neighbors who live in the same community. Moreover, the owner-founders typically take great pride in the products of their companies and therefore invest a high degree of craftsmanship in their work. Large customers often find these companies eager to please, just because their sizable accounts are so needed. Smaller customers usually find family businesses to be responsive and cooperative. For customers large and small, then, a family business provides that "personal touch" so important in today's frequently impersonal business world.

Adaptable to Smaller Markets. Small, specialty markets often provide greater opportunities than larger, mass markets do. And the company that first makes a name for itself in such a market is usually left alone by other competitors. Thus these markets can be quite profitable for the lucky few who know how to use them. The small business is eminently suited to take advantage of such market opportunities. For most of them, specialty products are a source of profit. In contrast, big businesses often will not give specialty markets a second glance, believing that they are not worth the time and trouble. A number of consumer product companies will not even do serious research on items that promise less than $100 million of potential sales. This attitude leaves smaller firms a good deal of room to make their mark in such products as pita bread or pickled pigs' feet. Markets like these allow one firm to master the distribution system and create brand awareness for consumers. That sort of protection creates high profit margins.

Investing in People. One of the oldest clichés about business is also among its truest: good people are a company's best asset. As a result, big and small businesses alike invest time and money in improving their personnel. They offer training programs, weekend seminars, time off for professional societies, even funding for further formal education. But it is the smaller companies and privately owned firms that gain the highest return from such an investment. Their employees tend to develop long-term loyalties, becoming "part of the family." Their owners have the pleasure of personally managing employees whose growth they have encouraged. This prompts energetic and committed work on both sides; frequently, that bond helps protect the private business owner from unionization as well. This is illustrated by a study (Ward, 1983) that showed that privately held companies are significantly less unionized than publicly owned firms—about one-third less.

Can Ignore Conventional Wisdom. Everyone pays lip service to the importance of innovation and creativity. But in reality a new idea is a "tough sell" in many businesses, especially big ones. If a proposal does not reflect the conventional wisdom, it is subjected to intense scrutiny. So, many managers simply stick to the tried and true. Examples of the rules they try to obey include "invest only in fast-growth markets," "automation is better than labor," and "the more you produce, the cheaper it gets."

Conversely, the smaller, privately controlled firm is much freer to follow its own instincts. It can install that specialty manufacturing procedure that turns out products at low volume but also at high quality, thus winning acceptance among customers. It can find a slow-growth market that it can profitably corner while others are looking elsewhere. Or it can hire fine craftsmen, who are often a more important drawing card for customers than automated machines.

A unique idea, in fact, is often the most profitable kind of idea because it provides a valuable competitive advantage. The profit premiums inherent in this course of action exist only for those willing to do things differently from the dictates of conventional wisdom. As a result, swimming against the tide is often the more appropriate course—and one more easily adopted by smaller firms.

Strong Culture. Family businesses typically exude a camaraderie that extends to nonfamily members working in the business. They all usually live in the same community, often working at one location for years. They form strong bonds with the company as well as with its owner. In such a closely knit environment people know the standards and know what is expected of them. Those standards—loosely termed the *corporate culture*—are reinforced in a thousand ways, from wall photographs and company folklore to special needs. Such clear standards make it easier to establish business direction and to get everyone pulling together in that direction, thus increasing a company's chances of success.

Confidentiality. Family businesses are usually private and need not disclose much financial information to the public. This often affords a considerable advantage, especially if publicly held competitors must publish reports that then double as a source of competitive intelligence for other companies. The plans and performance of public companies often lie in full view, while the details of private companies remain relatively hidden.

To be sure, the smaller family business does have some disadvantages. Those are important to recognize because good strategy rests upon minimizing weakness, as well as exploiting strength. These weaknesses may stem from the business's size, its role in the market, and the number of public competitors in its industry. Smaller size, less diversity, and limited financial resources, for example, make the family business vulnerable to technological change and market turmoil. These same characteristics also often discourage investments in speculative markets or new technologies. They make those directions riskier for a small company than for a larger, more financially stable concern.

The potential disadvantages of a small family firm may be summarized as follows:

1. Because they lack sophisticated cost accounting systems, small companies frequently do not know how much it actually costs to turn out their products.
2. The lack of advanced management systems and philosophies can make small companies unwilling to challenge old patterns or set new, aggressive goals.
3. Often tending to trust only their own employees, small companies may decline to participate in joint ventures that could infuse their businesses with new ideas and innovative technology.
4. Small companies frequently focus on one product or one market, a practice that does not permit the kind of cross-fertilization that multiproduct, multimarket companies enjoy.
5. Scarce capital resources do not allow for a high degree of automation and rapid expansion of small companies.
6. Small companies often have fewer economies of scale and, as a result, often bear higher costs than competitors.

These disadvantages may be overcome with a finely honed strategy that plays up a company's best qualities. But companies that see their weaknesses in this list should not ignore them. Knowing their weak spots will also help them highlight their strengths.

Handcrafting Business Strategies

The strengths and weaknesses discussed above have clear implications for the strategic direction of any family business. Suitable strategies include exploiting smaller markets, market niches, ethnic or regional markets, declining or more mature markets that may yield profit through extra personal effort, and emerging markets. Smaller companies might also emphasize craftsmanship and customization of service or products.

All these suggest that the small, private family business does best by seeking out "the hidden customer"—the buyer somehow overlooked or ignored by others. To spot such customers, companies must work closely with their sales force and distributors, seeking information about the market. They must also pay attention to comments from dissatisfied customers. The reasons for their dissatisfaction may suggest a broader market need not yet filled by anyone.

Reaching these customers, however, requires a good deal of careful planning. Marketing to such specialty groups often requires labor-intensive techniques, as does developing and manufacturing products for them. In all these areas, a family company must keep in mind that the key to penetrating any specialty market is customizing the item for the customer. That requires a good deal of extra work and personal attention, but these are details the family firm is well able to supply. Marketing techniques, for example, might include frequent point-of-purchase changes for individual markets. Again, the company could sponsor a special computer program or training classes for individual customers. It could make special sales presentations for a specific customer, targeted to a certain region or the location of the customer's purchase. Or it might use product service features as added attractions—features such as maintenance programs, waste disposal services, or data services that provide marketing feedback to their customers on the customer's activities.

The same principle holds true in operations and research. Many family businesses spend years developing new products with specially crafted and unique features rather than invest in advanced research and development. They work to constantly, incrementally improve the way the product is made rather than make one major breakthrough and freeze its design to accommodate large, capital-intensive production systems. These businesses work continuously to reduce costs and increase quality or improve flexibility and delivery performance. They stay alert to larger competitors' research breakthroughs and quickly copy the better ideas. This nimbleness allows them the best of both worlds—the benefit of advanced research by competitors and the advantage of extra effort in process engineering. As with the marketing techniques we described, these processes rely more on people than on machines. Individuals can customize products and services to specific customer needs. That is the key strength of the smaller family firm.

Not every small family firm follows these principles, of course. Some may concentrate on achieving major breakthroughs in research and make commitments to capital-intensive production. But most emphasize advantages inherent to the well-run family company: quality, specialization, flexibility, and personal service by employees eager to serve. A comparative study (Ward, 1983) of about 50 large, well-established family companies and 200 public companies, comparable by size, profit, and sophistication, confirmed this. The profitability of the two groups as a whole was near the national average of 22 percent ROI, with the family-controlled companies slightly ahead of the public ones (26 percent versus 21 percent). The family firms competed in smaller, more regional, and more mature markets—especially markets that benefited from extra personal effort. They were less unionized but paid their employees relatively more compensation than the larger firms did. They offered a broader product line and also served widely diverse customers who demanded customization and a variety of special features.

These family companies were also more clearly geared to

the long term. They spent proportionately more than public companies on research and development, marketing, and capital investment; in other words, they spent more on the future. And during economic and profit downturns, the family business maintained higher spending levels on projects for future benefit than did their public company peers. Public companies are often accused of cutting these expenses to improve earnings during downturns. Private companies, our research shows, chose to sacrifice short-term profits rather than cut back marketing and research programs. (More background on this research and its methodology is presented in Appendix G.)

Changing Times

To be sure, changing times threaten many of these successful strategies and the underlying relative competitive strengths of the smaller, family business. So many new entrepreneurs have entered the fray in recent years that these marketing and operational emphases have come to abound, thereby dulling the competitive edge they formerly gave. Moreover, new technologies enable much bigger businesses to "act small." Computerized data services speed the details of customers' individual requirements from the salesperson to the production floor. There, new flexible manufacturing equipment and processes turn out a wide variety of custom products, rapidly and at low cost. These enable large cost-conscious companies to be more experimental and to act more like job shops. These same technologies also permit very close attention to product and service quality.

Such capabilities have made many larger companies eager to "act smaller." They are eliminating layers of bureaucracy and developing more autonomous business units. They are struggling to encourage an entrepreneurial spirit. They espouse the message of such books as *In Search of Excellence* (Peters and Waterman, 1982) that urge larger businesses to adopt the attributes long associated with smaller, family businesses.

As a result of these forces, all companies—large and small —are now competing more with increasingly similar techniques. They are building fresh marketing programs around technological strengths, production processes, or distribution systems. They are seeking customers who want what they have, and they are staying close enough to those customers to meet their changing needs. They are introducing new products at a rapid rate and investing in flexible manufacturing and service systems in order to keep pace with all these changes. Hence, what *special* strategies are left for smaller companies, especially those that cannot afford such costly programs? What can the smaller, family business do to increase leverage against bigger, richer, and more powerful companies?

We would suggest that smaller businesses must now turn the tables and begin to learn from their larger competitors. They should consider developing more sophisticated support systems for their efforts. Methods of financial control, legal advice, strategic planning, marketing research, and information systems are all available to the smaller company through outside professional services. In fact, accounting and law firms, banks, educational institutions, and large commercial data networks are courting the smaller firm as never before. The managers of these smaller businesses can avail themselves of this expertise and create the affordable equivalent of sophisticated in-house staffs and financial services. Such support systems will offer the smaller firm fresh thinking, state-of-the-art market research, low-cost financing, and new insights into management and administration. In effect, smaller companies now can have access to the talent and information once available only to very large firms.

Second, small businesses must remember that while big businesses may have become better at acting small, they are still only acting. Responsiveness, flexibility, customized service, and other requirements of today's marketplace are all more easily achieved by the smaller family business. Thus these traditional strengths still work. Family firms have only to be better at them, and more faithful to them, than they were before in order to compete with the bigger businesses in their markets. And they must continue to emphasize those particular traits that big business, no matter how hard it tries, can never completely match.

Ability to Respond. No matter how decentralized large firms become, they will still be more bureaucratic than the smaller or owner-managed firm. They will have more layers of managers, more people protecting careers, and more red tape to be cut by anyone who wants to carry out an innovative project. In contrast, business owners who are in close, informal contact with all their managers can respond quickly and spontaneously. By emphasizing rapport, trust, and frequent contact among employees, they can keep paper work at a minimum. By promoting the family continuity of the business, they can minimize office politics. By staying in touch with customers and salespeople, they can receive direct feedback from the field.

Personal Involvement of Owner. Business owners often mislead themselves into thinking that their time is best spent in making decisions and refining and testing new information. And yet spending time this way often means that they will have little time to coach their employees, cheer them on, and consult with them. This is the most valuable—and often most underutilized—resource that a chief executive of a smaller family business has. He or she knows every aspect of the business, from the source of raw materials to the final destination of shipments. Customers like to be able to talk to the person in charge; they especially like to be able to talk to someone who knows the entire operation. Contact with the chief executive seals their loyalty to his or her product or service.

The chief executive's personal involvement with employees also heightens the power of corporate culture. By spending time with them, he or she can instill in them the key elements of the company's culture. Employees can daily assimilate the ideals and values of the company, not just read about them once in a while in company publications. All this provides a smaller company with a competitive edge over large companies.

Location. Proximity is still very important to customers. And smaller firms, often physically close to their customers, come naturally by this trait. This simple fact leads to many extra services that the family firm can provide. It can deliver a product speedily in an emergency, for example. Or it can keep track of a customer's preferences, calling when an item that the customer might like arrives. This is only one of numerous ways to cement customer loyalty.

Summary

The selection of a strategic direction for the future depends in part on an assessment of the industry environment and the strength of the business. We have proposed a list of alternative directions and suggested which match up best with what business circumstances. We have also argued that family considerations will substantially influence the final choice of strategy. The depth of the family's commitment, its available financial resources, and its vision of the future are the three critical points to keep in mind.

The exact nature of the final plans will depend on the company's distinctive strengths and weaknesses. Thus, we discussed the relative competitive strengths and weaknesses of smaller and/or family-owned businesses and presented the implications of these for final strategy refinement or development.

The final step in working out a successful strategy for the family business is to ensure that successors understand the strategic planning process, business and family assumptions, and the lessons that can be drawn from the past of the company. In the final chapter we will discuss how the successors can become effective strategic leaders who will keep the family business healthy.

EIGHT

The Transition to New Leadership: Promoting a Revitalized Business Vision and Strategy

The family's strategic plan should pave the way for the company's revitalization. As we noted in Chapter One, revitalization is often accomplished when a new leader takes over the company. In a family business, this new leadership means the successors: the senior family team of the next generation. The "team" might consist of only one inheritor, or it might consist of many—all the shareholder cousins and siblings. They will have been chosen by one of the several methods outlined in Chapter Three.

Whatever method of selection the family uses, however, it will be the successors' job to foster the new business life cycle and develop the organization professionally. Specifically, the successor or successors will (1) help develop the new strategy, (2) add formal management systems, and (3) build the new management team.

In many ways, such tasks are even more difficult than the process of selecting the strategic direction. For they will lead to *implementing* the new strategy, not merely choosing it. Under ideal conditions, successors will assume this responsibility with the full faith and support of the outgoing generation, who will have laid the groundwork for them. This is probably the single most important contribution that the outgoing generation can make as the family approaches the transition to new leadership.

In other cases, however, successors will not be able to simply *continue* the job of professionalizing the company and revitalizing its strategy but will find themselves faced with the necessity of *beginning* these tasks. Sometimes they may be able to work with the company's current leader. But if the leader of the past generation has chosen to maintain the status quo, successors will find themselves entirely on their own.

Whatever role the outgoing leader chooses to play, he or she will likely cast a powerful shadow. That of course makes it difficult for successors to establish their own presence. The challenges of new leadership are sharpened further when successors find it necessary to integrate old and new strategies and blend their own ways of doing business with earlier ones. They must manage a business that has probably become larger, more complex, more formal. In most family businesses, only the successor will know what it will take to accomplish these tasks. The previous generation implemented entrepreneurial strategies by instinct and the need to survive; successors, in contrast, must use planned and conscious administration. As a result, it is up to successors themselves to design a program that will teach them the necessary skills.

As we have noted, however, in the best of all possible worlds, successors—and their developmental programs—will have the support of the preceding generation. Such a healthy transition is illustrated by the example that follows:

> A Midwest entrepreneur, aged fifty-two, is shifting both control and ownership of his $8-million-a-year retail business to his twenty-eight-year-old son. He made the decision to do so when he saw his son outselling every other salesman in the company while also attending college full time. That feat was accomplished under the tutelage of a senior sales manager eager to teach the son all that he could. Father and son now work side by side, sharing business responsibilities. The father, looking ahead to retirement, occasionally takes long trips in his recreational vehicle. The son

has full authority to run the business in his absence. When the father returns, he does not undo what has been done. Instead, he typically praises his son's efforts.

"I remember how many mistakes I made when I was his age," this entrepreneur and family man says philosophically. "It's part of the learning process."

This anecdote exemplifies four traits common to successful transitions:

- A founder enthusiastic about passing on the business
- A successor who can handle responsibility at a young age
- Trust between founder and successor
- Commitment to work things out together

The attitude of the outgoing generation clearly has much to do with achieving a smooth transition. However, as we can see in the above example, that attitude is often influenced by the successor's willingness to take responsibility for his or her own development. In this chapter, we will discuss how successors can cultivate positive management traits. This effort involves two primary activities for successors: (1) establishing a personal development plan; and (2) systematically studying the company's past history, strategy, philosophy, and culture. Such a program is designed to provide a successor with an understanding of the challenges to strategic change, while helping him or her win the respect of the organization. But these activities should rest on a foundation that was laid years ago, in the way in which the successor was raised by his or her parents.

Successor's Progress

From childhood until roughly eighteen years of age, successors should be instilled with positive attitudes toward business challenges and taught good work habits. It is chiefly their families that should do this. In Chapter Three, we cited additional lessons that can be taught, such as the importance of sharing decisions and saving money. We also recommended several years of outside job experience for successors and specific job responsibilities when they return to the family business. We emphasized the importance of a mentor to guide their early years in that business. Such practices not only lay a strong foundation for successors' future roles but serve as "tests" of their capabilities and potential for leadership. Once they have passed these tests and are clearly the heirs apparent—and once the family has decided that the business is to remain in the family—successors may begin to take responsibility for the development and implementation of strategy. At this point, successors are usually between thirty and forty years of age.

This time line of career development is illustrated in Table 15. The table shows that after family socialization in business values, successors typically spend the next ten years attending college and gaining outside work experience, all the while developing their personal capabilities and self-confidence. They perhaps join the family business in their late twenties, and during the next five years or so they gain functional expertise and experience at making decisions. This stage blends into that of the "heir apparent." Now they take responsibility for one or more profit centers in order to acquire general management skills. Beyond this, they must begin to explore outside resources that will allow them to continue their professional development.

To be sure, successors' development will not always follow such a smooth course. For some successors, early death or disability of the parent rushes development. Because they have not yet acquired the proper skills, these young heirs are forced to act more like entrepreneurs than like professional managers. They learn to do what is necessary through instinct and the sheer need to survive.

Other successors—those in very large, complex companies —usually must pass through at least two "mentoring" stages. The large number of organizational layers and senior managers requires them to spend more time climbing the corporate ladder. In such circumstances, a nonfamily member or another

Table 15. Successor's Career Development Time Line.

Stage	Child: Home Upbringing	Young Adult: Learning Outside the Family Business	Professional Manager: Mentored Within the Family Business	Successor: Known as Heir Apparent	Leader: Chief Executive or Member of Family "Senior Management Team"
Age	0 to 18	18 to 28	25 to 35	30 to 40	35 to 45
Developmental Goals	Positive attitude toward business challenges; good personal work habits	Higher education; developing personal capabilities and learning lessons of organizational life	Functional expertise; decision-making experience	General management and profit center responsibility	Outside resources for stimulation and continuing education

older relative often serves in the chief executive's role between generations. That gives offspring enough time to develop.

The third and, sadly, most common exception involves a successor who is stalled behind an aging parent—a parent uninterested in relinquishing control. This is probably the most frustrating and stressful circumstance that can occur in a family business. At the point such reluctance becomes clear, it is usually too late for the successor to leave the family business for a new career. It also becomes impossible for the successor to realize his or her full management potential.

Some successors faced with this problem find that the only way to cope is simply to *take* responsibility rather than wait for it to be assigned. In this manner, they hope that they will win authority by default. They go ahead and make personnel changes. Or they buy a computer system. Or they develop a new product. Some even establish a new company to pursue new strategies, while continuing to remain with the family business. Other successors simply develop a personal rationale to help them weather near-term conflict and stress. In a survey of 120 successors (Holton, 1983) who were asked to list their reasons for remaining in the family business, the following rationales (in order of frequency) were voiced:

1. The business will be mine someday.
2. My parents expect it of me.
3. I am secure here.
4. It is too late to start over elsewhere.
5. I like my family; I am proud of it and the business.
6. My family has dynamic, trustworthy people that make good partners.
7. I want to protect my family's interests.
8. The family business is my heritage.
9. Working for the company is a good financial move.

In difficult times, any reinforcing rationale will do. Yet some are not as good as others in sustaining successors. "It is expected of me" and "I am stuck," for example, are extremely negative reasons for remaining in a family business. These state-

ments reflect the feelings of a person who is not in control of
his or her own destiny; ironically, they may not even reflect
what parents want for their children. "I will be secure" and "I
can protect my family's interests" and "It is a good investment"
are less negative reasons. Still, they are somewhat neutral as a
sustaining force. "I can have my own business," while offering
strong motivation to any successor, is a reason that may be
placed at significant risk by the participation of siblings in the
business. Their presence means the business may never truly be
the successor's after all, and that could undermine his or her interest in it.

These neutral and negative reasons are unfortunate. For
in a family business, it is the family-oriented motivations that
work to build cohesion and establish long-term perspectives.
Reasons 5, 6, and 8, all involving family motivation, provide the
most positive and compelling rationales a successor could have
to last out difficult times. They are unselfish, they help bond
family members, and they reflect a philosophy that will benefit
future generations. Such rationales will not directly solve the
emotional problems that frustrate many transitions, of course.
But they will certainly ease the pressure by helping successors
focus on the long-term promise instead of on daily dilemmas.
Coupled with a personal development program, these rationales
move a successor from asking such troubling questions as "Why
doesn't Dad believe in me?" or "Why doesn't Dad let me make
decisions?" to taking responsibility for his or her own growth.
(For more discussion of the survey of rationales, see Appendix G.)

Personal Development Plan

No matter what situation a successor finds himself or her-
self in, a personal development plan is useful. Such a plan pre-
pares the successor for leadership and thus helps to smoothe the
shift of power from one generation to the next. It can also provide enormous personal satisfaction and help the successor recall long-term goals in the face of short-term setbacks.

An effective plan for successors must (1) inculcate the

skills they will need to run the company and (2) allow them to develop their own identity by progressively gaining managerial responsibility. At best, it also provides for outside evaluation or clear accountability. The plan includes developing skills that complement a parent's capabilities; running a profit center; building one's own organization; setting goals, preferably with outside review; continuing professional education; and finding support groups. Successors can undertake many of these initiatives on their own. Others, such as running a profit center, will need the blessing of the outgoing generation.

Complement Parent/Owner's Interests

Successors should try to structure their skills so that they can avoid areas already staked out by the parent. Such structuring is especially important when the time comes to transfer power from one generation to the next. Emotions often run high when leaders feel that the company is slipping from their grasp. Some conflict is almost inevitable, but wise successors will seek ways to lessen it. They will try to make the transition to leadership without infringing on the territory of others.

One way to accomplish this is by *complementing* the boss instead of *competing* with him or her; that is, learning to be strong where the boss is weak. This tactic is not only good for founder-successor relations, it is also good for the business. The entrepreneur who dislikes record keeping, for example, has probably kept inadequate or incomplete records, thereby lessening the company's ability to control costs and budget expenses. By acquiring accounting and data-processing skills and improving these financial systems, the successor can (1) strengthen the business, (2) gain new abilities, and (3) increase the likelihood of avoiding conflict with his predecessor.

Learn Formal Business Skills. Founders tend to run their operations informally. They often take a seat-of-the-pants approach not only to record keeping but to such managerial tasks as inventory control, market research, and forecasting. These oversights make delegation of authority and accountability for results very difficult to implement. Hence, these are areas that successors might concentrate on, bringing capabilities to the business that it may badly need. Successors may carry out these tasks themselves or assign them to others who may be better prepared to execute them. Such activities typically include:

- market segment analysis
- departmental effectiveness measures
- productivity measures
- cost accounting systems
- inventory control systems
- forecasting
- personnel training programs
- company communications
- budgets and plans (operating, capital, and strategic)

Emphasize Technology. If a company already has one or more computers, the successor can move it into the next stage of computerization. If the company has no computers, the successor might consider introducing them slowly, buying one machine for one small task and thus gradually demonstrating the value of computerization. The computer will facilitate the professional analyses just cited. It will speed up current calculations and make new ones possible. It will also afford successors additional opportunities. People who take responsibility for computerizing a company gain access to important information concerning salaries, expenses, and performance trends. They gain a chance to teach employees new skills, thereby strengthening organizational relationships. They are also given an opportunity to alter a company's traditions, thus associating themselves with progress and cultural change.

Practice External Thinking. Successors may also make a valuable contribution through "external thinking"—that is, through exploring the market for clues to future growth and profit. Founders will likely have withdrawn from this habit years ago. They may no longer call on customers or track competitors' moves as closely as before. Without the insights gained through these activities, they may have become insensitive to market shifts. Successors who take these activities upon themselves will begin to learn what people think of the company's product or service and whether changes should be made. They can hunt for new entrepreneurial opportunities that might benefit the business. While they may not be able to immediately execute their ideas, they will acquire the habit of keeping close to the market, which is the key to running a business strategically.

In the meantime—as appropriate—the successor may patiently share insights with the parent and key managers. This is a way of testing the validity of these insights and also a way of sensitizing people to a change in leadership. Such nonthreatening questions as "Are customers asking about our follow-up servicing?" or "Why do we have more employee turnover on the day shift than the night shift?" can be quite effective.

Run a Profit Center

Successors often remain in one functional area such as marketing, operations, or finance for a long period of time. They then acquire the role of chief operating officer or executive vice president. The intent of this progression is to allow the successor to help the company in an area of need before assuming the president-elect's role. Yet such departmental positions teach little in the way of self-sufficiency. Even as the second-in-command, successors are still "responsible for everything and accountable for nothing." No accomplishment or failure is clearly theirs; their job is primarily to support the chief executive. And that does not necessarily prepare successors to take over the job themselves.

Alternatively, the most valuable training for the top manager's role is the management of an independent profit center. This may be a store, a sales region, a corporate division, or a particular line of products and services—anything that generates profit as a stand-alone unit. Here, at the head of their own "minicorporation," successors will learn leadership and strategy.

Build Own Organization

During the shift of power from parent to offspring, the successor should begin to develop his or her own management team. This ensures an orderly transition. The first step is to allow successors who have been assigned a department, branch, or sales territory to hire their own people for that unit. In that way, they can begin to create a loyal following. Employees will also begin doing things in the successor's style, an important desideratum for sound future management. The second step entails giving the successor some hiring responsibilities for the entire company. For example, he or she might be named head of data processing or head of personnel—a controller, a sales manager, or plant manager. These positions will also complement the successor's efforts to bring formal management skills to the organization.

None of this means sweeping the predecessor's team aside. Loyal key employees who have been part of the owner's team for many years are almost certain to stay on. If the parent has shaped the organization well, these people will constitute a vigorous, vital force. If the parent has not done this, the successor must probably accept them anyway since they will long ago have achieved tenure.

In the latter case, it will be necessary to create a "dual organization," in which the founder has one team reporting to him and the successor has another. Obviously, the duties of some people will overlap. A controller might perform some functions similar to those of the vice president of finance. A sales manager might share some duties with the marketing manager. These overlaps will probably be confusing and costly, and they can also provide occasions for emotional conflict between successors and their parents. Yet we believe the benefits outweigh the costs. These steps create continuity. They help a successor build rapport within the company, preparing her for the eventual day when her team will be at the top. It also develops people who can serve the successor's goals for growth in a manner compatible with her management style. When the founder's team does retire—its members will usually all reach retirement age at about the same time—the organization is then saved the tremendous costs that come from having to find a large number of new people all at once. Their replacements will have learned the business before they actually must take over the top positions.

While this is going on, the successor should be moving

through a series of positions: product or plant manager, vice president and/or division manager, executive vice president, chief operating officer, and, finally, president and chief executive officer. As she does so, more and more areas of responsibility—the personnel staff, the sales force, the finance department, production areas, the purchasing department—will begin to report to her. This gradually transfers authority from one generation to the next and reassures employees that the transition is progressing in an orderly fashion. Finally, it prevents time-consuming disruptions when the former president does retire.

Successors who for one reason or another do not have an opportunity to hire their own staff can still *prepare* themselves for this task. They can collect résumés of prospective employees and gather business cards of people who might lead them to prospective employees. They can learn what salaries they will have to pay to attract good people and what kinds of backgrounds to look for. All these activities help to establish a network of contracts that will serve them well later.

Set Goals with Outside Review

Establishing goals has many benefits. It gives successors a chance to define job responsibilities and to see that they are actually making meaningful contributions to the business. Goals can be established within such areas as sales and manufacturing performance, hiring, personal development, and business analysis. Targets might include:

- Hire a salesman in the second quarter
- Buy and install new equipment by the end of the year
- Design a preventive maintenance program
- Attend one or two management seminars each year
- Do an analysis of plant productivity, new market needs, or the image of a new product

Sharing these goals with such qualified outsiders as board members, accountants, lawyers, or organizational consultants also has benefits. Such outsiders can comment on the degree of ambition and realism that the goals reflect. They can also help define goals in ways that lessen their ambiguity and enhance their measurability.

Continue Professional Studies

Learning to "be the president" is not part of anybody's traditional education. Yet the skills required are formidable. The would-be president must be familiar with everything from formal management analysis techniques to business etiquette. He or she must be prepared to assume leadership roles in the business, the family, and the community. Often, the best way to acquire these capabilities is from peers: presidents and presidents-to-be. Many trade associations sponsor young executive groups for this express purpose. A popular alternative is the Young Presidents Organization. Based in New York City, this group holds workshops, seminars, and meetings and in general offers young presidents the opportunity to fraternize with one another. Membership, however, is open only to those who have become presidents of medium-sized businesses before their fortieth birthdays. Thus, many family businesses purposely pass on the presidency before successors turn forty so that they can gain access to such unique professional development.

Some skills can perhaps best be acquired through formal education. The graduate business schools of Yale University and the University of Southern California now offer for-credit courses in family business. Several other universities offer seminars on the same subject: Wharton School of the University of Pennsylvania in the East, Loyola University of Chicago in the Midwest, and Oregon State University in the West. Other schools, broadening the topic somewhat, offer professional development programs to executives of small businesses. Two of the best are Harvard University's Owner/President Management Program and Stanford University's Executive Program for Smaller Companies.

Find Support Groups

Successors' problems are unique to successors: no one else knows what working for one's father or mother, or gaining enormous business power at a young age, is really like. Thus, while support groups can offer intellectual stimulation and provide emotional support, only other successors can provide the special camaraderie that stems from similar experiences. And only other successors may be able to suggest solutions to some of the problems that are bound to occur when power is passed from one generation to another in a family business.

A variety of such "succession" groups exist outside educational circles. The best known of these is the "Sons of Bosses" or "Family Business Councils" (the name of the group is different in different cities, and most chapters now include daughters). In industries made up mostly of family businesses, Young Executive Societies (Y.E.S. groups) are also forming. Organizations that bring together business owners from a variety of industries are now spawning similar groups of successors such as Executive Committees. These committees are popular in Wisconsin, Illinois, and California. Most common of all is a small, informal support group put together by successors themselves. They seek each other out and then meet regularly for monthly breakfasts or lunches. One group in Chicago, for example, consists entirely of daughter successors who meet monthly at one another's businesses.

Respect for the Corporate Culture

This development program will ensure that successors gain self-confidence and the skills necessary to lead their businesses. But to truly prepare successors to direct the future of the family business, more is necessary. Successors must also spend time learning to appreciate their company's past, since that will have a critical effect on their ability to bring about change. Many successors, however, rebel against past business practices instead of trying to understand them. The company's management seems stale to them and its way of doing things outmoded. They eagerly propose new systems, seeking to introduce changes that reflect their own identity. Indeed, most of the programs we have just mentioned encourage this.

And yet organizations have deeply ingrained attitudes

about the way things should be done (Dyer, 1986), and trying to alter them overnight might be destructive of the success that the company has already achieved. Building a business typically calls not for *revolution* but *evolution*: a process of gradual, relatively peaceful movement from one stage to the next. It builds on the best of what has gone before, and it lets the rest gradually disappear.

Managing change in this way calls for a thorough understanding of both the past and the present. That, in turn, requires a systematic study of the company's history, strategy, creed, and values. These are the building blocks of corporate culture, the ideas that underlie the daily actions and attitudes of every employee in the company. Managers who seek to fundamentally change those actions and attitudes must change the underlying culture if they wish to achieve a lasting change. The extent of their ability to do so will determine, in many ways, the success of their plans for future strategic regeneration.

Insights into a company's culture are best obtained from sources such as the founder, long-term employees, old-time suppliers, trusted bankers or lawyers, and older family members. Awkward as it may sound, successors should actually interview these people and record their interviews on paper or tape. They might then consider setting their observations down on paper— producing a written corporate history, for example, or a documented summary of the company's past strategies—and reviewing this document with key sources to assure accuracy and refine their insights. Such documents can either be placed in the family business archives for posterity or disseminated throughout the business by means of the company newsletter, employee manuals, or customer brochures.

Successors who take the time to do this will not only gain insights into the nature of the business but will also find that this is a pleasant, productive way to talk business with their parents. They may also come to conclusions like the following:

1. Corporate change occurs slowly.
2. Meaningful change requires the implementation of bold new ideas regarding the business's strategy and philosophy

—ideas such as developing a flexible manufacturing capability to serve customers' unpredictable needs or formalizing a policy that allows employees to share in profit.

3. Change requires subtle, persistent, and consistent salesmanship by the chief executive.

Such lessons have significant implications for the activities of a successor. They suggest that rather than become bogged down in debates about sales commission rates or the choice of suppliers, he should try to take the long view. He should not try to influence the day-to-day decisions made by his parent but instead work to shape the general thinking of the organization. The successor wants to gradually focus employees' thinking so that in the future they will analyze decisions in a certain way. In this manner the successor can begin to influence *what* decisions come to the table, instead of *how* individual daily decisions are made. That is much more important to the future. With this goal in mind, a successor should begin a formal process of learning about the company. He or she needs to look at four areas: the company's history, strategy, creed, and values.

History. The history of the business may be the greatest educational tool available to the successor. He or she will almost always have fewer decades of business experience than the previous generation, and learning the lessons of history is the fastest way to close the gap. To be sure, every successor has doubtless already heard the business history in bits and pieces. But stringing these fragments together usually provides only a sketchy chronological account. That is insufficient for the purpose at hand. What the successor needs instead is an interpretive history that will explain not only what happened but, more importantly, *why* it happened. Some of the important questions in an interpretive history are: How was the business founded? How were decisions made in the beginning? What threats did the business have to face? When? How did the business respond to these threats? How was the business organized at the start? How has the organization changed? Who left the company and why? Where did they go?

Knowing how to ask follow-up questions is as important

as knowing what to ask initially. In many of these areas, for instance, it is only the second, third, or fourth query that will yield the desired information. Thus, in answer to the question about how the business was founded, successors will probably first be given the little thumbnail sketch that they have heard since childhood. But if they ask additional questions—how did the founder first come to see a business opportunity? how many people said his efforts were sure to fail? what convinced him or her to go ahead anyway? what was going on in his or her personal life at the time?—a true picture will begin to emerge. Once the successor begins to understand what really happened, he will be in a position to learn from those events.

Interviews that answer these questions provide nonthreatening learning opportunities. The successor and the founder do not start to argue about what should be done with the business *now*. Instead, they discuss what has already happened. That is more neutral subject matter. With any luck, successors will be able to learn from the previous generation's mistakes. They will gain experience vicariously, they will deepen their sense of the company's heritage, and they will acquire valuable perspective and judgment. Cultivating the corporate history accomplishes one other purpose. It shows the founder that the successor has some respect for what has gone before. Nothing could ease relations between them more.

Strategy. A strategy, as readers may recall, is the company's recipe for success. Earlier in this book we discussed a rather precise method of determining the ingredients of that strategy. Yet even companies that have not gone through that process will still have an implicit formula for creating profit. This formula develops decision by decision. A customer might ask that a product be manufactured in a slightly different way. A plant foreman may seek permission to design a new piece of equipment. A salesman might request a new line of merchandise. The acceptance or rejection of these requests gradually develops a pattern, circumscribing the company's overall strategy. Strategy formed this way is usually implicit and, not being written down, likely to drift over time.

Discerning a strategy that has been determined through

the processes outlined in this book will be a relatively easy task for successors. Much of the work will have been done for them. Unraveling the threads of a strategy determined in spontaneous fashion, however, is a quite complex process. The successor must then systematically attempt to examine his or her company's policies on the following:

- products
- markets
- distribution
- promotion
- price
- competitive advantage
- product development
- manufacturing operations
- financing
- administration

In examining promotional policy, for example, a successor would inquire into which forms of promotion are prevalent and why; what level of expense is customary and why that amount makes sense given competitors' policies; and what result the promotional effort is intended to have. All these policies taken together, whether they are stated or implied, will make up the current promotional strategy of the company.

Talks on such topics will be far more productive than most talks between successors and predecessors, which ordinarily focus on social trends, what motivates people, how to evaluate people, what is good or bad about the business, or *who* is good or bad in the business. These topics do not necessarily evoke conflict in themselves. But they often deteriorate into a debate on management styles—and on whose style is better, the successor's or the parent's. *That* can set off fireworks.

Corporate Creed or Philosophy. Successful entrepreneurs have at least four things in common. All had one or more great ideas. All had luck. All worked very hard. And all had deeply held philosophies about how to conduct business. These philosophies usually focus on the company's attitude toward its constituents: customers, employees, suppliers, investors, family, and community. They spell out what it takes to be successful. As a result, they form the business's creed and summarize the activities that a company must carry out successfully so that everything else—from sales to profit—will follow. Examples of corporate creeds include:

- Marshall Field & Co. (a department store): "Give the lady what she wants."
- ServiceMaster Industries (a service concern): "To honor God in all we do, to help people develop, to pursue excellence, and to grow profitably—precisely in that order."
- Leo Burnett Company (an advertising agency): "When you reach for the stars you may not quite get one, but you won't come up with a handful of mud either."

Such creeds become institutionalized through speeches, wall plaques, employee manuals, and other documents. At Leo Burnett, for example, a little hand reaches for the stars on all letterheads. Others expand their "one-liners" into full-blown corporate statements that capture the rules by which the company would like employees to live. J. C. Penney's "The Penney Idea," written in 1913, reads as follows:

1. To serve the public, as nearly as we can, to its complete satisfaction.
2. To expect for the service we render a fair remuneration and not all the profit the market will bear.
3. To do all in our power to pack the customer's dollar full of value, quality, and satisfaction.
4. To continue to train ourselves and our associates so that the service we give will be more and more intelligently performed.
5. To improve constantly the human factor in our business.
6. To reward men and women in our organization through participation in what the business produces.
7. To test our every policy, method, and act in this wise: "Does it square with what is right and just?"

Such creeds, however, are far more likely to be spoken than written in most first-generation companies. They are not hard to spot. The same sentences, with a few variations, will crop up again and again in speeches and conversations, memos, and meetings. The creeds likely originated with the company president or founder; as a result, they recall for the listener the very *idea* of the company.

Understanding these creeds, expanding their meaning, and adding to them are all ways for successors to build upon the corporate culture for purposes of achieving strategic regeneration. They must try not only to capture the "ring" of slogans but also to arrive at their correct interpretation. That means considering what characteristics of the company's environment originally made a slogan meaningful. One company's "Take a Risk or Take a Walk" slogan, for example, reflected the owner's desire to encourage spontaneous, decentralized experimentation. Sometimes the passage of time makes such original intentions obsolete. Far more often, however, messages remain valuable for generations. As a result, successors will do well to institutionalize them on formal wall plaques, business cards, posters, or banners.

Values. A company's culture is best described as a collection of beliefs or values. These cover a wide range of subjects, including attitudes toward risk taking, communicating with people, participation in the business, learning, and even money. Whatever the value system, it is typically shared throughout the company. Like the creed, it is highly visible. It shows up in a thousand tangible ways: in speeches, ceremonies, awards, even patterns of dress and conversation. These values bond people together, creating a corporate spirit and identity. Any attempt to change them quickly would be fought by long-time employees, who might interpret such an attempt as an attack on the founder himself.

As a result, successors owe it to themselves and the company to try to understand its culture, with an eye to preserving what is of value in it. This is a difficult task, to be sure. It means that successors must take an objective, even impersonal, look at some very familiar aspects of their lives. But knowing what to look for helps. Successors can identify the business's values by:

- observing office design and decoration.
- watching how the company treats visitors.
- analyzing the company's work ethic and decision-making style.
- discussing the question "Why are we successful?" with employees.
- drawing a mental profile of the typical person that the company hires and promotes.
- examining archives, including files, minutes of meetings, reports, employee handbooks, and training programs.
- reading employee handbooks and training programs.
- collecting corporate stories, legends, and myths.
- observing corporate ceremonies and rituals.
- noting what kinds of achievements the company rewards with formal awards and plaques.

As they watch and listen, successors should keep these questions in mind: How is our business different from others? What do those who like to work here have in common? What do people remember best about the founders' attitudes? When they have finished their inquiry, successors should be able to define the culture of the business in a few paragraphs.

Some businesses, for example, have a fast pace and bias to action as their primary values. Qualities of this kind are critical to success in such industries as wholesale distribution, and they will be reflected in a variety of ways. Visitors and vendors will be met and dispatched without much ceremony. Employees will work in shirt-sleeves and slacks. The minutes of meetings will be terse lists of things to be done. Corporate myths will feature heroes who put in long hours and never missed a day of work. Other businesses—those in the professional service industries, for example—place more value upon the considered, thoughtful response. This creates a somewhat formal atmosphere. Employees are referred to as Mr. or Ms. by subordinates. Elegance and subtlety reign in office decoration. Dresses and three-piece suits are worn. Meetings are recorded in detail. Employees speak in low and graceful tones; loud, vulgar employees do not last long.

In each case, cultural dictates suggest who to hire, who to promote, how to behave toward customers and employees, how to conduct business debates, and how to arrive at decisions. Those who want to begin shaping these dictates will find that culture is a powerful managerial tool. Skillful manipulation of its outward manifestations (legends, awards, employee handbooks, and so on) increases control. They transmit values and beliefs, communicate a management philosophy and develop commitment. They guide the progress of the company as distinctly as does the customer's demand for its product.

Special Roles

All the activities we have discussed here pertain to the entire senior family management team. But unless the family has decided to replace the company president with a group, it will fall to a single successor to become the company's primary leader. This successor will have a special role to play in implementing fresh business strategies.

The successor who presides over brothers, sisters, and cousins must be aware that each relative needs a distinct, accountable area of responsibility within the business. That gives everyone an area in which to take pride and satisfaction. Decision making should be shared, too. Then all can feel part of the managerial process and committed to implementing its various aspects.

These two tactics—sharing decisions with all family members and seeing that each member has his or her own niche—will help preserve harmony within the family and the business. Even with such measures in place, however, some family members will find it difficult to take orders from a sibling or cousin. They may also feel uneasy having to depend on relatives of the same generation for recognition, advancement, and compensation. The suggestion here is that these issues be addressed and reconciled through choice of a family model. The family member who succeeds the chief executive has a special responsibility to ensure that such reconciliation occurs.

The successor's parent—the current leader and, in many

cases, the founder of the company—also has a special role to play in implementing the new strategic direction. His job, difficult as it may be, is to relinquish his hold on the company in a graceful way and to support the successor's efforts at strategic implementation. There are many activities that can help accomplish this. A parent-owner may suggest that his successor begin a personal development program, for example, or support his successor's own initiatives along those lines. He can help facilitate matters here by identifying a profit center in the company for the successor, including the successor in hiring and recruiting activities, or urging her to join trade and professional societies. A parent can also begin to collect historical mementos and write personal letters outlining his business philosophy. He can also make himself available to respond to a successor's questions in this regard.

Most importantly, however, a parent can begin to plan what he will do after leaving the company. He may be interested in writing a book, starting a new business venture, or simply going fishing. Whatever the activity, parental enthusiasm for the period ahead is one of the most critical factors in a successful transition. Otherwise, the business leader tends to cling to the company, and that will stall implementation of the plans outlined in these chapters. In the end, it is up to the parent to set the tone and pace of succession. If he performs this task well, nothing could better assure the future success of his company as the next generation takes over.

Summary

Successors hold the key to the future of a company. Yet it is the members of the outgoing generation who must give successors their start. They can do so with a wide range of practices, from childhood lessons to strategic planning. Together, parents and offspring, business owners and successors can lay the foundation for revitalizing the family business. Companies in which this happens successfully possess four characteristics: (1) a founder who is enthusiastic about passing on the business, (2) a successor who deserves authority at a young age, (3) trust between founder and successor, and (4) a firm commitment to work things out together.

Successors cannot singlehandedly bring these characteristics into being. But they can encourage their development by taking responsibility for their own growth and designing personal development programs that will inculcate the proper skills. It is important, too, that they show respect for the business's past. Members of the outgoing generation can also facilitate the transition process in many ways. Their most valuable contributions would be (1) responding at length to a successor's questions and (2) allowing the successor time to pursue developmental plans. Such attitudes on both sides will help successors fulfill their new role: promoting a strategy and vision that will pave the way for the company's revitalization.

EPILOGUE

Making the Commitment
to Plan for Future Generations

As more business families begin a new generation of leadership, the family business stands at the most significant crossroads in its history.

The stories of their successions are full of drama and human interest; as a result, the media have recently found the family business an appealing topic. Professional service firms have also put the spotlight on the family concern, and smaller and mid-sized private enterprises have become the focal point of marketing strategies by banks, accounting firms, law firms, and financial planning and consulting organizations.

Meanwhile, society has chosen to champion the entrepreneurial business. Economic stagnation, doubts about the value of mass production techniques, and merger mania are just a few of the forces that have generated fast-growing interest in careers in smaller enterprises. Governments on all levels are increasingly recognizing the critical importance of small business development, and public policy is beginning to create a positive aura for the smaller business. Clearly, the family business is an old idea whose time has come.

The family businesses at the center of such attention are, for the most part, well-established, mature businesses that face common challenges. They must operate in a rapidly changing world—a world characterized by new technologies, new competitors, and new attitudes on the part of suppliers and customers. It is a world that demands, among other things, increasingly professional management techniques and approaches. As a result, family business leaders must plan for organizational change and make new efforts to build strong management teams. They will also need new business strategies and a means to plan them.

Strategic planning is the best methodology for developing both new strategies and strong managers. We have set forth this methodology in the preceding chapters as a way of helping the family business secure its future. Since our research suggests that attention to the family is at least as important as attention to the business, we have also uniquely applied the techniques of formal strategic planning to the *family*. We propose that this serves several indispensable purposes. Thus, family strategic planning

- provides broad business education for the entire family
- fosters an articulated commitment to keeping the company in the family
- provides the opportunity to develop a family vision for the future
- identifies key business issues the family must address through programs to achieve its objectives
- integrates the next generation of owners and leaders into the family vision, while simultaneously developing their effectiveness for implementing future business strategies.

The strategic planning process also provides family businesses with the opportunity to recognize and exploit their unique strengths. Their competitive advantages, which include a dedication to quality, craftsmanship, and the "personal touch," are especially effective in today's environment. To be sure, these inherent advantages are often neutralized by family conflicts. Members may begin to argue about salaries, responsibilities, and promotions; these arguments are intensified by the very familial relationships that should be sources of strength. Such families need a clear, overriding philosophy that will help them resolve these and other issues. Some families, for example, may decide to place family equality above everything else. They will then arrange jobs and compensation in accordance with that belief. Other families may choose the standard business principles of meritocracy and competition. Still other families will work hard to creatively balance both family and business interests—a philosophy that we have come to term "the family enterprise" approach.

We recommend this third approach, believing it best serves the cause of perpetuating the business into future generations. Still, any of these philosophies, as long as it is clearly and fairly applied, will help keep conflict under control. The planning process allows families to develop the philosophy that is best for them.

Planning also helps address the process of transferring leadership and ownership from one generation to the next. Here, too, many obstacles can make their appearance. But the planning format we recommend, reflecting as it does the experience of other families that have negotiated these transitions successfully, will help identify problems in advance. When successors have established themselves as heirs apparent, for instance, the plan calls for parents to offer a "verbal contract," or commitment, that specifically outlines the specific timing and conditions of ownership and leadership transfer. It also suggests that parents prepare themselves emotionally to release the business. Typically, this requires enough forethought so that life *after* retirement will remain as enjoyable as it was before. This takes time and deliberate planning, but it is one of the most important keys to a successful transition.

As presented, then, strategic planning is a *way of thinking that focuses on the future*. There are many ways to start developing this specialized way of thinking. The important thing is for business families to *begin*—anywhere!

The format we suggest in this book, however, reflects our own belief that it is best to begin with a general family commitment to continue the business. After making this statement of commitment, which will be refined and, it is hoped, confirmed throughout the planning process, the family should next identify the issues that need attention. For this purpose, we propose that a meeting be held to assess the overall condition of the business and determine the issues that require attention, such as the need for family education or the need to resolve family rules for participation. Some of the analyses undertaken at this meeting will reveal whether the future of the business is already being compromised as a result of the family's financial practices. We also propose that a family meeting be held to consider family concerns.

The agenda for additional discussions will emerge from these two meetings. Continued meetings within the family and management group will help develop a picture of what the business and the family will look like in the future—anywhere from five to twenty-five years ahead. Ultimately, these views of the business and the family will converge into a single vision, but the family's interests will likely be the dominant factor in shaping it. This vision will be motivating. It will provide direction. But it will also provide room for individual differences and for unforeseen but inevitable changes in circumstances. It will create a general philosophy that will limit day-to-day conflict among family members, as well as between business requirements and family needs.

Once this vision and its philosophical foundation are established, fewer unnecessary conflicts will occur and fewer family resources will be wasted. It is therefore helpful to begin developing this vision long before children become adults and enter the family business. Professional advisers to the family business may play a special role in this process. It is sometimes easier for such outsiders to see the big picture. They can be more objective, and they can contribute the lessons of their experience with other families. Those related experiences will ease discussion, making sensitive issues appear more natural and normal. The purpose of this book, then, is to share the strategic planning way of thinking with family business members and their advisers.

Businesses and families are social groups that have their full share of human emotion. Directing that emotional energy constructively is the key to keeping the family business healthy. To keep the *business* moving forward requires a spirit of reinvestment: a confident eagerness to commit funds for the sake of future rewards. To motivate the *family* requires a compelling vision of the future—a commitment to a family dream, shared by all.

We have outlined the many, many challenges to sustaining this positive emotional energy from generation to generation. We have suggested financial and market analyses to recognize the possible need to regenerate the business' condition. We have suggested ways to manage the family's affairs that stem from our studies of successful family firms. We have offered a variety of models that the business-owning family can use for portraying its vision. In this manner it can come to better understand the compromises it will have to make.

Most importantly, we have urged that the key to success is deliberate planning. Planning may begin as soon as the owning family first glimpses the prospect of founding a multigenerational family business. When the family's allegiance to this goal is secure, formal planning then provides the means to shape the future. Planning for the future creates the motivation to sustain the family and business through inevitable differences in individual values and perspectives. Then, tremendous energy will be available to fulfill the challenging dream—the dream of creating a healthy family enterprise for the next generation.

 APPENDIXES

A. Family Business Values Questionnaire

B. Sample Financial Analysis of Business

C. Strategic Planning Worksheets

D. Sample Business Strategic Plan

E. Sample Family Strategic Plan

F. Democratic Capitalism

G. Note on Research on Family Businesses

Appendix A: Family Business Values Questionnaire

For almost every business, the choice of strategy depends a great deal on the personal values of key decision makers. As a result, open discussion of those values is as essential to business planning as it is to family and management harmony. Such discussions can be difficult to get started and keep going. Yet without them, managers often pay the price of thinking they are debating facts, when in reality they are debating differences in values and personalities. This tends to lead to conflict and prevent resolution of the issue at hand.

The following questionnaire is designed to help reveal the value orientations most likely to influence business strategic planning. It explores values as they affect business goals, willingness to take risks, and perceived keys to business success. Its benefits are the promotion of dialogue and the recognition that personal values may differ and are important to business decision making. As a result, some find it valuable to have the spouses of key family member managers complete the questionnaire along with shareholders and key managers. Once individuals have completed the questionnaire, they should share answers and discuss differences of opinion and the implications of those differences.

Family Business Values Questionnaire

I. *Goals for the Business*
    1. Rank and compare your preference for business per-
        formance measures (1 = highest, 8 = lowest):
        _____ Market Share
        _____ Sales Growth Rate
        _____ Return on Sales Now
        _____ Return on Assets Now
        _____ Return on Sales in Five Years
        _____ Return on Assets in Five Years
        _____ Profit Stability/Consistency
        _____ Reputation for Excellence in Your Industry
    2. What do you believe to be appropriate numerical goals
        for your company?
        _____ Annual Sales Growth Rate
        _____ Market Share in Five Years
        _____ Minimum Return on Owners' Equity
        _____ Desired Return on Owners' Equity
        _____ Maximum Debt-Equity Ratio
        _____ Desired Debt-Equity Ratio

II. *Willingness to Accept Risk*
    1. What is the biggest bet (commitment of funds) our
        business can afford to lose? $ _____
    2. What percentage of the business's cash requirements
        for growth should be funded internally from opera-
        tions and what percentage from new debt?
        Internal   _____ %
        New Debt   _____ %
    3. What percentage of company profits (cash flow)
        should be reinvested in the business and what per-
        centage should be shared with ownership via bonuses,
        salary and perk increases, and dividends?
        Reinvested   _____ %
        Paid Out   _____ %

4. How would you rate the following people as "risk takers"?

	Very High	Moderate	Low
Owner(s)	/ / / / / / /		
Successor(s)	/ / / / / / /		
Key Managers	/ / / / / / /		

5. In your opinion which is the best "teacher"?
    (   ) Experience under close direction
    (   ) Opportunity to experiment in an independent area

III. *Keys to Business Success*
    1. The greatest strategic threat to a healthy, successful business is:
        (   ) *Deviation* from what made it successful in the past
        (   ) Inability to *adapt* to new opportunities as they occur
    2. Check which of the following you consider to be the critical threat or threats to the future of your business (check no more than three):
        _____ New Competition
        _____ Aggressiveness of Current Competition
        _____ Declining Market(s)
        _____ Labor Demands
        _____ Changing End User Desires (Final Customers)
        _____ Changing Immediate Customer Desires (Immediate Customers)
        _____ Aging Assets
        _____ Inadequate Cash Flow
        _____ Declining Product/Service Quality
    3. Rank the following management tools according to their importance to your business (1 = first, 10 = last):
        _____ Forecasting
        _____ Market Research
        _____ Variable Budgets

_____ Standardized Costs
_____ Computer Simulation
_____ Financial Analysis
_____ Discounted Cash Flows
_____ Materials Requirement Plan
_____ Inventory Order Models
_____ Capital Budgeting

4. Rank which of the following are the key areas for success in your business (1 = first, 8 = last):

    _____ Production
    _____ Purchasing
    _____ Marketing
    _____ Distribution
    _____ Research and Development
    _____ Engineering
    _____ Organization
    _____ Finance

5. Rank the following as keys to business success (1 = first, 6 = last):

    _____ Attention to Detail
    _____ Consistent Execution
    _____ Creative Thinking
    _____ Aggressive Decision Making
    _____ Experimentation
    _____ Happy Employees

6. Where is your business "leaving the most money on the table" for others to grab?

    _____

    _____

7. Score the following statements as to how much you agree or disagree with them (10 = agree completely, 1 = disagree completely)

    _____ Growth in sales would solve most of our profit goals.
    _____ Our costs are mostly fixed costs.
    _____ Marginal pricing (by variable cost) is necessary.
    _____ Prices should be based on competition.

_____ Prices should be based on desired profit margin.

_____ Our market is not very price sensitive.

_____ We should spend more money on competitive and market research.

_____ Our hourly labor force is satisfied with their jobs.

_____ We have plenty of plant capacity for growth.

_____ Our people are productive.

_____ Our competition will react quickly to any changes we make.

_____ We should spend more money and time learning our true product and/or process costs.

_____ The physical appearance of our administrative offices is very important.

_____ Our people want employment and personal security more than take-home pay.

_____ Increasing our product line increases our average costs significantly.

_____ Salesmen are mostly motivated by money.

Appendix B: Sample Financial Analysis of Business

Income Statement	1984	1985	1986
Sales Revenues (all $ in millions)	$10.0	$11.0	$12.0
Less Cost of Goods Sold	6.0	6.8	7.3
Gross Margin	4.0	4.2	4.7
Marketing Expense	1.0	.9	1.0
Research and Development Expense	.5	.4	.4
Depreciation	.5	.6	.7
Other General and Administrative Expense	1.0	1.1	1.2
Net Income	1.0	1.2	1.4

Balance Sheet	1984	1985	1986
Cash and Securities	1.0	1.3	1.4
Receivables	1.0	1.3	1.6
Inventories	1.0	1.7	2.2
Net Plant and Equipment	3.0	2.9	2.8
Total Assets, Liabilities, Equity	6.0	7.2	8.0
Payables	1.0	1.3	1.5
Borrowings/Debt	1.0	1.4	1.5
Owners' Equity	4.0	4.5	5.0
Total	6.0	7.2	8.0
Number of Employees	200	210	220
Real Market Growth		+3%	+3%

Step One: Calculate Traditional Performance Measures

	1984	1985	1986
Sales Revenues		+10%	+ 9%

$$\frac{\text{Sales }1985 - \text{Sales }1984}{\text{Sales }1984} \qquad \frac{11.0 - 10.0}{10.0} = .10 \text{ or } 10\%$$

Market Growing		+ 3%	+ 3%

Return on Sales	10%	11%	12%

Net Income ÷ Sales:	1984	1.0 ÷ 10.0 = 10%	
Return on Assets	16%	16%	18%

Net Income ÷ Total Assets:	1984	1.0 ÷ 6.0 = 16.67%	
Return on Investment	20%	20%	22%

Net Income ÷ (Total Assets − Current Liabilities): 1984 = 1.0 ÷ (6.0 − 1.0)
or
Net Income ÷ (Equity + Long-Term Debt): 1.0 ÷ (4.0 + 1.0)

Return on Equity	25%	25%	25%

Net Income ÷ Owners Equity; 1984 1.0 ÷ 4.0			
Sales per Employee	$50,000	$52,381	$54,545

Sales ÷ Number of Employees; 1984 $10,000,000 ÷ 200 = $50,000

Conclusion: Most traditional performance measures (sales growth, return on sales, return on assets, return on investment, return on equity, and sales per employee) are strong and improving!

Step Two: Translate Income Statement Figures into Percentages
To See Trends

	1984	1985	1986
Sales	10.0 (100%)	11.0 (100%)	12.0 (100%)
Purchases/Materials	3.0 (30%)	3.4 (31%)	3.5 (29%)
Manufacturing/Labor	2.0 (20%)	2.2 (20%)	2.4 (20%)
Operating Overhead	1.0 (10%)	1.2 (11%)	1.4 (12%)
Gross Margin	4.0 (40%)	4.2 (38%)	4.7 (39%)
Marketing	1.0 (10%)	.9 (8%)	1.0 (8%)
Research and Development	.5 (5%)	.4 (4%)	.4 (3%)

	1984	*1985*	*1986*
Depreciation	.5 (5%)	.6 (5%)	.7 (6%)
Other General and Administrative Expense	1.0 (10%)	1.1 (10%)	1.2 (10%)
Net Income	1.0 (10%)	1.2 (11%)	1.4 (12%)

Conclusion: Profit is hurt by increasing overhead but more than compensated for by reducing the percentages of marketing and research and development (profit increasing +2%, overhead increasing +2%, marketing decreasing −2%, and research and development decreasing −2%); therefore, company is harming the future but showing improving current profit while also decreasing overhead productivity.

Step Three: Translate Balance Sheet Figures into Percentages To See Trends

	1984	*1985*	*1986*
Sales	10.0 (100%)	11.0 (100%)	12.0 (100%)
Cash and Securities	1.0 (10%)	1.3 (12%)	1.4 (12%)
Receivables	1.0 (10%)	1.3 (12%)	1.6 (13%)
Inventory	1.0 (10%)	1.7 (15%)	2.2 (18%)
Net Plant and Equipment	3.0 (30%)	2.9 (26%)	2.8 (23%)
Payables	1.0 (10%)	1.3 (12%)	1.5 (13%)
Borrowings	1.0 (10%)	1.4 (13%)	1.5 (13%)
Owners' Equity	4.0 (40%)	4.5 (40%)	5.0 (41%)

Conclusion: Sloppy cash management with borrowings up more than cash (+3% vs. +2%), receivables up (+3%), inventories up (+8%); increasing working capital financed by threatening business future via declining plant and equipment (−7%) and increasing payables (+3%).

Step Four: Calculate Effects of Inflation on Accounting Information

	1983-84	*1984-85*	*1985-86*
Assume:			
Price Increases	+10%	+10%	+10%
Purchase Costs	+10%	+15%	+10%
Wage Increases	+ 8%	+ 7%	+ 7%
Then:			
Real Sales$_{84}$	10.0 (100%)	10.0 (100%)	9.9 (100%)
	11.0 ÷ 1.10	12.0 ÷ 2.20 ÷ 1.10	
Real Purchases$_{84}$	3.0 (30%)	3.0 (30%)	2.8 (28%)

Appendix B: Sample Financial Analysis of Business 225

Real Labor$_{84}$	3.4 ÷ 1.15 2.0 (20%)	3.5 ÷ 1.15 ÷ 1.10 2.1 (21%)	2.2 (21%)

	2.2 ÷ 1.07	2.4 ÷ 1.07 ÷ 1.07
Real Sales Growth	+ 0%	− 1%
Real Market Growth	+ 3%	+ 3%

Conclusion: After consideration of inflation effects, it becomes apparent that sales are not growing while the market is growing (+3%), representing a decline in market share; also illustrates that productivity may be declining, since real labor as percentage of sales is increasing from 20% to 21%.

Step Five: Further Calculation of Productivity Measures

(A)	1984	1985	1986
Labor	2.0	2.2	2.4
Labor % Sales	20%	20%	20%
Real Labor$_{84}$	2.0	2.1	2.1
Real Labor$_{84}$/Real Sales	20%	21%	21%

(B)	1984	1985	1986
Sales	10.0	11.0	12.0
Purchases	3.0	3.4	3.5
Value Added	7.0	7.6	8.5
Real Sales	10.0	10.0	9.9
Real Purchases	3.0	3.0	2.8
Real Value Added	7.0	7.0	7.1
Number of Employees	200	210	220
Real Value Added/Employee	35,000	33,333	32,273

Conclusion: Calculation of real value added per employee confirms that business is losing productivity from $35,000 per employee to $32,273 per employee.

Step Six: Calculate Sources and Uses of Cash

Sources	1984	1985	1986
Net Income	1.0	1.2	1.4
Income Tax	.3	.4	.5
Net After Tax	.7	.8	.9
+ Depreciation	.5	.6	.7
Cash from Operations	1.2	1.4	1.6

	1984	1985	1986
Payables	1.0	1.3 (+.3)	1.5 (+.2)
Borrowings	1.0	1.4 (+.4)	1.5 (+.1)
Total Sources		2.1	1.9

Uses

	1984	1985	1986
Cash and Securities	1.0	1.3 (+.3)	1.4 (+.1)
Receivables	1.0	1.3 (+.3)	1.6 (+.3)
Inventory	1.0	1.7 (+.7)	2.2 (+.5)
Capital Budget		+.5	+.6
Dividends	.2	.3	.4
Total Uses		2.1	1.9

Other Analysis

	1984	1985	1986
Capital Budget	.4	.5	.6
vs.			
Depreciation	.5	.6	.7
÷	80%	83%	86%
Dividends (and so on)	.2	.3	.4
vs.			
Net after Tax Income	.7	.8	.9
%	29%	38%	44%

Conclusion: Calculation illustrates in another way how funds generated by profits and depreciation and slowing payables are being consumed for increasing inventories and receivables; in the meantime dividends are growing at a faster rate than profits, and the capital budget is growing less fast than depreciation.

Appendix C: Strategic Planning Worksheets

Many find worksheets to collect planning data useful for gathering facts, prompting discussion, and retaining and comparing data over the years to observe trends. The following worksheets are those we have found most helpful:

- Table C-1 suggests how to categorize sales and gross profit data in order to identify and evaluate *market segments.*
- Table C-2 suggests an outline to record lost and gained customers and thus identify segments and evaluate *relative competitive advantage.*
- Figure C-1 offers an example of *mapping* market segment information to help identify which are better and who competes in which segments.
- Table C-3 suggests a preliminary listing of some possible *critical success factors* for customers and recommends identifying which segments demand which success requirements. The insights for this list will be prompted by the analysis of lost/gained accounts in Table C-2.
- Table C-4 explains how to formalize and quantify the critical success factors for each significant market segment relative to competitors. This quantification has several advantages: (1) it promotes more productive planning discussion, (2) it allows for tracking "scores" over time, and (3) it offers insights on how different groups (known as strategic groups) of competitors compete similarly and dissimilarly.
- Table C-5 provides a summary of the market segment information developed through Figure C-1 and also asks for iden-

tification of *selling strategy* per segment and per competitor.

- Table C-6 outlines characteristics to help determine how attractive an *industry structure* is.
- Table C-7 outlines characteristics to help determine how attractive a *market environment* is.
- Table C-8 outlines characteristics to help identify business *strengths and weaknesses.*

By using these worksheets, the business should be better able to distinguish market segments and determine marketing strategy through selecting segment priorities, appropriate competitive advantages, and target competitors. They also help in evaluating industry and market attractiveness and the relative strength of the business. All this information will aid the business in arriving at a final choice of direction for strategic growth.

Table C-1. Identifying Market Segment by Sales History.

	Years													
	19 —						19 —						19 —	
Category	Sales ($)	Sales (Units/ Orders)	Sales (Rank)	Gross Margin (%)	Gross Margin (Rank)	Sales ($)	Sales (Units/ Orders)	Sales (Rank)	Gross Margin ($)	Gross Margin (Rank)	Sales ($)	Sales (Units/ Orders)	Sales (Rank)	Gross Margin (%)	Gross Margin (Rank)
Type of Product														
Type of Customer														
Top 20 Customers														
Geography														
Selling Method														

Table C-2. Identifying Market Segments by Gained/Lost Accounts.

1984		1985							1986					
Top 20 Accounts	Sales ($)	Now Top 20 Accounts	1984 Rank	Why gained? From whom?	Lost Top 20 Accounts	1984 Rank	Why lost? To whom?		New Top 20 Accounts	1985 Rank	Why gained? From whom?	Lost Top 20 Accounts	1985 Rank	Why lost? To whom?

Figure C-1. Market Segment Map.

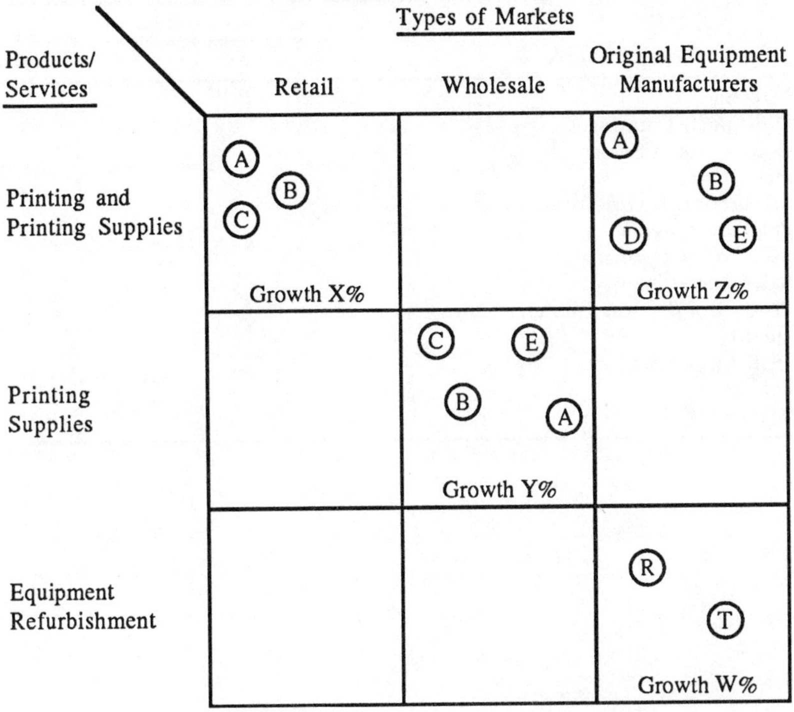

Note: A, B, C, D, E, R, and T are competitors. Some prefer to make the size of the circles approximate to the relative size or market share of the competitors.

Analytical Questions To Consider

- Why different growth rates in different segments?
- Why different competitors in different segments?
- What differences among competitors in their choice of segments? Why?
- What are the benefits of serving more than one segment?
- If you were only in the business of one segment, what would you do differently and how profitable could you ideally be?

Table C-3. Critical Success Requirements of Market Segments.

	Segment			
Keys to Success	Sa	Sb	Sc	Sd
Materials				
Quoting/Estimating				
Economies of Scale				
Design/Art				
Production Technology				
Product Range/Variety				
Sales Force Quantity				
Sales Force Quality				
Promotion/Personal Relationships				
Quality				
Distribution/Delivery				
Service				
After Service				

Table C-4. Critical Success Factors per Segment Relative to Competition.

Key Customer Requirements	Weighted Overall Importance in our General Market	Competitors					Total Weighted Points for Requirement
		AAA	Best	Fly-By-Nite	A Best	Our Firm	
1.	.10	25	20	20	10	25	10
2.	.20	30	15	15	20	20	20
3.	.10	20	20	20	20	20	10
4.	.25	30	15	15	20	20	25
5.	.20	40	15	10	10	25	20
6.	.10	40	15	15	15	15	10
7.	.05	20	20	0	30	30	5
8.	.0	—	—	—	—	—	—
9.	.0	—	—	—	—	—	—
Total	1.00	31.0	16.25	14.25	17.0	21.5	100

Total weighted points by competitor

Instructions

A. List key competitors and key customer success requirements identified earlier.

B. Weight the relative importance of each key customer requirement (totaling 100%).

C. Distribute 100 points among the competitors (including Our Firm) for each key customer requirement according to how well they fulfill requirement.

D. Calculate each competitor's overall strength by summing up the result of multiplying the weight of each customer requirement times the points attributed to the competitor.

E. The more total weighted points a competitor has, the stronger the competitive position of the competitor. Total points for all the competitors should total 100.

F. Do some analysis and interpretation of the results. For example, in this case:

1. Competitor AAA is excellent, Our Firm a strong but distant second, Best and A Best about the same, Fly-By-Nite very weak.

2. The most important key customer requirements are factors 2, 4, and 5.

3. Our Firm is especially strong in the relatively unimportant factors 1 and 7. Are there some customers or segments that we should specialize in?

4. If Our Firm wants to take a customer from A Best, the best customer requirement to emphasize is 5; Our Firm is most vulnerable to AAA on requirements 5 and 6, and so on.

G. As a result of this kind of analysis, how to sell against whom can be formed and the key elements of a marketing strategy identified.

Table C-5. Segment Summary and Priority.

Segment and Rank	Critical Success Factors	Attractiveness Score	Our Market Share	Key Competitors and Shares	Our Selling Advantage per Competitor per Segment
1					
2					
3					
4					

Table C-6. Characteristics Affecting Industry Attractiveness/Unattractiveness

Buyer Power	Attractive	Unattractive
• Rivalry Among Buyers	Low	High
• Profitability of Buyers	Low	High
• Significance of Purchase to Buyers	High	Low
• Threat of Backward Integration by Buyer	Low	High
• Costs for Buyers to Switch Suppliers	High	Low
• Number of Customers	High	Low
Supplier Power		
• Rivalry Among Suppliers	Low	High
• Profitability of Suppliers	High	Low
• Significance of Purchase	High	Low
• Threat of Forward Integration by Suppliers	Low	High
• Supplier's Ability to Differentiate	Low	High
• Costs of Switching Suppliers	Low	High
• Supplier's Dependence on Us	High	Low
Rivalry of our Industry		
• Number of Competitors	Less	More
• Equality of Competitor's Size	Less	More
• Market Growth	Fast	Slow
• Fixed Costs	Low	High
• Additional Capacity Increments	Small	Large
• Chronic Excess Supply	No	Yes
• Perishability of Product	Low	High
• Our Differentiability	High	Low
• Producers' Backgrounds	Similar	Diverse
• Ability to Add Value	High	Low

Barriers to Enter Our Industry	Attractive	Unattractive
• Customer Loyalties	High	Low
• Capital Required	High	Low
• Age of Assets	Old	New
• Patents or Control of Key Labor/Materials/Processes	High	Low
• Economies of Scale	High	Low
• Frequent Changes in Technology	Few	Many
• Exclusivity of Distribution	Yes	No
• Other Aggressive Companies Serving Same Customers with Related Products	No	Yes
• Other Companies Doing Same Thing in Other Geographies	No	Yes

Table C-7. Characteristics Affecting Market Attractiveness/Unattractiveness.

Characteristics	Attractive	Average	Unattractive
Total Potential of Served Market	$1 Billion	$100 Million / $10 Million	$1 Million
Stage of Product Life Cycle	Emerging	Mature / Fragmented	Declining
Annual Growth of Units	15% more than GNP	5% more than GNP / Equal to GNP	Less than GNP
Market Diversity (Number of Potential End Customers in Served Market)	Many	Some	Few
Significant (5% of volume) and Distinguishable (channels or buying behavior) Segments	Many / 10	Some / 6 to 8 / 2 to 4	Few / 1
Real Annual Growth Rates of the Segments	Several much faster than total market	One or two faster than total market	None faster than total market
Regional or International Export Opportunities	Plentiful	Few	None
Customer "Professionalism" (pay bills, appropriate expectations, pleasant)	High	Above average / Below average	Low
Cyclicality of Demand	No	Low / High	Very High
Seasonality of Demand	No	Low / High	Very High

Table C-8. Capability Analysis: Skills and Talents and Resources.

Item	Assessment/Discussion	Overall Strength (s) or Weakness (w)	Significance 0 → 10 Highest
Pricing Skill			
Promotion Skill			
Delivery Capability			
Distribution Productivity			
Operating Productivity			
Technical Equipment			
Transportation Equipment			
Production Equipment			
Knowledge of Customers			
Competitive Intelligence			
Supplier Relationships			
Selling Skills and Tools			
Production Supervision			
Personnel Policies			
Compensation Policies			
Union Status			
Employee Morale			
Management Development Programs			
Human Resources Development			
Financial Resources			
Financial Relationships			
Information Availability and Timeliness			
Quality Control			
Innovation Spirit			
Teamwork and Cooperation			
Organizational Structure			
Management Skills			
Supervisory Skills			
Technical Competence			
Others:			

Appendix D: Sample Business Strategic Plan

We believe our business has an exciting, challenging, and rewarding future. Since our founding in 1907, we have gained the confidence of our suppliers, our customers, our employees, and our community. We gain tremendous advantage from proving to our suppliers, customers, and community that we are committed to a long-term relationship as "partners in business." This assures them of fair treatment and of our eagerness to serve their interests as well as our own.

We would not have enjoyed our success to date if it were not for the dedicated service that generations of employees have provided us. We take great pride that many of them have brought their children and their friends into our company. We owe them the confidence that our firm will prosper economically and will retain its key values: loyalty; concern; opportunities for personal advancement; and fair, frequent performance review.

We believe we have the fortunate, invaluable advantage of a family of shareholders unanimously committed to the long-term perpetuation of the business as a private entity. Private ownership provides us with the freedom to invest in the future and to accommodate short-run variations in the economy without disturbing our valued relationships.

We are also fortunate that capable family members have joined the business each generation. This participation helps assure everyone that our future business resolve remains firm.

Our Business

We are in the business of distributing specialty goods to retail food establishments in the Midwest. Historically, we have sold only to grocery stores. No one is able to identify new, exciting consumer food products better than we are. We owe our strength to a team of innovative merchandisers. They know that they significantly affect our success, and we are committed to sharing our successes with them. We also owe our strength to our operations team, which is comprised of hardworking, customer-oriented people conscientiously dedicated to superior customer service. They accept no excuses for imperfection.

Our Long-Term Goals

Specialty food products are growing faster than the food market as a whole. We expect to grow at least 10 percent per year in real terms. Half of our growth will come from effectively promoting our current product line, half from introducing new products.

We expect to continuously increase our share of our customers' food purchases. We owe our shareholders and the future of our business a fair return on the money invested in the business. We expect to earn a 15 percent aftertax return on equity. The high profitability of our products and the modest rate of growth we seek allows us to finance that growth with internally generated funds. Our shareholders will earn a 4 percent dividend yield on their investment as long as the business return exceeds 15 percent.

Our Strategy

We believe that the following are the critical success factors for the future of the business:

- Identification of exciting new products
- Effective promotion of our products to our customers and to their customers
- Reliable delivery and mistake-free service to our customers
- Development of new career merchandisers
- Hedging against possible food price deflation
- Continuous development of our computerized marketing analysis of product promotions for our customers

- Development of a way to serve the eat-away-from-home market.

Our Policies

The following policies support our goals and needs:

Product Policy. We will distribute only new products not yet available to our customers. New products must have the promise of a return on investment greater than the average we now enjoy. All products must be of the highest quality and without any known evidence of unhealthfulness. Current products will be continuously monitored as to viability. We will eliminate every year those products that yield the lowest returns up to a maximum of 10 percent of our total sales volume.

Pricing Policy. We will assure our customers that our products will promise them margins in the upper quartile of their product lines. We will aggressively promote new products for them to prove that they will create customer acceptance.

Promotion Policy. Innovative, fresh, responsive promotion is our most important strength. We will be ever alert to new promotional ideas. We will experiment aggressively with all forms of promotion except electronic media advertising. Our products do not lend themselves to television and radio advertising. We prefer in-store promotions—especially those that portray our products as healthy and of high quality. Ten to fifteen percent of our gross profit will be spent on promotion.

Operations. Our order entry and warehouse and delivery systems are dedicated to fulfilling every customer request. We promise forty-eight-hour fulfillment. This limits our market definition to a 200-mile radius. We pledge to our customers 99.5 percent success in meeting their expectations. We will develop and maintain our systems to provide each customer with detailed performance feedback. For employees we will provide an environment that makes it unnecessary for them to seek outside representation of their interests.

New Growth. We have formed a "Restaurant Task Force" to identify which of our products might best serve that growing market segment. When the task force has completed its assessment, we will form another task force from operations to determine the best means of distribution and customer service. We will commit $200,000 to this effort over the next two years. If it is breaking even in the third year, it will be a success.

Organization. Our people deserve the best of working conditions. They also deserve every opportunity for personal development and career advancement. We believe in the posting of new job openings with preference for hiring from within. We also will support each employee in any accredited education program that he or she may undertake after business hours. We will give our merchandisers 1 percent of their gross profits for travel expenses to assure good vendor relations and identification of new products. Our merchandisers deserve to share in the profitability of their product lines. The remainder of our organization will participate in companywide profit sharing.

We hope every employee will join a "work team" to meet together weekly to provide senior management with feedback on how we can improve our business performance. We are an informal organization that requires delegation of responsibility to assure quick and creative decision making. We trust our people but owe them quarterly performance reviews to help them develop and to learn from their experiences.

Each department will annually develop plans to support our strategy. These plans will be reviewed before final budgets and forecasts are presented.

Budget and Forecast

The 1986 Budget and 1987–1989 Forecast and Strategic Expense outline are attachments to this plan.

Appendix E: Sample Family Strategic Plan

To all in our loving family,

We are fortunate to have a privately owned business in our family. The business provides family members opportunities that are difficult to replicate: opportunities to earn financial independence, to learn the skills of business and leadership, to contribute actively to others in the community, and to share in common family interests. To work productively is to grow, to respect humility, to know the realities of life. Not to work is an unhealthy state. Maintaining the business in the family and seeking to expand and strengthen the business will help assure that our family will have productive work rather than live off the accomplishments of past generations. We are committed to the long-term success of our family business for the benefit of our future generations.

The business must be run as a business. In that way family members will know that they have earned their personal successes; those that work for us will know that their careers and families will be secure. It is not easy to run a family business like a business. Family members will inevitably have needs and turn to the business to fill them. For that reason we, as a family, have all openly pledged to help one another when one is in need from our personal resources—not from those of the business. We have provided an estate apart from the business to assure some comfort and security for each family member; we hope family members will forever prolong the prudence our family has always practiced by saving these funds rather than spending them.

All family members are welcome in the business. We are fortunate to be a large enough business to have ample opportunities. As in the past, however, family members may be asked to withdraw if their contributions and business circumstances so require.

We hope one or more family members will qualify to be able future leaders of the business. For our business that will require excellent skills and excellent educational backgrounds. We wish a family member to serve as chief executive and to assume the traditions of our business and family, as well as ensure by example that it remains a working business for the family—not a passive investment.

To help ensure that the family acts as one and works hard to formulate common plans and ideals, we have established a voting trust. Three members of the family will be elected as trustees for three-year terms—one each year. No family member may serve as trustee for more than two consecutive terms. The trust will represent the family shareholders.

Business decisions will be aided by a board of directors comprised of the three trustees and four others who are neither family members nor employees. If we are to run ourselves like a business, we should be able to convince the outside directors of the rightness of our business plans and goals.

The trustees will also accept informal roles as family leaders. In that position they will be available to help any family member in need or to counsel family members on matters of financial orientation. The trustees will help identify investment opportunities for all family members to share in (voluntarily). These nonfamily business investments will provide one form of common family interests.

Individual family members may suggest any agenda item to the trustees on a confidential basis. The trustees will make every effort to examine and resolve family differences.

In the end, this plan is no stronger than the will and love of the entire family. Together we can provide great opportunities for ourselves and our children and even their children. It has been done before. Surely we can do it now. Why not?

Appendix F: Democratic Capitalism

Years of Business

For the family example presented here, consider that there are four children of the owning parents: two enter the business in 1975 and 1980, respectively; two do not enter the business at all. The $2 million business value earned between 1955 and 1975 belongs to the parents and, in their estate, would be shared equally among all *four* offspring ($500,000 each); this is their "blood equity." The $1 million increase in value from the founder's complete retirement in 1985 to 1987 clearly belongs only to the two offspring leading the business ($500,000 more each). The increase of $2 million from 1975 to 1985 is at least partially a result of the offsprings' contribution. Some arbitrary percent of that belongs to them—say 5% per year involved. So for the first entrant who was in the business 10 years he has rights to 50% (5% × 10 years) of the appreciation; the second entrant 25% (5% × 5 years). The remaining 25% of the $2 million appreciation would be shared as "blood equity" among all four offspring equally—$125,000 each. In sum, the following values have been attributed:

First entrant	2,125,000
Second entrant	1,625,000
Inactive third child	625,000
Inactive fourth child	625,000
	$5,000,000

Figure F-1. Determining "Blood Equity" Versus "Sweat Equity."

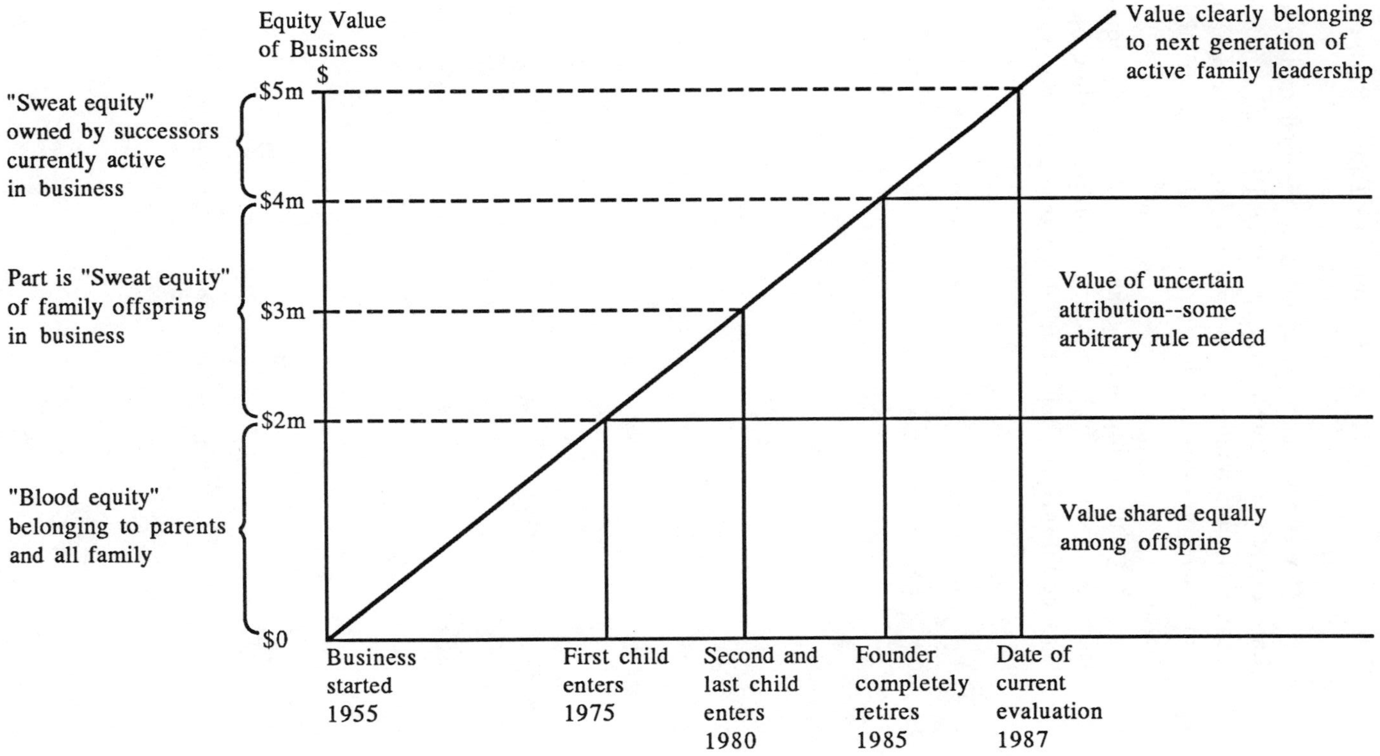

Equity Value of Business

Value clearly belonging to next generation of active family leadership

Value of uncertain attribution--some arbitrary rule needed

Value shared equally among offspring

Business started 1955
First child enters 1975
Second and last child enters 1980
Founder completely retires 1985
Date of current evaluation 1987

$5m
$4m
$3m
$2m
$0

"Sweat equity" owned by successors currently active in business

Part is "Sweat equity" of family offspring in business

"Blood equity" belonging to parents and all family

It was arbitrarily assumed that the first and second born share equally in "sweat equity" after 1985; they could just as easily share unequally based on some business criterion (that is, salary, sales volume generated, profit center contributions, and so on).

Eventually buy-sell agreements will likely liquidate the holdings of the third and fourth children if they have stock. They could receive their "fair" interest in other forms as well.

Appendix G: Note on Research on Family Businesses

Research on family businesses is a young but rapidly growing field. Before 1980 there was scarcely a doctoral dissertation on the topic; now, several appear each year. 1985 marked the first year that "for credit" academic courses were offered, and Jossey-Bass will begin publishing a journal on the family business in 1987. A doctoral program on family businesses has just been implemented at the Fielding Institute in California. The Academy of Management has recently included symposia and papers on the family business, and the Chicago Family Business Council has established the first award for outstanding research on the family business. The newly formed Family Firm Institute, under the direction of Barbara Hollander in Pittsburgh, is dedicated to developing the study of family business into a well-recognized field.

As in any new discipline, the opportunities, needs, and challenges for future research into family businesses are abundant. The purpose of this appendix is to begin to identify some future research directions and methodological issues. To that end, we first provide more background on the research presented in this book. Then we propose some critical questions as possible future directions for research. We conclude with a brief discussion of some of the methodological issues for family business research.

Background of Our Research

Seemingly, the most frequently asked questions about passing on a family business are: How long do family businesses usually last and how many succeed? To address these questions, we studied 200 Illinois manufacturing companies from 1924 to 1984, as summarized in Chapter One. The 200 businesses were selected randomly from the 1924 *Illinois Manufactures Guide*. That source was used because it listed the names of the officers of the companies, the founding dates of the companies, and the number of their employees. To assure that the businesses were well enough established to continue, two criteria were arbitarily selected: the business had to have at least twenty employees, and it had to be at least five years old in 1924. Conventional wisdom suggests that most fragile businesses do not last more than five years.

These 200 businesses were then tracked for the next sixty years through the same source, and the pattern of officers and directors, the number of employees, and the date the business "disappears" from the reference were noted. When the business disappeared, we tried to determine what had happened to it by checking bankruptcy court records, yellow pages in telephone books, sales of businesses, business name changes, and local public library records. In the case of businesses that disappeared from the guide in recent years, we attempted to call the former officers and owners. Sometimes we could not determine the actual reason for the disappearance of a business. We are now interviewing owners of those businesses that remained family businesses throughout the sixty years.

This research has several limitations, of course. First, our sample was only Illinois manufactures—no better historic record was identified. (Dun and Bradstreet, for example, did not begin its business history data base until the 1950s.) Finding historic records was necessary, as examining businesses that exist now or disappear now gives us no insight into survival rate. Finally, the data in this guide were voluntary and self-reported.

Second, what has happened over the last sixty years is not necessarily indicative of what will happen to family businesses into the future. Pursuing research on family businesses into the future similar to the research we undertook over the past sixty years will remain somewhat difficult, as no convenient public records on family businesses indicate who owns how much of the stock and how the stockholders may be related. It seems that the best possible data base for future research would be one that is personally developed by the researcher rather than one that depends on public records.

A third limitation to the research reported here is that we do not know how many family businesses failed in the years before 1924. In other words, we studied businesses of various ages that already existed in 1924 instead of focusing our study on all businesses founded in 1924. The reason we selected businesses of various ages that existed in 1924 was that we wanted to understand what happened to the family businesses of 1924 rather than to the new businesses founded at that time. In this way we could study businesses that became third, fourth, or fifth generation businesses as well as those that might reach just the second or third generation.

This research involved many frustrations. Bankruptcy records are quite difficult to find and, once found, difficult to comprehend. Many publications providing business information went out of business or did not publish during the Depression and World War II. There are no good records on businesses sold or on those that changed names until recent years.

There is good opportunity for more research. Such future efforts may examine the relationships between ownership structure and family roles in leadership compared to the firm's financial performance. Such an effort has been begun by John Dairs at the University of Southern California.

A second study we have undertaken, as reported in this book, is an examination of the strategies and performance of family businesses as compared to the strategies and performance of nonfamily public companies. This study utilized the PIMS (Strategic Planning Institute) data base. The PIMS data base has several unique advantages. More than any other available data base it reflects actual financial performance. It also provides valuable but confidential data on a company's strategic profile: market share, marketing expenses, degree of competitive differentiation, and so on. It also provides all this information in a consistent way over several years—often five or more years. Finally, it reports data on a line of business (SBU) basis.

While these are the best data available, they are limited by the nature of the firms included. It is a private cooperative data base including only PIMS member companies. Consequently, it comprises mostly larger businesses that are interested in strategic planning and analysis. In all, we studied nearly 300 corporations of which about 20 to 25 percent were privately owned. A more complete description of the research methodology and results appears elsewhere (Ward, 1983).

In Chapter Seven we proposed that family considerations shape final strategic choices more than business considerations do. This belief was partly based on a study of the strategic planning process and choice of strategy in twenty family businesses.

These twenty firms were part of a structured workshop in strategic planning that followed the planning methodology outlined in Chapter Five. After top family managers had assessed their strategic situation, they were asked to identify their current strategy and to note the "best" strategic direction for the future based on their planning analysis. Seventeen of the twenty said that their current strategies were not as aggressive as they collectively agreed they should be. They then were interviewed to determine what caused them to choose such strategies. This research effort was limited by its use of a small and nonrandom sample.

The other data presented in Chapter One on why parents wish to pass on their family business and why successors wish to succeed are also a result of surveys of family business members who attended family business seminars. These questions and many others need to be addressed to a more scientifically selected family business sample. And, in fact, some excellent research into the succession patterns, success, and goals in family businesses is now being undertaken by Ivan Lansburg of Yale University.

Future Research Questions

Because the study of family businesses is so young, the variety of questions for future research is limited only by one's imagination. Different people with different perspectives may propose different questions. Tax and legal people may study the structure of estate plans; behavioral scientists may study family relationships and personal motivations. We will attempt to suggest some possible research directions from our perspective of strategic planning.

Some Common Underlying Presumptions. In the recent flurry of magazine and newspaper articles about how to manage family businesses, several "truths" are proposed. While these presumptions have been tested only by observation, not by research, it might be helpful to list them here:

- The primary tool of family business negotiations is power.
- The primary motivator is money.
- The perpetuation of family businesses is good for society.
- Inherited wealth is demotivating.
- U.S. tax laws make it difficult to pass a family business from one generation to another.
- Daughters will not remain active in a family business and make it their career.
- In-laws do not get along well.
- Mothers hold the family and its business together.
- A business needs a single chief executive.
- Family businesses have difficulty attracting and retaining excellent professional managers.
- Voting stock should remain with family members who are actively involved in management.
- Ownership should be consolidated over the generations.
- Successors should begin their careers with work experience outside the family business.
- "Business first" rules of conduct are preferred.
- Outside directors on the board are desirable.

Some Critical Questions for Family Business Continuity. The following questions address some of the issues we have found to be critical to long-term family business success. Designing research to examine these questions would be a fruitful contribution to understanding family business behavior:

- Why do some chief executives have the continued motivation to grow and change their businesses?

- How do family businesses contribute to our national economic well-being and to the welfare of our communities?
- Why do some offspring choose careers in the family business while others do not?
- What criteria should be used to select the best long-term successor(s)?
- How do family culture, ethnic culture, and national policy affect family business health and continuity?
- Do the lessons learned from wealthy, highly visible, and larger family businesses also apply to smaller and less wealthy ones?
- What forms of equity ownership (for example, employee stock ownership plans or multiple classes of stock) are most conducive to family business success?
- How is the organizational culture of the family business different from that of nonfamily businesses?
- What forms of intervention (for example, family systems, strategic planning, organizational development) are of most help in what family business situations?
- What rules of family member compensation and participation are best in different situations?
- How long should a person serve as business chief executive of a family business?
- Are family business organizations more or less adaptable than traditional bureaucratic organizations?

Methodological Issues

Research on family business faces several methodological challenges. The first and most obvious challenge facing a family business researcher is defining *what is a family business.* We define a family business as one that will be passed on for the family's next generation to manage and control. But some define a family business as one that includes two or more relatives, and others define it by its culture or by its form of ownership. Besides defining the business as a family business it is also important to define who are members of the family.

The second methodological challenge involves access to

data. To date there is no family business data base—the best is a small-business data base being adopted by John Davis of the University of Southern California for family business research. Gaining access to data about family businesses will always be difficult. Not surprisingly, such companies want to keep information on strategy, financial performance, and family relations private and confidential. For this reason, most research and study so far have been based on those few businesses that are willing to talk openly for the public record and on the personal, confidential consulting experiences of those who write about family businesses. Case research has been very fruitful so far.

The third challenge is to measure and control the necessary variables, including personal, family, and business variables. Research here is difficult for two reasons. First, how many variables do you attempt to control at once (that is, ownership structure, size, and age of the company, family relations and personal goals)? Second, how do you measure some of the important but "soft" variables, such as personal values, personal competence, family health, quality of strategy, and so on?

One of the purposes of this book was to provoke further research on the family business. Hence, we set forth many "propositions" throughout the book and also presented the results of some of our research. The nature of our research efforts was varied. Some of these efforts involved empirical longitudinal studies of random samples of family businesses. Some involved quantitative comparisons and contrasts of the business behavior of family and nonfamily businesses. Others were surveys of self-selected family business participants. It is hoped that these several different efforts will stimulate further questions for research and further ideas on how to design effective research procedures.

As the rapidly emerging field of research on family business continues to proliferate, we can expect that the chances of successfully perpetuating family business will continue to grow. We will be able to test many of the prescriptions and opinions expressed in this book, and we will learn to ask much better questions. But academic research into a field is not without its risks. Typically, academic research is better at identifying the limits of our knowledge than at spelling out what works. Academic research is usually written for other academics rather than for practitioners. Academic research is sometimes accused of focusing more on what is easily measured than on what is critically needed. Probably in few other fields of business research are human needs and hopes so apparent. Hopefully, those who do future research on family business will not only try to improve the use of scientific method in the research but will also try to focus on research questions that will help resolve the personal desires and needs of those who own and work in family businesses.

References

Aaker, D. A. *Strategic Market Management.* New York: Wiley, 1984.

Adizes, I. "Organizational Passages—Diagnosing and Treating Life Cycle Problems of Organizations." *Organizational Dynamics,* 1979, *8,* 3–25.

Adler, A. *Education of Children.* Chicago: Henry Regnery, 1970.

Alcorn, P. *Success and Survival in the Family-Owned Business.* New York: McGraw-Hill, 1982.

American Institute of Certified Public Accountants. "Small Companies Hire More Women, Young, Elderly." *CPA Client Bulletin,* May 1984, p. 1.

Andrews, K. R. *The Concept of Corporate Strategy.* Homewood, Ill.: Dow Jones-Irwin, 1980.

"Back to Work." *Wall Street Journal,* Jan. 24, 1985, p. 17.

Becker, B., and Tillman, F. *The Family-Owned Business.* Chicago: Commerce Clearing House, 1978.

Berenbein, R. "From Owner to Professional Management: Problems in Transition." Conference Board, Report no. 851. New York: 1984.

Birch, D. L., and MacCracken, S. *Corporate Evolution: A Micro-Based Analysis.* Cambridge, Mass.: MIT Press, 1981.

Birely, S. "Succession in the Family Firm: The Inheritor's View." Working paper, Cranfield School of Management, Bedford, England, 1985.

Blotnick, S. "The Case of the Reluctant Heirs." *Forbes,* 1984, *134,* 180.

Brandt, S. C. *Strategic Planning in Emerging Companies.* Reading, Mass.: Addison-Wesley, 1981.

Buzzell, R. D., Gale, B. T., and Sultan, G. M. "Market Share—A Key to Profitability." *Harvard Business Review*, 1975, *53*, 97-106.

Chasman, H. *Who Gets the Business?* New York: Farnsworth, 1983.

Christensen, C. R. *Management Succession in Small and Growing Enterprises.* Boston: Division of Research, Graduate School of Business Administration, Harvard University, 1953.

Danco, K. *From the Other Side of the Bed—A Woman Looks at Life in the Family Business.* Cleveland: University Press, 1981.

Danco, L. *Beyond Survival.* Cleveland: Center for Family Business, University Press, 1975.

Davidson, W. R., Bates, A. D., and Bass, S. J. "The Retail Life Cycle." *Harvard Business Review*, 1976, *54*, 89-96.

Davis, J. "The Influence of Life Stage on Father-Son Work Relationships in the Family Firm." Unpublished doctoral dissertation, Graduate School of Business Administration, Harvard University, 1982.

Dreikurs, R., and Saltz, V. *Children: The Challenge.* New York: Hawthorn Books, 1964.

Drucker, P. F. *Innovation and Entrepreneurship.* New York: Harper & Row, 1985.

Dyer, G. *Cultural Change in Family Firms.* San Francisco: Jossey-Bass, 1986.

Fraker, S. "High-Speed Management for the High-Tech Age." *Fortune*, 1984, *109*, 62-68.

Gale, B. T. "Balancing Capital and Labor Productivity." *Pimsletter*, no. 21, Strategic Planning Institute, Cambridge, Mass., 1979.

Gale, B. T. "Beating the Cost of Capital." *Pimsletter*, no. 32, Strategic Planning Institute, Cambridge, Mass., 1984.

Gilman, H. "The Last Generation." *Wall Street Journal*, May 20, 1985, p. 29C.

Gluck, F., Kaufman, S., and Walleck, S. "Strategic Management for Competitive Advantage." *Harvard Business Review*, 1980, *58*, 154.

Greiner, L. E. "Evolution and Revolution as Organizations Grow." *Harvard Business Review*, 1972, *50*, 37-46.

Herschon, S. A. "The Problem of Management Succession in Family Businesses." Unpublished doctoral dissertation, Graduate School of Business Administration, Harvard University, 1975.

Hollander, B. S. "Family-Owned Business as a System: A Case Study of the Interaction of Family, Task, and Marketplace Components." Unpublished doctoral dissertation, School of Education, University of Pittsburgh, 1983.

Holton, L. "Emotional Ties Keep Generations Working in the Family Business." *Chicago Sun Times,* Aug. 8, 1983, p. 83.

Isenberg, D. J. "How Senior Managers Think." *Harvard Business Review,* 1984, *62,* 81–90.

Kotler, P. *Marketing Management—Analysis, Planning, and Control.* Englewood Cliffs, N.J.: Prentice-Hall, 1976.

Kotler, P., Fahey, L., and Jatusripitak, S. *The New Competition.* Englewood Cliffs, N.J.: Prentice-Hall, 1985.

Lansberg, I. "The Succession Conspiracy: Mapping Resistances to Succession Planning in First-Generation Family Firms." Unpublished paper, Yale University, 1985.

Levinson, D. J. *The Season of a Man's Life.* New York: Ballantine Books, 1978.

Machalaba, D. "Newhouse Chain Stays with Founder's Ways, and with His Heirs." *Wall Street Journal,* Feb. 12, 1982, p. 1.

McNeill, W. H. *The Origin of Civilization.* Oxford, England: Oxford University Press, 1968.

Miller, D. "Structural Change and Performance: Quantum Versus Piecemeal-Incremental Approaches." *Academy of Management Journal,* 1982, *25,* 867–892.

Mintzberg, M., and Waters, J. A. "Of Strategies, Deliberate and Emergent." *Strategic Management Journal,* 1985, *6,* 257–272.

Olson, D., Portner, J., and Lavee, Y. *Faces III.* St. Paul: Family Social Science, University of Minnesota, 1985.

O'Toole, P. *Corporate Messiah.* New York: William Morrow, 1984.

Peiser, R. B., and Wooten, L. M. "Life Cycle Changes in Small Family Businesses." *Business Horizons,* 1983, *26,* 58–65.

Peters, T. J., and Waterman, R. H., Jr. *In Search of Excellence.* New York: Harper & Row, 1982.

Porter, M. E. *Competitive Strategy.* New York: Free Press, 1980.

Posner, B. G. "The 100-Year-Old Start-Up." *Inc.,* September 1985, pp. 79-85.

Quinn, J. B. *Strategic Change: Logical Incrementalism.* Homewood, Ill.: Richard D. Irwin, 1980.

Richman, T. "Super Market." *Inc.,* October, 1985, pp. 115-120.

Rosenblatt, P. C., de Mik, L., Anderson, R. M., and Johnson, P. A. *The Family in Business: Understanding and Dealing with the Challenges Entrepreneurial Families Face.* San Francisco: Jossey-Bass, 1985.

Rothschild, W. E. *Strategic Alternatives—Selection, Development, and Implementation.* New York: AMACOM, 1979.

Salter, M. S. "Stages of Corporate Development." *Journal of Business Policy,* 1970, *I,* 23-27.

Schere, J. L. "Tolerance of Ambiguity as a Discriminating Variable Between Entrepreneurs and Managers." *Academy of Management Proceedings,* 1982, *42,* 404-408.

Small Business Administration. *Handbook of Small Business Data.* Washington, D.C.: Small Business Administration, 1983a.

Small Business Administration. *The State of Small Business: A Report to the President.* Washington, D.C.: Small Business Administration, 1983b.

Steiner, G. A. *Top Management Planning.* Ontario, Canada: Collier-Macmillan Canada, 1969.

Stevenson, H. "Defining Corporate Strengths and Weaknesses." *Sloan Management Review,* Spring 1976, *17,* 51-58.

Sturdivant, F. D., Ginter, J. L., and Sawyer, A. G. "Managers' Conservatism and Corporate Performance." *Strategic Management Journal,* 1985, *6,* 17-38.

Thompson, P., DeSouza, G., and Gale, B. T. *Pimsletter,* no. 33. Strategic Planning Institute, Cambridge, Mass., 1985.

Trow, D. B. "Executive Succession in Small Companies." *Administrative Science Quarterly,* 1961, *6,* 228-239.

Walsh, F. *Normal Family Processes.* New York: Guilford Press, 1982.

Ward, J. L. "The Impact of Family Business Ownership on Marketing Strategy and Performance." In G. Hills and others (eds.), *Marketing and Small Business Entrepreneurship*. Washington, D.C.: American Marketing Association, 1983.

Ward, J. L. "Perpetuating the Family Business." In C. E. Arnoff, R. B. Good, and J. L. Ward (eds.), *The Future of Private Enterprise*. Atlanta: George State University Press, 1986a.

Ward, J. L. "Siblings and the Family Business." *Loyola Business Forum*, 1986b, *6*, 1–3.

Wharton Entrepreneurial Center. *Post-Acquisition Experience of Family-Held Companies*. Working Paper Series, no. 75. Philadelphia: University of Pennsylvania, 1975.

Zaslow, J. "New Nepotism Calls for Junior To Earn Stripes Away from Home." *Wall Street Journal*, January 14, 1986, p. 35.

Index

261